Human–Computer Interaction and Complex Systems

Computers and People Series

Edited by
B. R. GAINES and A. MONK

Monographs

Communicating with Microcomputers: An introduction to the technology of man–computer communication, *Ian H. Witten* 1980

The Computer in Experimental Psychology, *R. Bird* 1981

Principles of Computer Speech, *I. H. Witten* 1982

Cognitive Psychology of Planning, *J-M. Hoc* 1988

Formal Methods for Interactive Systems, *A. Dix* 1991

Edited Works

Computing Skills and the User Interface, *M. J. Coombs and J. L. Alty (eds)* 1981

Fuzzy Reasoning and Its Applications, *E. H. Mamdani and B. R. Gaines (eds)* 1981

Intelligent Tutoring Systems, *D. Sleeman and J. S. Brown (eds)* 1982 (1986 paperback)

Designing for Human–Computer Communication, *M. E. Sime and M. J. Coombs (eds)* 1983

The Psychology of Computer Use, *T. R. G. Green, S. J. Payne and G. C. van der Veer (eds)* 1983

Fundamentals of Human–Computer Interaction, *Andrew Monk (ed)* 1984, 1985

Working with Computers: Theory versus Outcome, *G. C. van der Veer, T. R. G. Green, J-M. Hoc and D. Murray (eds)* 1988

Cognitive Engineering in Complex Dynamic Worlds, *E. Hollnagel, G. Mancini and D. D. Woods (eds)* 1988

Computers and Conversation, *P. Luff, N. Gilbert and D. Frohlich (eds)* 1990

Adaptive User Interfaces, *D. Browne, P. Totterdell and M. Norman (eds)* 1990

Human–Computer Interaction and Complex Systems, *G. R. S. Weir and J. L. Alty (eds)* 1991

Practical Texts

Effective Color Displays: Theory and Practice, *D. Travis* 1991

EACE Publications

(Consulting Editors: *Y. WAERN and J-M. HOC*)

Cognitive Ergonomics, *P. Falzon (ed)* 1990

Psychology of Programming, *J-M. Hoc, T. R. G. Green, R. Samurçay and D. Gilmore (eds)* 1990

Human–Computer Interaction and Complex Systems

Edited by

GEORGE R. S. WEIR
JAMES L. ALTY

Scottish HCI Centre,
Strathclyde University,
Glasgow, UK

ACADEMIC PRESS

Harcourt Brace Jovanovich, Publishers
London   San Diego   New York
Boston   Sydney   Tokyo   Toronto

ACADEMIC PRESS LTD.
24/28 Oval Road,
London NW1 7DX

United States Edition published by
ACADEMIC PRESS INC.
San Diego, California 92101-4311

A catalogue record for this book is available from the British Library

ISBN 0-12-742660-4

Printed in Great Britain by St Edmundsbury Press Ltd,
Bury St Edmunds, Suffolk

Contents

List of Figures

Authors

James L. Alty, Scottish HCI Centre, University of Strathclyde, George House, 36 North Hanover Street, Glasgow G1 2AD, UK

Lisanne Bainbridge, Department of Psychology, University College, London WC1E 6BT, UK

Paul A. Booth, Department of Computing, Manchester Polytechnic, John Dalton Building, Chester Street, Manchester M1 5GD, UK

Bernd-Burkhard Borys, University of Kassel (GhK), Laboratory for Man-Machine Systems, Postfach 10 13 80, Mönchbergstraße 7, D-3500 Kassel, West Germany

Pietro C. Cacciabue, Commission of the European Communities, Joint Research Centre, Ispra (VA) 21020, Italy

Françoise Decortis, Commission of the European Communities, Joint Research Centre, Ispra (VA) 21020, Italy

Veronique de Keyser, University of Liège Sart-Tilman, 4000 Liège 1, Belgium

Ernest Edmonds, LUTCHI Research Centre, Loughborough University of Technology, UK

Jenia Ghazikhanian, LUTCHI Research Centre, Loughborough University of Technology, UK

Simon Grant, Scottish HCI Centre, University of Strathclyde, George House, 36 North Hanover Street, Glasgow G1 2AD, UK

Erik Hollnagel, Computer Resources International, Bregnerødvej 144, DK-3460 Birkerød, Denmark

Pertti Järvinen, University of Tampere, Department of Computer Science, P. O. Box 607, SF-33101 Tampere, Finland

Morten Lind, Institute of Automatic Control Systems, Technical University of Denmark, DK-2800 Lyngby, Denmark

Terry Mayes, Scottish HCI Centre, University of Strathclyde, George House, 36 North Hanover Street, Glasgow G1 2AD, UK

Russell A. Ritchie, Scottish HCI Centre, University of Strathclyde, George House, 36 North Hanover Street, Glasgow G1 2AD, UK

Giuseppe Volta, Commission of the European Communities, Joint Research Centre, Ispra (VA) 21020, Italy

George R. S. Weir, Scottish HCI Centre, University of Strathclyde, George House, 36 North Hanover Street, Glasgow G1 2AD, UK

David D. Woods, The Ohio State University, 1971 Neil Avenue, Columbus, OH 43210, USA

Foreword

The principal concerns of this book are human-computer interaction (HCI) and complexity. The former is an increasingly well-established discipline, attending to the characteristics of human users and the computer-based systems with which they interact. The latter is a quality of such systems, present to a greater or lesser degree by virtue of system scale, nature of application and available forms of interaction, and, of course, influenced by user characteristics.

HCI and complexity are intimately linked. Increasing use of computer-controlled equipment within industry, the office, leisure and the home, exposes humans to ever more sophisticated, elaborate and, often, incomprehensible interactive systems.

Here, technology plays a dual role. Firstly, by extending the range of available interactive devices and thereby, the demands placed upon human operators, technology contributes to the complexities faced by these users. Secondly, in contrast, technology provides a means whereby the difficult (complex) may be made more manageable [244]. Thus, technological factors contribute both as a source of problems associated with the design and use of complex interactive systems, and, in some measure, to their solution.

Although the incidence of human interaction with machines is driven by technological 'progress', such progress is rarely founded upon principled (theoretical) bases [44]. Consequently, end-users are exposed to widely divergent 'standards' for interactive systems. The manner in which system designers choose to accommodate users as necessary partners in human-machine interaction is not circumscribed. Thus, part of the complexity facing today's end-user is *knowing what to expect* of new technology. Indeed, this problem is compounded when confronted with tools (technological systems) that make little or no concession to their human users. Inevitably, such lack of system transparency, combined with inexperience or human frailty, leads to misunderstanding and errors on the part of the end-user. (Systems may vary greatly in the degree of their tolerance and support for such situations.) A potential resolution to this difficulty lies in a move from 'tool-driven to problem-driven approaches to the application of computational power' [250].

Thus, much of what follows concerns itself with the difficulties of accommodating human operators when designing interactive systems—how to provide interactive systems that naturally support users in addressing task-based problems. With any interactive device, the operator has to ascertain what can be achieved in this domain (what is possible), and how it can be achieved (the means available). Thus, one concern is with methodology for development of systems that can make such information transparent.

Work on the analysis of accidents and the nature of human error [169, 193] suggests that operators are prone to recurrent problems in handling complex systems. Indeed, Reason [193] argues that many operator errors arise 'from a mismatch between the properties of the system as a whole and the characteristics of human information processing'. Although a ready solution to this inherent problem is not easily found, a longer-term strategy is recommended, *viz.*:

> it is necessary to go back to the drawing board and create a new generation of systems with the basic properties of human cognition firmly in mind from the outset [193, p.10].

In the chapters that follow are discussions and proposals which address this concern and which seek to further our understanding of how human users operate with complex systems and how the interactive efficacy of such systems may be improved. Although this is a multi-author work, the foci of its authors combine to provide a broad image of this world of HCI and complex systems. Thus, in Chapter 1—*Living with complex interactive systems*—we begin with a gentle (relatively untechnical) overview of problems and pitfalls in the design and use of familiar interactive systems. Specific attention is given to the behaviour of interfaces and its relation to overall system complexity. In this light, a perspective on the development of human-machine interaction is proposed which describes a role for technology in the transition from simple command-based interfaces, through intelligent (automated) control, intelligent dialogue (automated program elicitation), toward dialogue expertise. Technology is portrayed not solely as a cause of complexity but as a potential solution.

Continuing the theme of capturing interface behaviour, Chapter 2—*An algebraic approach to interface specification analysis*—focusses on describing user system interaction. Here, emphasis is placed upon the use and analysis of interface specifications (means for describing a system's interactive behaviour), which hold potential for the design and testing of interfaces. Claims for the efficacy of interface specification and analysis are given practical support in the form of an example interface description facility. This is detailed, in conjunction with a technique, based upon matrix algebra, for algebraic analysis of such specifications. The result is a convincing case for early design specification and analysis prior to final implementation for interactive systems.

Following Chapter 2, we begin to consider specific problems in user interaction. An often ignored yet key feature is that of time. Chapter 3—*The temporal dimension of man-machine interaction*—moves away from the earlier technical approach to system development, to address the role of time in human-machine interaction. With specific attention to operators in process control, this chapter discusses ways of accommodating the human perception of temporal aspects of tasks, and, in particular, describes how such factors contribute to human error.

Often, operator error in human-machine interaction is indicative of a system's success in design. Yet, in the world of large-scale technological systems, where unanticipated incidents may lead to adverse environmental or personal injury, scope for performance error gives serious cause for concern. Chapter 4—*The phenotype of erroneous actions: implications for HCI design*—begins with a discussion on the nature and complexity of HCI before addressing the arena of human error. This chapter presents a taxonomy of error 'phenotypes'. An operator support system ('response evaluation system'), based upon such phenotypes, is also described.

Since task structure and task representation play a crucial role in the performance of any interactive system, Chapter 5—*Modelling the user: user-system errors and predictive grammars*—discusses the use of 'predictive grammars' as a basis for analysing task complexity in system design. The claim is that user performance and significant errors, play a major role in determining the efficacy of any such predictive design techniques. This is illustrated by an end-user study of a *Memomaker* package.

Many of the descriptive/analytical techniques described in Chapter 5 embody presumptions about the nature of human operators and the characteristics that they bring to task performance. Such focus upon the contribution played to interaction by the human agent underpins the place for cognitive psychology in HCI. Patently, a methodology that allows system designers to accommodate more adequately the cognitive characteristics of their user population should yield great dividend. A burgeoning approach is that termed 'cognitive task analysis'. Here, theorists attempt to capture the cognitive demands and potential cognitive contributions that can be expected of human operators using specific interactive system designs. However, there is some ambiguity in the scope and nature of this enterprise. Thus, Chapter 6—*Cognitive task analysis?*—evaluates approaches to cognitive task analysis.

Cognition and the nature of human information processing accounts for much of operator performance in human-machine interaction. The vital role of information processing leads us to emphasise aspects of display design and utilisation. Thus, effective design of an information delivery system needs to consider the manner and form in which information is structured and presented to the end-user. Several of the following chapters address these aspects.

In chapter 7—*The cognitive engineering of problem representations*—the manner in which human agents handle abnormal situations and, in particular, the way in which information presentation techniques may assist operators, or exacerbate problem situations, is addressed. This concern is further detailed in Chapter 8—*Multiplexed VDT display systems*. Here, the nature and role of human skill is considered and a framework for good practice is outlined.

The design of interface systems that adequately accommodate the needs and limitations of the end-user is a prime objective in HCI research. While the foregoing chapters emphasise the nature and limits for the final operator, Chapter 9—*Ways of supporting ergonomically and technically correct display design*—describes the use of expert systems technology to provide a practical support for display design.

The theme of display design is continued in Chapter 10—*Representations and abstractions for interface design using Multilevel Flow Modelling*. Here, a methodology is described that supports the description of complex systems at differing levels of abstraction. Among its potential uses, Multilevel Flow Modelling promises a means for design of interfaces based upon system functions and possible goals, thereby allowing for better reflection of system characteristics at a variety of abstract levels of description.

User-system *cooperation*, as a contrast to mere user-system interaction, is an ambition described in Chapter 11—*Cooperation between distributed knowledge-bases and the user*. The context here is the increasing use of knowledge-based systems as a technology for interface design and support. A specific technique is described for communication between human users and a number of separate system knowledge-bases. Such a facility may provide a basis for adequate integration of knowledge-base interaction and more conventional system components.

This collection ends on a philosophical note with a consideration of work by the Finnish systems theorist Alvin Aulin. The implications for HCI research from Aulin's account of system dynamics are discussed in Chapter 12—*Human-Computer Interaction research in the light of Aulin's Foundations of Mathematical Systems Dynamics*. The conclusion expressed is that study of dynamic systems indicates precise (and limited) approaches toward improvement in HCI.

Taken together, these chapters present the arena of human-computer interaction in the world of complex interactive systems, where human operators and domestic end-users meet devices which are technologically ever more advanced and diverse in application.

Acknowledgements

Several acknowledgements are due. Primarily, our thanks go to Simon Grant for his critical reading and extensive support in manuscript preparation, using LaTeX. Without Simon's concern, unselfish assistance and dedication, this work would have suffered considerably.

Professor Andrew McGettrick, through the Department of Computer Science, University of Strathclyde, provided financial support for a workshop on HCI and Complex Systems, for which most of the present chapters were originally prepared. Finally, our thanks to the contributors for tolerating the painstaking process from original drafts to final publication.

G. R. S. Weir
J. L. Alty
Glasgow

Chapter 1

Living with Complex Interactive Systems

George R. S. Weir

1 Introduction

Complex interactive systems are manifest in many areas, including nuclear
power generation, aircraft flight control, brewing and oil refining. Such application domains, like many others, embrace sophisticated control techniques,
in combination with human operators, as means for achieving the particular
goals of the system.

   In their complexity and safety requirements, the scale of such domains
places rigorous design demands upon control equipment and upon the interface afforded to the system operators. Naturally, such constraints require
specialists in control and reliability. Yet there are valuable lessons to be
learned by the non-specialist from less elaborate and more common systems
which reside closer to home and, certainly, outside the world of industrial
process control.

   Although smaller in scale than the average power plant, many of the devices we meet in daily life are interactive and complex. The purpose in this
chapter is to highlight general problems in the design and operation of complex systems, with special reference to the relationship between interface and
control, as evidenced by familiar small-scale interactive systems. In the belief
that there are lessons to be learned from the commonplace which have bearing upon more exotic large-scale environments, the viewpoints portrayed here
provide a convenient means of underlining some of the fundamental design
difficulties which determine the joint performance of any combined man and
machine system.

HUMAN–COMPUTER INTERACTION
AND COMPLEX SYSTEMS: ISBN 0-12-742660-4

2   The locus of complexity

Obviously, the degree of complexity inherent in any domain will determine
the difficulty in design and the resultant quality of any interactive system
which aims to exploit that domain. Woods [245] identifies several dimensions
of world complexity: the degree to which the task domain proves dynamic, is
composed of many interconnected parts, suffers a high degree of uncertainty,
or bears high levels of risk (see also [247]). The latter two dimensions are
specific features of the cognitive complexity facing operators, being intimately
concerned with operators' behavioural capabilities.

While Woods' classification serves to focus attention on factors which
contribute to the complexity of 'dynamic worlds' (op. cit.), it is useful to
consider complexity in terms of its locus, i.e., where it arises in such worlds.
The sole relevance of these factors is their contribution to the prospects for
design or control. Thus, we can go some way towards partitioning factors by
their role in the world, conceived in terms of their effects upon the possible
operation of a particular dynamic system.

For systems in which some process is contained and controlled (many
interactive applications) we may identify three sources of complexity:

- complexity of the domain itself;
- complexity of the control requirements;
- complexity of the required user/operator interaction.

Each of these facets is described in detail below.

2.1   Domain complexity

Firstly, the domain may itself be complex, i.e., it may embody many critical
variables and a large number of possible states. In such cases, the behaviour
of the process is not determined by a few discrete factors but by a compound
of interrelated variables [158]. (This would include aspects of Woods' second
dimension of complexity: the degree to which the world is composed of many
interconnected parts.) Further, the degree of inherent dynamicity within the
domain provides a dimension to its complexity (*pace* Woods).

Of course, the complexity of a domain is defined to some extent in terms
of the goals ascribed to the system by its designers or users. The purpose of
those who wish to manipulate the domain will determine which factors are
relevant. Thus, a system whose purpose is the distribution of water through
several rooms in a home is less complex than a water-based room heating
system. Although these two domains are very similar in their physical bases,
only in the latter case will water temperature and conditions for thermal
transfer be relevant factors. Of course, other variables, such as water pressure,
may be pertinent in both systems.

2.2 Control complexity

The range of determinant variables in the physical domain of the process also affects the degree of complexity at the level of control. Thus, if our system is intended to provide room heating and several factors affect the overall efficacy, then controlling the system's performance *vis-à-vis* this goal may require control facilities on many of the affecting variables. The number of 'hooks' we require on the process will depend upon how 'closely coupled' are these variables. If both water pressure and water temperature affect system performance (i.e., the desired product of system operation) it may be sufficient to provide a control mechanism which directly affects temperature and thereby indirectly affects pressure. While domain complexity will generally correlate with control complexity, i.e., the manipulation of constraints (variables) that determine overall system performance, the complexity of control requirements should be seen as a function of system purpose on domain complexity.

2.3 Interaction complexity

A third locus of complexity for interactive systems lies with the requirements placed upon system operators. The greater the demands on the end-user the more complex is the overall system. This may take the form of demands upon the operator's physical responses (ergonomic constraints), e.g., to interact often in ways which may be physically awkward, or as demands upon cognitive capacities (comprehension, planning capabilities, memory load, etc.). Both the ergonomic and cognitive requirements will be determined in part by the means (and modes) of interaction made available to the operator via the man-machine interface. This embraces means whereby operators effect changes on control facilities as well as provisions for the elicitation or delivery of information on the status of the man-machine system.

In a simple sense, the hardware and software of the system interface determines the interaction complexity. However, for individual operators, complexity of interaction is determined in part by what they as operators (and, indeed, as human information processors) bring to the interaction. Generally, the complexity of interaction will correlate to the control complexity, since the requirements imposed by the operator's tasks will inevitably reflect the capacities of the control facilities.[1]

2.4 A pyramid of complexity

Seen in terms of their loci, factors which contribute to the complexity of a dynamic system are better apprehended for the part they play in shaping

---

[1] Nevertheless, with automation, the density of control activity may be high whilst the requirements for operator interaction remain low.

prospects for design, control and operator interaction. In this light, the dynamic world of process control is itself viewed from three perspectives: the confines of the physical system; the possibilities of affecting the organisation of this physical system (control); and the available means of accessing this domain (the man-machine interface). Clearly, the aspects of complexity identified by Woods cut across these perspectives. Furthermore, Woods' factors are themselves interrelated; for example, with the degree of uncertainty and the task dynamicity contributing to the level of risk. A clearer sense of the role played by such factors is exhibited by mapping their position against the loci mentioned above. Figure 1 presents this as a 'pyramid of complexity'.

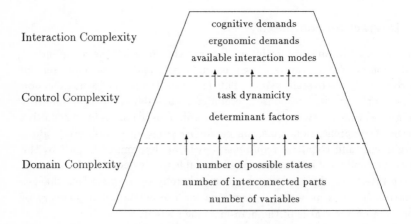

Figure 1: Pyramid of complexity

This pyramid represents several aspects of complex man-machine systems. Its base holds the physical world constituents of the process to be controlled. Built upon this, comes the plant control equipment, used to monitor and manipulate this subset of the physical world. Finally, on top of the control equipment, facilities are provided to allow human operators to organise information from the lower level and also facilitate interaction with the control equipment and thereby effect changes on the process.

Clearly, domain, control and interaction complexity are not insular aspects of any dynamic system but are closely interrelated. In terms of overall system complexity, the pyramid diagram represents the influence of each factor percolating upward from the level of the process domain, through the task and control level to the arena of man-machine interaction, finally revealing itself to operators at the man-machine interface. The factors listed provide an increase in level of abstraction; from the domain, through control, to the level of interaction, with each layer able to modify or compound the final degree of complexity. Thus, the number of variables (at the domain level) contributes to the number of interconnected parts, which contributes to the number of possible states, which will influence the task dynamicity, and so on, up through the levels.

At the top-most level of man-machine interaction, the complexity is principally determined by the transitivity of influences from the lower levels of the system. This being the case, we can also view the structure of the process control domain in terms of these physical levels. The operator sits at the apex of a pyramid, faced with a layered process control system, and the tide of complexity which rises from these layers (see Figure 2).[2]

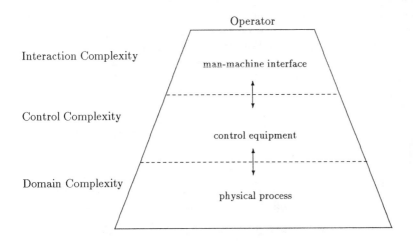

Figure 2: Man-machine system viewed as a pyramid

In what follows, I suggest that this classification provides a framework within which we can better appreciate the primary roles of technology in process control.

---

[2] This is an abstraction of the real situation in which there may be several operators and a number of subsystem interfaces.

3   The role of technology

3.1   Bringing system functions to the operator

A primary factor in the efficacy of any interactive system design is the effectiveness with which opportunities for the control of key factors in the system
domain are made accessible to the operator. The simplest, although often the
least supportive, strategy is to afford direct user manipulation of the application environment in a one-to-one mapping from interface to control facility
and thence to effect on the domain.

An example of this approach is evident in the design of some electric
cookers. In one instance, the cooker boasts an integral grill and oven. The
oven itself has three heating elements, as well as a grill and a fan for heat
distribution. With such a system, a vital design issue is how to provide control
facilities for the system functions.

As usual, the oven should include a thermostat facility and the grill requires the possibility of finely adjusting its setting. Curiously, the combination
of this range of functions leads to unusual control features.

Three control dials are provided on the fascia of the oven. The first (grill
power) sets the grill in a range of 0 to 9 (see Figure 3). The second (element
switch) allows for selection of specific heating elements within the oven (either
fan-assisted or fan-off), and the third (thermostat) sets the oven temperature,
above which the oven will automatically switch off and below which it will
automatically switch on.

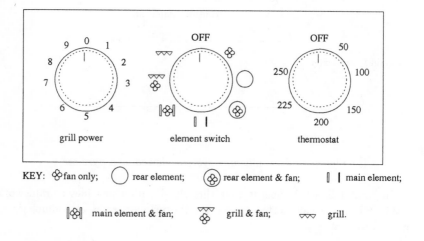

Figure 3: Control interface for integral oven and grill

Nothing too strange so far, until one realises the implications of these three control mechanisms. Since the grill is an integral element within the oven, it can only operate when selected by the element switch. Furthermore, since its heat will affect oven temperature, the grill must also be under the influence of the thermostat. These are direct consequences (one might suppose, reasonable consequences) of the design strategy which treats the oven as a single control domain. The inconvenient consequence arises when one wishes merely to make toast.

Firstly, the element switch is set to grill. Next, the grill power switch selects the appropriate setting on the 0 to 9 scale. Yet this is not sufficient, because the thermostat control must be set to a sufficiently high temperature to allow the bread to toast without the grill power being automatically cut. In order to perform a task which is ostensibly very simple, one must employ all three of the oven control switches. The result is that the user is not able simply to make toast, but, rather, must take over control of the whole oven.

In cases such as this, design has focussed on the integral effects upon the overall oven domain (manipulation of the key variables). The close coupling between the heat from the various elements and overall oven temperature represents a degree of complexity (or complication!) in the requirements for control (i.e., at the level of the control facilities). Unfortunately, this complexity permeates to the system interface, with its resultant peculiar requirements on operator (user) action. (Arguably, this design embodies a lack of attention to the specifics of particular operator tasks. A more convenient approach would provide a reasonable degree of control support for all levels of task. Thus, if only the grill is selected the thermostat may be overridden as superfluous to task requirements, or, in addition, the grill power dial might also act as an on-off switch for the grill. The existing system shows a failure to match end-user's tasks to the control facilities in the given domain.) A second example will suffice to make this point clear.

Comparison of two digital watches illustrates how different interaction and control operations are required of the user in the task of setting the alarm function. In the first case[3], the alarm time is set by selecting the alarm display, via the main function button (see Figure 4). A time-change button must next be pressed to enable alteration of the alarm setting. Thereafter, the desired hour and minute setting is achieved by a combination of the hours/minutes selector (main function button) and the counter advance function. Depressing the time-change button when the desired alarm time is displayed returns the watch to normal operation and activates the alarm.

This procedure differs in an important respect from the second watch.[4] Having only three control buttons, against the four buttons of the previous

---

[3] Casio AE-9W.
[4] Casio AQ-8W.

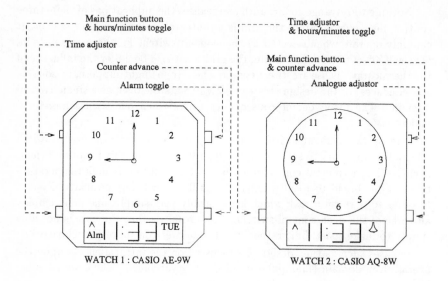

Figure 4 : Digital watch interfaces (simplified)

watch, selection of time-change mode is achieved by means of the same button as is used subsequently to select hours/minutes (see Figure 4). When selecting a specific alarm time the same number of key presses is required for either watch. But economy on the part of the latter device has a crucial effect on a related user task.

Having set an alarm time, the user may reasonably wish to de-select the alarm without losing the alarm setting. On the first watch this is achieved by selecting the alarm display mode and depressing the fourth control button (a two-step procedure). The latter action serves as an alarm toggle without affecting the preset alarm time.

Simply de-selecting the alarm on the second watch requires the user to perform precisely the same sequence of actions as for setting an alarm time (a six-step procedure) and includes the risk of accidentally altering the chosen alarm time *en route*.

In the latter case, we may reasonably assume that the final design is a deliberate compromise. This compromise emerges as a trade-off in locus of complexity, whereby complexity is greater at the interface so that complexity at the level of control functions can be minimised. Such a strategy has its rationale in economics, but this short-changes the user through inattention to the specifics of his likely tasks.

The above examples (oven and watch) illustrate partial design failure in the way that system functions are brought to the operator of the interactive system. We may see in such failings a tendency to disregard the *ease of execution* afforded by specific control facilities, i.e., a failure to deflect domain or control complexity from permeating the man-machine interface. In turn, this results in designs which lock the end-user tightly into the constraints of domain control. This is of concern not simply because of the overheads imposed upon operators in such systems but because these overheads increase the likelihood of errors by the end-user. Such *task-overhead errors* are insignificant in terms of digital watch control, less so for electric ovens[5], and considerably more serious for large-scale industrial plant. Notably, restrictive or inflexible interaction has been cited as a major problem, in the eyes of process control operators [8].

3.2 Bringing system information to the operator

Just as there are design issues in making system functions available to the operator, so there are related issues which concern the supply of pertinent information. Each interactive system makes demands upon its users. In order to manipulate the system appropriately, the operator must appreciate its current state in terms which are pertinent to the tasks before him. Once again, arcane examples serve to illustrate a point which has very serious ramifications for large-scale systems.

Although many familiar interactive systems display state information for the benefit of their users, such information is often not presented in an optimal (task-related) fashion. Even worse, the information may be inadequate or misleading to the operator. A simple case is the display on a digital radio tuner. When using such a radio, I often want to know which station I am hearing. Of course, the system is designed to provide such information, after a fashion.

In fact, the display shows the radio frequency in megahertz of the station to which I have tuned (e.g., 88.30). Like most reasonable people, I cannot recall the radio frequencies of all the stations I might require. Hence, although the available information correctly reflects the state of the system, it does not satisfy the user's immediate information needs. The mere fact that state information is correct does not render it useful or even usable. Here, with the aid of a printed reference guide, I can 'translate' from displayed frequencies to radio station names. But this is a concession to the domain of the radio system and a compromise on system comprehensibility.[6]

Arguably, such restricted information is the best that the system can provide. Yet, other examples underline the pitfalls of presenting system state

---

[5]It is easy to overlook one of the three controls when switching off the grill.

[6]There are now radios on the market which allow the user to predefine station names against particular frequencies. Thereafter, the radio can display either radio frequency or radio station name.

to the user. Whilst staying abroad in a large hotel, I had occasion to take the lift from the thirteenth floor to the lobby. The lift system comprised a suite of three separate lifts and above each lift was an indicator light. Upon pressing the call button, I looked to the lights as indication of which lift would arrive. Almost immediately a light came on above lift number one. So I stepped toward the appropriate door. Instantly, the light went out, and no lift arrived. Shortly, the light above lift number three came on and I stepped toward its door, only to find that this light also expired without lift arrival. Eventually, when two lights lit simultaneously, I realised the significance of the information being provided. Counter to my initial assumption, the lights did not indicate which of the lifts would arrive. Rather, they reflected which of the lifts was in motion at any instant.

Clearly, knowing which lift is moving is pertinent to knowing which will arrive. (Motion is a necessary condition for lift arrival.) But this information is inadequate as a guide to which lift will arrive. (Motion is not a sufficient condition of lift arrival.) Presumably, the information actually presented by this lift system is easily afforded, whereas determining and indicating the specific lift that will answer a particular call is more complex. Curiously, which lift will arrive is precisely what users want to know in such circumstances. Most lift systems avoid the described problem by indicating simply which lift has arrived (seconds before the corresponding doors open). In the end, the available information merely shows that the lifts are operational.

This gives us a further prime example of the problem of information relevance. Clearly, the ready availability of state information is not in itself a good reason for presenting it (unsolicited) to the end-user. Rather, available information should bear relevance to the operator's goals or objectives. Otherwise, the resultant mismatch between what information the operator requires and what is provided may result in misinterpretation and error.

Similar issues of relevance arise in the context of display design for many complex control tasks. Potential problems for the operator may be exacerbated by traditional design practices such as the use of elemental display techniques (cf. Woods, Chapter 7), wherein individual data from the process or control system are assigned to individual values in display. Such a trend is a variety of information overkill which aims at quantity of information but may ignore the quality (i.e., its relevance to the operator's perceived context).

The tendency in process environments to employ alarm annunciators on as many individually significant plant components as possible further exacerbates the problem of information management. Thus, Rasmussen notes that

> In a plant designed by bringing together standard equipment and subsystems, the alarm system is typically the conglomeration of the warning signals which the individual suppliers consider important for the mon-

itoring of the state of their piece (as the basis for performance guarantees). Hundreds of alarm windows presenting the state of individual physical parameters may overload the operator's information capacity during disturbances [186, p. 180].

Operator's will generally have concern for the performance of the plant at a coarser level of detail than is represented by warning signals on such individual components. Furthermore, status information may mislead if signals reflect the condition of control equipment but not whether such apparatus has performed as expected. Thus, in the notorious incident at Three Mile Island the solenoid component in a valve operated correctly yet failed to close the valve. Unknown to the operators, the valve status indicator reflected the operation of the solenoid and not the valve. In consequence, the open valve remained undetected for several hours while operators sought elsewhere for the locus of trouble [24].[7]

4 Applying technology

4.1 Making progress

The design features highlighted above illustrate difficulties in bringing together a manipulable application domain and its operators. In the cases cited, either the quality of an operator's access to system functions or to system information is suboptimal.

Through application of technology we are able to tackle the loci of system complexity mentioned above. Control equipment and control theories have rendered manageable the most hazardous of domains and made possible the design of ever more sophisticated devices. Thereby, applications (processes for control) are potentially more complex in their constitution; we can manage more elaborate dynamic environments through advances in control technology (with its resultant increase in complexity at the control equipment level).

Although, as users and operators of interactive systems, we may reasonably expect benefits from progress in technology, it would be naïve to suppose that the role of technology is solely that of simplification. Advances through technology may reasonably come in three forms:

- Increasing functionality: whereby newer systems embody a greater range of functions (or greater utility) than their predecessors;

- Simplified control: whereby equivalent functionality may be controlled with greater ease;

---

[7]As if this was not sufficiently problematic for the design of information display systems, Sanderson has recently indicated further potential pitfalls within the semantics of displays [203].

- Improved interaction: whereby the quality of man-machine interaction is enhanced.

There are many possible examples of systems whose utility has increased as a result of technological progress, although this does not always entail simplification.

Ostensibly, my present washing machine is more complicated than that used by my grandmother twenty years ago. Her washing machine was designed to clean clothes in the most practical and efficient manner then available. To this end, the machine came with four basic functions: heat, wash, rinse and spin. In operation, the user selected each of these functions in turn, thereby performing a 'washing cycle'.

One might expect today's technology to afford washing machines with a wider range of functions than those of my grandmother's day. In fact, precisely the same range of primitive options is provided on my automatic washing system. The basic function set has not increased (presumably because there is no additional apposite function).

On the other hand, the manner in which the basic functions are combined has become more sophisticated. Whereas older machines operated a single washing cycle (heat, wash, rinse and spin) under manual selection, modern machines provide a range of preselectable cycles to suit a variety of washing requirements—supporting a range of washing temperatures, spin strengths, and sequential combinations of the basic functions.

While the number of possible different wash cycles has greatly increased, today's machines are physically easier to use than the twin-tubs of yesteryear. User intervention at each phase in the cycle is no longer required. So, technological progress is also exhibited here as a simplification of the user-required actions.[8] This example seems to embody two of our three potential benefits through technology. The system utility has increased and the quality of user interaction is greatly enhanced, yet at the level of system control the equipment required for handling the wider range of user options is more elaborate and complex. In general, washing systems have increased in the complexity of their control over the washing environment.

4.1.1 The task-artifact cycle

Progress in washing machine technology has given us finer grain control over the precise execution of functions within the basic washing cycle. Such refinement in control also reflects a refinement in user objectives. Carroll *et al.* [44] view such development as the essence of evolution in human-computer interaction, *viz.*:

---

[8] Admittedly, a corollary of the increase in choice of washing cycle is a new need for the user to comprehend and make decisions on the available alternatives.

> The evolution of HCI technology is a co-evaluation of HCI tasks and HCI artifacts: a task implicitly sets requirements for the development of artifacts to support it, an artifact suggests possibilities and introduces constraints that often radically redefine the task for which the artifact was originally developed. ...In each case, changed tasks suggest new needs and opportunities for further change. This dynamic relation, the task-artifact cycle, circumscribes the development activities of human-computer interaction.

In the present example, our artifact is the washing machine, and the possibilities are newly considered enhancements to system utility (e.g., the possibility of drying the clothes after washing). Such possibilities give rise to an extended set of tasks which the system should support (e.g., blow hot air through the clothes). In turn, these tasks impose requirements upon the artifact itself (e.g., the need for additional hardware and alterations to the existing control circuitry). Following each reincarnation of the artifact, the cycle resumes.

This task-artifact cycle represents the technological evolution of such systems (see Figure 5; taken from [44]). So it is that current automatic washing machines come to allow for the treatment of many different types of fabric and washers cum tumble-dryers are born. This is also a sense in which my washing machine has greater complexity than my grandmother's.

Winograd and Flores make a similar, though more general, observation on the source of technological innovation, *viz.*,

> We are concerned with what happens when new devices are created, and how possibilities for innovation arise. There is a circularity here: the world determines what we can do and what we do determines our world. The creation of a new device or systematic domain can have far-reaching significance—it can create new ways of being that previously did not exist and a framework for actions that would not previously have made sense [239, p. 177].

4.2   Intelligent control

A naïve response to the systems described above would point out that end-users have to live with the constraints of whatever application they wish to control; that designers of interactive systems can do no more than provide facilities to control available features in the domain. Underlying this assumption may be the simplistic view that the mapping from operator control action to effect on the domain must be one-to-one. Yet we have already seen from our automatic washing machine that the actions required on the part of the operator may be simple while the effects upon the application domain remain

REQUIREMENTS

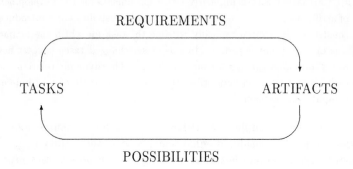

TASKS   ARTIFACTS

POSSIBILITIES

Figure 5: The task-artifact cycle

complex. The mapping from user action to domain action may be one-to-many.

The possibility of reducing the complexity of user interaction is evident in many familiar interactive systems. Aside from washing machines, domestic video recorders have grown increasingly sophisticated in the support they offer for user control of the video-cassette domain. A prime example, which I have detailed elsewhere [231], is a facility termed index-search.

This facility allows the operator to locate the start point of any recording made previously. When the appropriate button on a remote control handset is pressed, a display light marked 'index' is toggled. If the index facility is enabled and the user switches the VCR to rewind, the machine rewinds the tape until the next previous start-of-recording point is located.[9] Upon reaching the first previous recording point, the VCR switches to play, then immediately to fast scan forward. If the user does not switch the system to play or to stop within 30 seconds, the VCR switches from fast scan back to rewind, until it finds a start-of-recording point prior to that first located. Thereafter, the above sequence repeats. If the user does not interrupt this searching before the system reaches the beginning of the tape, the search sequence resumes in fast forward mode. The sophistication of this 'range of behaviour' is illustrated in Figure 6.

Such a facility provides a high degree of interpretation from the operator's actions at the machine interface to control actions on the application. The index-search option facilitates the user's objective, which involves a complex sequence of control actions on the domain, yet renders this as a simple in-

---

[9]The VCR automatically marks a record point on the tape whenever a recording is begun.

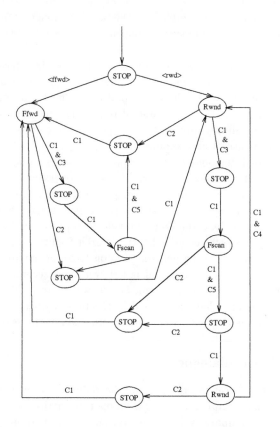

KEY :

User actions		Machine states	Conditions for state transition	
<ffwd>	fast forward	Ffwd	C1	index is on
			C2	end of tape
<rwd>	rewind	Rwnd	C3	index point
		Fscan	C4	2nd index point
			C5	30secs elapsed
		STOP	C1&C3	conjunction

Figure 6 : State transition diagram for 'index search'

teraction at the operator's interface. In so doing, this represents a complex mapping from user interaction to actions at the control level. Effectively, the complexity embodied in accomplishing the task is no longer imposed upon the user but is embraced by the system and managed by a facility for *intelligent control*.[10]

In response to a few simple actions at the user interface, this facility 'interprets' the user requirements and effects a range of behaviour at the control level (see Figure 6). The same point is true for the automatic washing machine. No longer is the user required to specify each step in the washing cycle. The system simply interprets the type of wash required in terms of the appropriate sequence of user actions.

This form of intelligent control responds to sparse user actions by initiating predefined complex sequences of control operations. A further step in sophistication would permit the user personally to define the control sequence. This would be a major step forward in interface flexibility. Once more, VCRs seem to lead the domestic field in sophisticated control. Latest models of video cassette recorder boast a search facility that allows the user to specify an operation to be performed upon locating the appropriate index point. Thus, the 'search' command is followed by a second command from the 'standard' set (play, stop, rewind, fast-forward, etc.). The search operation only commences when the second instruction has been registered. This second command is then executed upon completion of the search.

4.3   Intelligent dialogue

The complexity of user interaction may be reduced by such intelligent control; supporting a complex mapping from operator actions to control actions. By such means, comparatively few operations at the man-machine interface can result in a sophisticated series of actions at the control level. Thereby, complicated (but standard) tasks can be accomplished by the operator with ease.[11]

Sadly, much of the inherent complexity of human-machine interaction remains unaffected by facilities for intelligent control. Ironically, enhancements to the flexibility of control facilities (such as the previous VCR example) can actually increase demands upon the operator by virtue of the need for pre-planning of user direction. Happily, technology can assist further in easing the burden of interaction through support for man-machine dialogue.

The term 'dialogue' is used here to describe the active ingredients of interaction between human and machine. Included are all aspects of operator input at the machine interface and all manifestations of system-generated

---

[10]This is a fine example of what may be crudely termed 'automation'.

[11]See [232] for further discussion of such mapping in interaction.

output and responses. Excluded are physical components which make up the interface and the machine.

I would suggest that we should expect major improvements through technology to the quality of dialogue between humans and machines. Furthermore, the first step in this development is the transition from single-shot command interaction to intelligent dialogue. The available scope for such improvements may be more evident if we consider potential ingredients in man-machine dialogue, *viz.* :

- control flow ;

- display manipulation ;

- meta-dialogue.

Control flow. Primarily, the human-machine interface provides a means whereby users (operators) can affect the course or operation of the machine or underlying process. To this end, the interface affords opportunities for the input of control actions. Allied to such facilities, information must be provided which allows the operator to gauge the system state and the effects of his actions. These dialogue facilities are essentially tied up with *control flow*. Control flow dialogue includes all operator actions on the application and all status data, including results of operator actions. Clearly, such actions are the basis for intelligent control.

Display manipulation. A second desirable feature in man-machine dialogue is the possibility for operators to affect the manner in which system information is presented. This may affect either the mode of presentation or the position of presentation. In the first case, the user may be allowed to specify a preferred form of display. This might be dial outputs as opposed to digital readouts, twelve rather than twenty-four hour clock, etc. In the second case, operators may have discretion on the positioning of output information, e.g., whether default options appear on the bottom or top of the VDU screen. Notably, such interaction has no direct bearing on control of the underlying domain. Such display manipulation facilities are not present in all man-machine systems.

Meta-dialogue. Generally, the subject of meta-dialogue is control of the application. Such dialogue is 'meta' because it does not directly affect control flow. Rather, it covers support information or advice either directly on the subject of control or on relevant aspects of the application. Included within this category is any help facility, such as on-line manuals, event logs, data analysis facilities, etc.

Although a desirable feature of interaction, meta-dialogue is not evident in all man-machine systems. There is no such feature on the average washing machine, but video recorders and, often, compact disc players are privileged in this respect.[12] Thus, they support user interaction about how the system will behave at the control level.

In general terms, the combination of features in man-machine dialogue described above seems desirable for the joint performance of man and machine. Control flow dialogue may represent the *raison d'être* of the system interface, but the other aspects of interaction, especially meta-dialogue, are essential for effective operator performance on all but the simplest man-machine systems. Indeed, attempts to design explicitly for better dialogue and user support are apparent in recent user interface developments.[13]

Meta-dialogue is engaged when the system queries the operator in order to determine desired characteristics of control behaviour. This is a defining characteristic of intelligent dialogue. What makes such interaction 'intelligent' is, in part, its link to intelligent control, and the fact that by this combination (i.e., dialogue + control) the man-machine system, as a combination of operator and complex system, is better able to establish and accomplish system objectives. The other aspect of 'intelligence' is that the system overtly derives the information it needs from the operator by engaging in interaction which serves just this purpose. An example of intelligent dialogue from the VCR domain serves to make this clear.

4.3.1   VCR programming

The programming facility on video recorders involves a two-stage operation. In the first place, the user must enter the requisite items of information, i.e., day, channel number, recording start time and recording stop time. This is the 'program elicitation' phase of the operation. Subsequently, in a 'program execution' phase, the VCR handles the switching of control functions according to the values given by the user during program elicitation. Thereby, at the selected times the system is switched to record the appropriate channel and, thereafter, switched off.

This operation illustrates the combination of intelligent control (in the execution phase) and intelligent dialogue (in the elicitation phase). The hallmark of intelligent dialogue is the active (system-driven) interaction which serves to establish the precise nature of the operator's requirements. During program elicitation, the VCR follows a sequence of steps designed to secure

---

[12] Generally, these machines allow the operator to inspect the current program status, e.g., what tracks are selected for playing on the CD player, or which television channel is set for recording on the video recorder.

[13] Thus, User Interface Management Systems (UIMS) employ functional separation as a feature of the software architecture for interactive interface systems (see [99] and [142], for examples).

the data items it requires for timed television recording. The complexity of this phase, shown in Figure 7, may extend to 'dialogue excursions' which allow the operator to check previously submitted program information, or to correct prior entries.

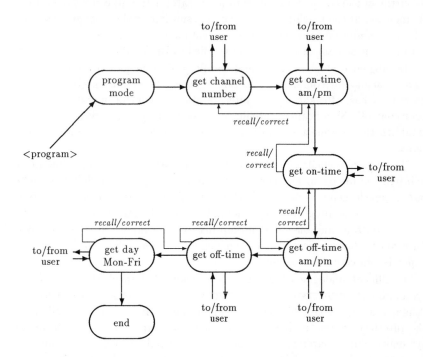

Figure 7: Program elicitation phase of VCR programming

5 Towards dialogue expertise

In the foregoing, we have recognised three generations of man-machine dialogue:

- single-shot command interaction;
- intelligent control;
- intelligent dialogue.

The first case, familiar to all, is characterised by a one-to-one correspondence between operator actions at a machine interface and responses at the level of control. Such actions have a single response.[14] This variety of dialogue takes its name from computer command language interaction, as found in traditional operating systems.

We have seen that intelligent control differs from single-shot interaction by virtue of the complex mapping from operator action to control operations. A single act at the machine interface may result in complex control behaviour. This is represented as an interpretative relation from the semantics of operator action to the semantics of control, as typified by the VCR index-search facility.

Intelligent dialogue is a natural corollary of intelligent control. Here, we have a facility for complex interaction between the system interface and the user, as a basis for subsequent interpretation as control operations (intelligent control). Significantly, intelligent dialogue is 'system driven'; seeking to establish the information required in order to perform precise control operations.

The program elicitation phase of VCR programming is a useful illustration of intelligent dialogue. Furthermore, this is an example of a 'difficult' aspect of human-machine interaction. Indeed, much ingenuity has gone into simplifying the task of video programming, leading to talking handsets, bar-code-reading remote controls, and on-screen prompting for data input. Here, we see scope for a major development in man-machine interaction—the need for 'dialogue expertise' in complex systems.

Intelligent dialogue addresses the problem of data elicitation from the system operator by systematically leading the user through an input routine. A major step beyond this requires enhancements in the means available to the interface system as it engages in such data input situations. Literally, systems require greater expertise for engaging in dialogue with their operators. The concept I have in mind—dialogue expertise—embodies the notion that such systems can *flexibly* engage their users in data elicitation. This entails, not merely a range of possible interaction modes (talking handsets, on-screen prompting, or whatever), but the use of meta-dialogue as a resource in support of the user. So, complex interactive systems should be capable of articulating the possible varying effects of alternative data inputs, in order to attain user-understanding for the context of elicitation.

Indeed, we can see a parallel between the evolution of dialogue in man-machine systems and developments in computer programming. Historically, assembly language provided a one-to-one mapping from programmer's instructions to machine instructions (as in single-shot command interaction). Subsequently, high-level languages such as Fortran and Pascal were evolved. These languages provide higher-level semantics, allowing interpretation from single-programmer instructions to many machine instructions (as with intel-

---

[14]The immediacy or mediacy of such responses is not important, only the mapping of actions from operator to control is the defining feature.

ligent control). The next development addressed the problem of supporting programmers in expressing what their program should do. Computer-Aided Software Engineering (CASE) tools assist in the task of program specification (as with intelligent dialogue).

As with the evolution of man-machine dialogue, computer programming has yet to realise the equivalent of dialogue expertise. This would entail software engineering systems that greatly shield programmers from detail in the final code, whilst producing programs that adequately satisfy requirements. In both cases, such progress can be realised only through the application of present and future technologies to handling the complexity of user-system interaction.

The aim of this chapter has been a better understanding of the intricacies of human-machine interaction, through an appreciation of how aspects of complexity affect this interaction, and how technology may help and hinder us in living with interactive systems. I have suggested that easier interaction will come through development of sophisticated dialogue facilities—beyond existing intelligent dialogue, toward dialogue expertise. There is indication of a research focus toward such facilities in current approaches to the design and analysis of dialogue (e.g., Alty and Ritchie, Chapter 2). I do not doubt that dialogue expertise will eventually be realised in commonplace systems. Furthermore, my money is on VCRs as the shape of things to come.

Acknowledgement

I am grateful to Simon Grant for comments on an earlier draft of this paper.

Chapter 2

An Algebraic Approach to Interface Specification Analysis

J. L. Alty and R. A. Ritchie

1 Introduction

Many authors have suggested that considerable benefits would arise from the use of formal specification techniques in interface design. Guttag and Horning [93] in an early often-quoted paper suggest the use of formal specification in the design process. They argue that more effort should be expended on getting the design *right* rather than on demonstrating the consistency of the resulting program (i.e., program verification). They view a system as a set of states and a set of mechanisms for changing between states and suggest that an *algebraic axiom* approach would be an effective way of analysing such systems. Their specification consists of operators, axioms and routines, where the operators are defined by an algebraic specification and are viewed as mathematical abstractions. Their goal was to develop a tool which could be used to derive, document and analyse an excellent interface design. A more recent formal approach has been proposed by Alexander [1, 2] based upon the specification language **Me Too** [103].

Since Guttag and Horning's paper was published, interest has developed in the design of User Interface Management Systems (UIMS), particularly those based on the Seeheim Model [176]. In such systems the dialogue component is separated from the presentation component and the application [69]. This enables decisions about presentation to be separated from consideration about dialogue. Such separation also makes dialogue specification easier. A number of UIMS have been proposed (for example SYNICS [71]; CONNECT [7]; ADDS [33]; [89, 101, 230]). These UIMS involve a number of different dialogue specification techniques: Transition Networks [112], Grammars [198, 210], and Event models [89].

HUMAN–COMPUTER INTERACTION
AND COMPLEX SYSTEMS: ISBN 0-12-742660-4

The Seeheim Model has recently been criticised for not properly taking account of semantic feedback and modifications have therefore been proposed [173]. More recent developments in UIMS have concentrated on the use of object-oriented programming techniques (GWUIMS [214]; CORAL [220]) where separation between the lexical, syntactic and semantic aspects of the communication are maintained. Specification however using object-oriented techniques is more problematic [172].

Although the UIMS approach offers significant prototyping advantages through the separation of dialogue from presentation, little has been reported on the advantages (or even use) of dialogue specification. Many authors claim it to be an advantage but do not give examples of actual analyses. Apart from a few trivial examples there appear to be no reported analyses of actual dialogues in real systems. The purpose of this chapter is to outline the GRADIENT approach to dialogue specification and to identify the advantages this realised.

2   The GRADIENT User Interface Management System

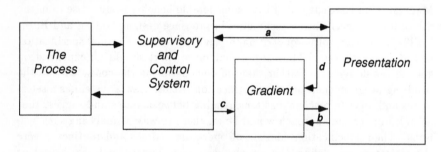

Figure 1 : A schematic representation of the GRADIENT system

GRADIENT (GRAphical DIalogue environmENT) is an ESPRIT-1 project which comprises the industrial partners Axion (Denmark) and Asea Brown Boveri (Federal Republic of Germany), and the Universities of Kassel (Federal Republic of Germany), Strathclyde (Scotland) and Leuven (Belgium). The main objective of the system is to provide knowledge-based support to operators of large dynamic systems and it has a heavy emphasis on graphical techniques and artificial intelligence. The system is intended to provide operators with advisory support when controlling complex systems both as a prosthesis and as a more passive advisor. At the heart of the GRADIENT system is a User Interface Management System and one of the key features in its conception was the ability to specify and analyse dialogues at the design stage. A schematic diagram of the GRADIENT system is shown in Figure 1.

The operator communicates directly (a) with the Supervisory and Control System (S&C System) which controls the process. Important S&C output is sent directly back to the presentation system. The GRADIENT system is therefore of an advisory nature and need never be used by operators. All operator input is read by the GRADIENT system (d) and it receives input about the current state of the process (c). Once invoked in an advisory context it talks directly with the operators (b). The system consists of a number of advisory modules and a dialogue system as shown in Figure 2.

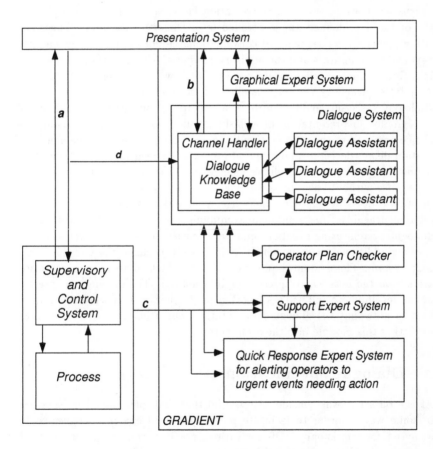

Figure 2: The functionality of the GRADIENT system

A number of advisory systems assist the operator when in difficulty. They operate under the following circumstances:

1. The Quick Response Expert System: when a serious error is detected in the system, the operator is warned of the condition and suggestions

are made for correction (or at least stabilisation).

2. The Support Expert System: this can be invoked by the operators to assist them in analysing and tracking down faults in the system, or to investigate possible scenarios.

3. The Operator Plan Checker: this system monitors the operator input and recognises unacceptable sequences or plans.

All these systems talk to the operator via the dialogue system which controls concurrent conversations. A conversation between an advisory module and the operator is defined and controlled by a Dialogue Assistant. These Assistants specify the sequence of conversational actions required and mediate between the operators and the advisory modules. Although they define what is to be communicated they do not specify how it is to be communicated. This latter aspect is the responsibility of the presentation system. Thus a Dialogue Assistant could require an alarm to be indicated—but this could be signalled in presentation as a flashing button or as a klaxon sound, the choice being up to the presentation designer. This presentation/dialogue separation delays decisions about actual presentation realisation to a later stage in the design process, and allows changes to be made in the light of actual experience without affecting the dialogue. It also simplifies the dialogue specification process by removing many irrelevant actions such as window moving or item dragging. Assistants can communicate with each other within the dialogue system using events to maintain consistency across conversations.

One additional development in GRADIENT is called the Graphical Expert System. This system is an expert system which advises the presentation system on the best way of presenting information. The system is at present under development and will not be discussed further here. It is however important to note that the dialogue/presentation separation approach is essential for fitting this module into the architecture.

3   Dialogue specification

At the outset it was considered essential that dialogues should be specified in some way in order to facilitate prototyping and enable dialogues to be analysed for consistency. Of the various possible representations outlined earlier we decided to use transition networks for the following reasons.

1. Since they are graphical in form they are amenable to analysis through graph theory.

2. They do capture one essential aspect of dialogue—that of sequence.

3. By using subnets the complexity can be contained.

4. Most of the event-driven aspects of the interaction will be handled in the presentation system.

The specification of a Dialogue Assistant consists of two separate specifications: an *environmental specification*, and a *procedural specification*. The procedural specification defines the procedural aspects of the Assistant (what is to be done next?) and the environmental specification the event-driven environment in which it operates (what can happen externally which affects this procedural specification or what events does the procedural specification cause in the external world?).

3.1 The environmental specification

During the execution of a Dialogue Assistant a number of actions can happen in relation to the external world. These could be:

1. a value of a variable could be changed by the application which might affect what should be done next in a conversation;

2. an event might take place in presentation (caused by the operator) which affects the dialogue;

3. something which the dialogue system has asked presentation to display might change;

4. something might change in presentation which needs to be communicated to the application or vice versa;

5. the Assistant itself may wish to cause a change in presentation or in an application variable.

These changes make up the environment in which the Assistant operates. The basic idea behind the environmental specification is shown in Figure 3.

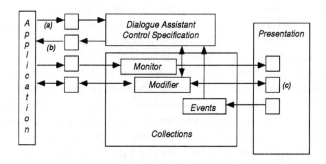

Figure 3: The environmental specification of an Assistant

The basic mechanism for communication is very similar to the active value concept in the object-oriented paradigm. An object (or slot) is defined as having interests in other objects so that when the object is updated it automatically sends a message to all interested objects. Thus, slots are used for communication between application and the dialogue system and dialogue system and presentation.

In the centre of Figure 3 the procedural specification (inside the shaded box) defines a dialogue sequence. This is a transition network which describes the actual conversation. During this sequence the Assistant will receive event interrupts because certain slots have been altered by the application through slot changes (a) or it will send changes to the application via the same mechanism (b). Alternatively the Assistant communicates with the presentation objects (c).

For communication with the presentation objects we require a more versatile specification than that with the application because we are dealing with communication with the outside world. One important concept is that of grouping. Objects in the outside world could be grouped together in some externally meaningful way (for example in a window or as a set of sounds). Although the Assistant does not care how the presentation realisation is achieved (for example visually or aurally) it needs to signal that a grouping is required. This grouping of objects is described by what we call *collections*.

In general, presentation objects within a collection can be connected to the *inside* world in a number of ways. They may continuously reflect the current state of some object in the inner world (for example a clock showing the time of day), they may generate events for the inner world (i.e., informing the Dialogue Assistant that an event has taken place), or they may be closely coupled with objects in the inner world so that a change in an inner world object is reflected in the outside world and vice versa (this allows input from presentation from an object which is currently being displayed). We call these three types of relationship—monitors, events and modifiers. Any collection is therefore a set of monitors, events and modifiers. A clock display would be an example of a monitor, a mouse-activated button an example of an event, and a valve icon which could be opened or closed and affects the internal state of the application would be an example of a modifier.

Let us consider the specification for a Dialogue Assistant which helps a user to save a file. The Dialogue Assistant is invoked by some user action (say activating a save action in a pull-down menu in another Assistant). The Assistant begins by instructing presentation to display a collection to the user which shows a current active filename which the user can alter, allows the user to complete the save or cancel the action and provides a message box for indicating the effect of the save (for example if the file exists the save will not take place and the user will be informed that a potential overwrite situation exists. The user can then decide to continue or cancel the action).

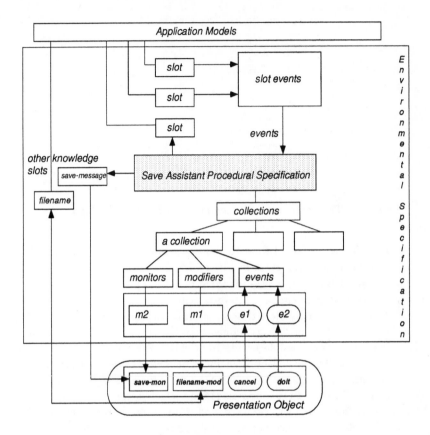

Figure 4: The environmental specification of a Save Assistant

Figure 4 show diagrammatically the environmental specification. One collection is shown and it consists of one monitor m2 (to display messages from a message slot), one modifier m1 (to display the filename and allow the user to alter it) and two events, E and F (to allow the user to save or cancel). The operator, therefore, can activate either of the two event buttons cancel and doit, has a continuous display of the save-message object (as save-mon, the message slot), and continuously sees the value of filename (as filename-mod, the box where the user enters the filename to be saved) which can be changed at any time. When a collection is opened the links are established between the relevant slots and the presentation objects. Once established the links are maintained automatically thereby avoiding placing a load on the dialogue system.

Whilst diagrams are useful, a specification is more powerful in language form. We have therefore defined a language to describe the environmental

```
ASSISTANT save-assistant ;;; start of environmental spec
  SLOTS    save-message VALUE CLASS string
           file-name    VALUE CLASS symbol
END ;;; of assistant slots

ROOT COLLECTION  Top-level-collection
  EVENTS cancel
         doit
  END ;;; of events
  MONITORS save-message-monitor SHOWS save-message
  END ;;; of monitors
  MODIFIERS file-name-modifier SHOWS AND ALTERS filename
  END ;;; of modifiers
END ;;; of root-collection
```

Figure 5: The environmental language specification for Figure 1

specification. To give a feel of what the language looks like, an environmental specification for Figure 4 is given in Figure 5.[1]

The Assistant is named **save-assistant** and has two knowledge slots— **save-message** and **file-name**. Interests will be defined in these slots so changes to these slots may alert the Assistant or the application. The Assistant drives a collection of objects named **top-level-collection** in presentation. It expects two possible events from this collection named **doit** and **cancel**. Additionally, the collection includes **save-message-monitor**, an object which continuously shows the value of the slot **save-message**, and another object in the collection, **file-name-modifier** which is connected to the slot **file-name**. If the value of **file-name-modifier** in presentation changes so does the slot object and vice versa. **save-message-monitor** therefore only shows the current value of **save-message**, but **file-name-modifier** can be used for input as well. How this collection is actually presented is a separate issue. It must merely have two event generators, a modifier and a monitor. A possible presentation realisation of the collection defined here could be that shown in Figure 6.

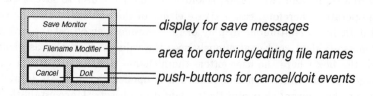

Figure 6: A possible presentation collection for Figure 5

---

[1] In Figure 5 comments are preceded by ;;;.

3.2 The procedural specification

The procedural specification is simply a set of named nodes connected by arcs on which the condition for selecting that arc is defined together with the action to be taken if selected. Figure 7 illustrates diagrammatically the procedural specification for saving the file which would operate in the environmental specification defined in Figure 5 on the previous page.

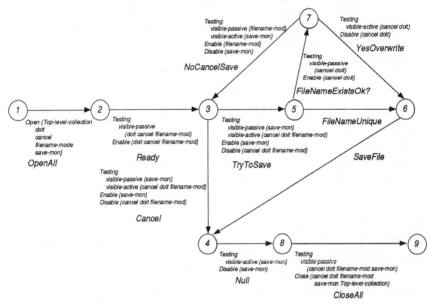

Figure 7: An example procedural specification (for saving a file)

All actions take place on the arcs. Arc actions are as follows:

1 → 2 Open `Top-level-collection` and all the objects contained within it. This causes the objects to be visible on-screen but passive, i.e., no interaction can take place with them.

2 → 3 Enable objects `doit`, `cancel`, and `filename-mod`, thus allowing interaction to take place. `filename-mod` will display the current value of filename. The Assistant now sits and waits for an event.

3 → 4 If event = `cancel` then disable `filename-mod`, `cancel` and `doit`, and enable `save-mon`.

3 → 5 If event = `doit` then disable `filename-mod`, `cancel` and `doit` and enable `save-mon`.

5 → 6 If `Filename` does not exist in directory then do nothing.

5 → 7 If `Filename` is in directory then set `Save-message` to "Overwrite filename ?". `save-mon` will ensure this is displayed. Enable `cancel` and `doit`.

7 → 3 If `event = cancel` then disable `save-mon` and enable `filename-mod`.

7 → 6 If `event = doit` then disable `cancel` and `doit`.

6 → 4 Set `Save-message` to "Saving Filename", again `save-mon` will ensure this is displayed. Replace value of `Filename` with entered filename. This will trigger the save automatically. Disable `cancel` and `doit`.

4 → 8 Disable `save-mon`.

9 → 9 Close all objects and `Top-level-collection` then exit.

This procedural specification will drive a collection in presentation which would look something like Figure 6.

We have also defined a language for describing these procedural specifications. Nodes in the procedural specification can be of two types: Event nodes and Condition nodes. At an Event node, the system waits for a set of possible external events. There will be an exit arc for each event. The first event to occur will cause a transition down its particular arc. At a Condition node one of a number of arcs is taken depending on the condition of a set of variables. A detailed discussion of the syntax is given by Mullin [165] and a full procedural specification of this Save Assistant is given in section 7.4.

The specifications are implemented in KEE (Knowledge Engineering Environment) on a Texas Instruments Explorer. A compiler automatically creates the KEE code from the specification language.

Having defined procedural and environment specifications, what can we do with them?

4 Specification analysis using algebraic techniques

4.1 The problem

In our control transition networks, the arcs contain all the important information in a label on the arc. The n nodes which make up the network are numbered $1, 2, 3, \ldots, n$ and are only used to define the topology of the network. The network therefore consists of a set of labels a_{pq} where p and q run from 1 to n. Thus, we can form a complete description of the network by using an $n \times n$ adjacency matrix A, which contains all the possible labels a_{pq}. Some of these labels will represent no connection in the network. We will call such a label the Zero Label and denote it by Φ.

What form can the labels take? The same network can be labelled in many ways, the labelling scheme being chosen to reflect some property of interest.

For example, if we were interested in the connectivity of the network, we might label all valid connections with a 1 and all non-connections with a 0 (i.e., $\Phi = 0$). If we wanted to find out the various paths through the network, we might label each arc with a unique letter $\{a\},\{b\},\{c\}, \ldots$, etc. with $\Phi = \{\}$. Figure 8 shows a simple network labelled in these two ways together with the adjacency matrices.

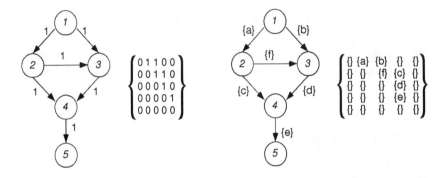

Figure 8: Different labellings of the same network

The above adjacency matrices carry information about adjacent nodes but what if we wished to know, say, whether there was connectivity between nodes 1 and 5, or the path label between 2 and 5? This can be seen by inspection in small networks but becomes difficult in complex networks. Since the adjacency matrix does contain all the information necessary to answer these questions, we need some way of operating on adjacency matrices to obtain answers of interest.

To do this, we need to know, given two sequential arcs, what is the combined effect of the two labels. In other words, how do we replace two sequential labelled arcs by a single arc with a composite label? Furthermore, we need to be able to do the same operation for two arcs in parallel. Figure 9 illustrates what we require.

For any particular labelling scheme, we can regard the labels on the arcs as words from some language. This language will have certain restrictions on what constitutes a valid word and there will be a complete set of all the possible words in the language. In addition, there will be rules (or operators) for combining words in series or in parallel. In particular, we can make some statements about these operators in order that they satisfy general rules we observe in dialogues:

1. sequential combinations will not usually be commutative;

2. parallel combinations will be commutative;

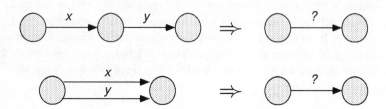

Figure 9: Arc label combinations

3. parallel combinations will be idempotent, that is, if we have two paths between the same nodes each with the same label then the result is a single path with that label;

4. both parallel and serial combinations will be associative.

4.2   Path algebras

An examination of the literature on graph theory reveals a technique called *path algebras* [43] which exactly fits the above requirements, and was noted to have potential for dialogue analysis [6].

A Path Algebra consists of a set of labels (our label language), two operators for combining words from the language in series or in parallel (called *dot*, denoted by ∘, and *join*, denoted by ∨, the two operations required in Figure 9) and two special labels - a Zero label (our Φ) and a Unit label (which we will call E). The whole form an algebra with the following properties:

join must be **commutative**, **idempotent** and **associative**, i.e.,

$$x \vee y = y \vee x$$
$$x \vee x = x$$
$$x \vee (y \vee z) = (x \vee y) \vee z$$

dot must be **associative**, and **distributive** over *join*, i.e.,

$$(x \circ y) \circ z = x \circ (y \circ z)$$
$$x \circ (y \vee z) = (x \circ y) \vee (x \circ z)$$

the Zero (Φ) and Unit (E) elements are defined by

$$x \circ \Phi = \Phi$$
$$x \vee \Phi = x$$
$$x \circ E = x$$

All these properties are what we require. These operators have a superset of properties defined in points 1 to 4 on the previous page.

As a simple example, if the arcs were labelled with distances between towns (the nodes), then if *dot* = **addition** and *join* = **minimum**, the algebra would yield path labels of minimum distance.

4.3 Application to whole networks

The above algebras enable one to simplify networks by progressively applying the *dot* and *join* operators across the network. For example, the network in Figure 10 can be reduced, as shown, to a single arc label which gives the effect of the whole network.

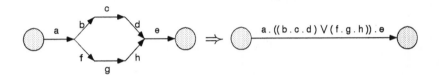

Figure 10: *Using path algebras to simplify labels*

Try putting distances for a,b,c, ... and using *dot* = **addition** and *join* = **minimum** to show that the final label is the minimum distance from the beginning to the end of the network.

However, it is tedious to reduce networks in this way. Carré [43] pointed out that if P is a path algebra and $M_n(P)$ is the set of all possible $n \times n$ matrices whose entries belong to P, then, given any two such matrices $X = [x_{ij}]$ and $Y = [y_{ij}]$, we can define two matrix operations *dot* and *join* resulting in a final matrix $Z = [z_{ij}]$ such that

$$X \ join \ Y \ = \ [z_{ij}] = [x_{ij} \vee y_{ij}]$$
$$X \ dot \ Y \ = \ [z_{ij}] = [\bigvee_{k=1}^{n} x_{ik} \circ y_{kj}]$$

i.e.,

$$[z_{3,5}] = \bigvee_{k=1}^{n} x_{3,k} \circ y_{k,5} = x_{3,1} \circ y_{1,5} \vee x_{3,2} \circ y_{2,5} \vee x_{3,3} \circ y_{3,5} \cdots$$

These operations are identical to those in conventional matrix algebra with + replaced by $\vee$ (*join*) and $\times$ replaced by $\circ$ (*dot*).

It then follows that for any path algebra P the set of matrices themselves $M_n(P)$ equipped with the definitions of *dot* and *join* above is itself a path algebra. The Zero Element in this algebra is an $n \times n$ matrix filled with Φ, and the Unit Element A^0 is an $n \times n$ matrix filled with Φ but with unit elements E on the main diagonal. Thus, we can *dot* and *join* adjacency matrices and this gives us a way of analysing effects on the whole network.

We can take the adjacency matrix A and *dot* or *join* it with itself. For example, $A \circ A = A^2$, and $A \circ A \circ A = A^3$, etc. What do these powers represent? A^2 represents two moves on the network, A^3 represents three moves on the network and A^n represents n moves on the network. We can also interpret multiple joins:

$$\vee_{k=m}^{n} A^k \text{ represents } m, m+1, m+2, \ldots, m+k \text{ moves on the network.}$$

Certain algebras (not all) exhibit a special property called closure. We form the *multiple join* by progressively joining ascending powers of A, starting at A^0

$$A^0 \vee A^1 \vee A^2 \vee \ldots A^k$$

At some power k, the resultant matrix stabilises and further joining of increasing powers does not alter the resultant matrix. This is called the Strong Closure Matrix A^*. There is also a Weak Closure Matrix $\hat{A}$ where the *multiple join* starts at A^1 rather than A^0. These matrices indicate important properties of the network as we shall see.

To analyse a network, we devise a label set (chosen to examine a property of interest), choose two operators *dot* and *join*, and work out what the Φ and E labels are from the formulae above. In order to make the analysis easier we have developed a path algebra analysis system called PATHOGEN [10]. The adjacency matrix is supplied and the designer defines the *dot* and *join* operator in LISP. The system will then work out powers, multiple joins and closure matrices. A library of standard *dot* and *join* routines which we have found useful is also supplied.

5   Three example algebras

5.1   A labelled path algebra (P6)

An algebra (called P6 by Carré) can be defined to find labelled paths through networks.

Let each arc initially be labelled with a set containing a single unique letter, e.g., $\{s\}$. Paths through the network will be labelled with concatenations of these letters, e.g., $\{sab\}$. Because there can be alternative paths between two nodes in a network the set may contain more than one member e.g.,$\{abc, def\}$. Thus a general path label will be a set of label concatenations.

The *dot* operation is defined as concatenation, e.g.,

$$\{a\} \circ \{b\} = \{ab\}$$
$$\{a,c\} \circ \{d,ef\} = \{ad, aef, cd, cef\}$$

The *join* operation is defined as set inclusion, e.g.,

$$\{a, bc, d\} \vee \{d, er\} = \{a, bc, d, er\}$$

The Zero element is the empty set ($\{\}$ or $\emptyset$) and the Unit element is the empty letter Λ. (i.e., $a \circ \Lambda = a$)

This algebra will find all paths through the network. However it will not exhibit closure if there are any loops because these can obviously concatenate for ever, always producing different longer results.

5.2 A simple path algebra (P7)

A simple path is one which goes through any arc only once. These can be found by a path algebra called P7 by Carré. The definition is identical to the one above in 5.1 with the addition that in the *dot* operation only one copy of a letter is allowed. If a *dot* operation causes a label with a repeat letter then the label is rejected. So $\{a\} \circ \{a\} = \emptyset$ and $\{ab, c, d\} \circ \{a, cf\} = \{abcf, ca, da, dcf\}$.

5.3 An elementary path algebra (P8)

An elementary path is defined as one which goes through any node only once. These can easily be found by an 'elementary' path algebra (P8 of Carré). The algebra is identical to the definition in 5.1 with an added restriction on the *join* operation. To understand this restriction we need to introduce the concept of an abbreviation. A label y is an abbreviation of a word w if y can be formed by removing any number of letters (including all of them) from w. Clearly if all letters are removed we get the empty letter Λ. Thus ab is an abbreviation of $asertb$, aab, $pqrafgb$ and $avfbnmy$.

join is therefore defined as set inclusion with the added restriction that the resultant set must not contain any labels whose abbreviations are also present, e.g., $\{a, bc, gh\} \vee \{g, jv, h\} = \{a, bc, g, jv, h\}$.

Figure 11 illustrates resultant closure matrices derived from applying these algebras to a network. The diagonal elements identify the loops in the network. A column of Zero Elements represents an input node, i.e., a node with no entrances, and a row of Zero Elements an output node, i.e., a node with no exits.

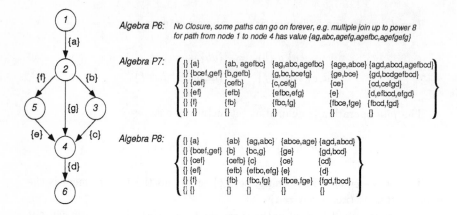

Algebra P6: No Closure, some paths can go on forever, e.g. multiple join up to power 8 for path from node 1 to node 4 has value {ag,abc,agefg,agefbc,agefgefg}

Algebra P7:

$$\begin{pmatrix} \{\} \{a\} & \{ab, agefbc\} & \{ag,abc,agefbc\} & \{age,abce\} & \{agd,abcd,agefbcd\} \\ \{\} \{bcef,gef\} & \{b,gefb\} & \{g,bc,bcefg\} & \{ge,bce\} & \{gd,bcdgefbcd\} \\ \{\} \{cef\} & \{cefb\} & \{c,cefg\} & \{ce\} & \{cd,cefgd\} \\ \{\} \{ef\} & \{efb\} & \{efbc,efg\} & \{e\} & \{d,efbcd,efgd\} \\ \{\} \{f\} & \{fb\} & \{fbc,fg\} & \{fbce,fge\} & \{fbcd,fgd\} \\ \{\} \{\} & \{\} & \{\} & \{\} & \{\} \end{pmatrix}$$

Algebra P8:

$$\begin{pmatrix} \{\} \{a\} & \{ab\} & \{ag,abc\} & \{abce,age\} & \{agd,abcd\} \\ \{\} \{bcef,gef\} & \{b\} & \{bc,g\} & \{ge\} & \{gd,bcd\} \\ \{\} \{cef\} & \{cefb\} & \{c\} & \{ce\} & \{cd\} \\ \{\} \{ef\} & \{efb\} & \{efbc,efg\} & \{e\} & \{d\} \\ \{\} \{f\} & \{fb\} & \{fbc,fg\} & \{fbce,fge\} & \{fgd,fbcd\} \\ \{\} \{\} & \{\} & \{\} & \{\} & \{\} \end{pmatrix}$$

Figure 11 : Closure matrices for P6, P7 and P8

6   Other matrix operations (Algebraic Circuits)

As well as path algebra operations it is useful to be able to carry out other operations on the adjacency matrix (and its powers). Such operations might be inversion, transposition or operating on each element with a function. These operations (with the algebraic operations) may also be combined in various way to form what we have defined as an *Algebraic Circuit*. Figure 12 illustrates the general idea.

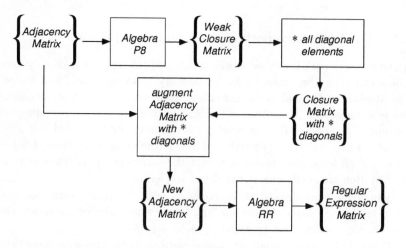

Figure 12: The Algebraic Circuit concept

This circuit provides regular expressions from an adjacency matrix. The original matrix is analysed by P8 to give simple paths. This will show any loops on the diagonals. These loops are starred using a function and are added using another function to the original matrix. This is then further analysed using the RR algebra. This will reduce each path to a regular expression describing the loops along the path. This provides us with a concise representation of the optional elements of an iterative dialogue.

Algebraic circuits enable complex problems to be approached relatively easily, where it is difficult (or impossible) to define a single algebra approach to solve the problem. They are also more understandable because the problem is decomposed into a series of simpler steps.

7 Use of algebras in dialogue analysis

Some of the algebras mentioned above have immediate applications. The computation of simple and elementary paths, for example, can be of considerable value. It is important to note that the designer can choose his or her own label set and operators thus providing a really flexible tool.

7.1 Regular expression reduction analysis

Regular algebras are particularly useful since they can show possible interface effects directly. For example we can use actual English words as arc labels and examine dialogue sequences. Consider the dialogue shown in Figure 13.

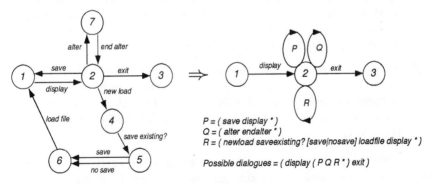

$P = (save\ display \ ^*)$
$Q = (alter\ endalter \ ^*)$
$R = (newload\ saveexisting?\ [save|nosave]\ loadfile\ display \ ^*)$

Possible dialogues $= (display\ (P\ Q\ R \ ^*)\ exit)$

Figure 13: A data modification dialogue

In this dialogue a user is displaying a data table, and can alter any elements or can load in a new set of data. The current table can be saved at any time. If a new set of data is loaded the option of saving the current data is offered. There is only one entry point (node 1) and exit point (node 3). Thus the only long-term interesting transformation is the label on arc 1 to 3.

By inspection the dialogue has three loops P Q and R and the possible dialogues are { display (P Q R *) exit }. Expanding P Q and R we get

{display((save display*)(newload saveexisting? [nosave|save] loadfile display*)(alter endalter*)*)exit}

where * means zero or more times. The three starred parenthetically grouped items can appear in any order or can be individually omitted.

A first sight this appears reasonable. However we notice that one possible path is { display (alter endalter *) exit } which would clearly lose altered data and indicates we should add a saveexisting? option on the exit path.

Regular expressions are very useful because they partition the optional sequences in a dialogue specification, and display them in a clear, concise manner.

7.2   Other useful analyses

The arcs of interest and the desired labelling will, of course depend upon the application. In the above example there was only one entry and exit arc. This is quite common for Dialogue Assistants and the key result from such a path algebra analysis is usually the label on the entry-exit arc. There can be two different desired results on such an arc:

1. we require the overall effect of the dialogue to be null (i.e., unit). Often we want Assistants to have no overall effect (i.e., leave things as they found them). For example we might wish to check that all collections opened are closed properly at the conclusion of the dialogue. We might want to check that all enabled events are properly disabled at dialogue conclusion. Such factors are not always easy to check in a complex Assistant with many possible paths.

2. we require the overall effect to have some definite value. We may require the Assistant to have a precise effect. For example, in the previous save example we wish the overall effect to be either null or save. In these cases the entry-exit arc label should have a label which specifies only this effect.

The determination of entry-exit arc values in single entry-exit dialogues is thus an important focus for the analysis. It might be thought that all the other arc labels in single entry-exit Dialogue Assistants would be of no interest. However this is not the case. The arc values for loops are particularly interesting (usually one would require them to be null or single-valued). Other arc values show what might happen if there were a system breakdown during execution of the Assistant and their values could identify restart options.

Furthermore, as a general rule, we usually do not allow any multivalued arc labels between nodes (apart from the entry-exit arc) since these mean that the same overall transition can have different effects and thus confuse the user.

Finally we can examine particular arc values to check that a desired situation has been reached at a particular node. In dialogues with a single entry point the paths of interest will typically be those from the entry node to other nodes.

7.3 Analysing context-dependent specifications

When specifying interfaces, it is desirable for the designer to be able to specify, in some sense, requirements or resources that must be present in order for some operation to be performed, or for some option to be offered to the user. Such resources might be windows on the screen or output available for display. Operations may be being offered in some context-dependent manner, such as an *Open File* option on a menu only being offered when no file is currently open. Even in only moderately complex systems with simple functionality the relationships between requirements and operations can quickly become complex and prone to errors of specification.

Unfortunately, the formal definition of path algebras, and previous examples, give no obvious means of communicating information about context-dependent issues between arcs. Indeed the whole point of path algebra analyses, and the foundation upon which the technique is built, is the idea that individual arc pairs are examined in isolation, with no positional knowledge of their location in the network. This is perhaps one of the most difficult ideas to convey to designers unfamiliar with the technique.

7.4 Labels with a notion of state can solve this problem

The solution is to equip each label with a notion of its state, and examine this state for the desired context-sensitive properties. Typically the label will be a set of label elements, each having four parts: *state, tests, changes* and *actions.*

State is the ambient *state of the world* place-holder for this arc,

Tests is the (possibly empty) set of tests that should be applied to *state* in order to determine whether this is a valid arc or not. This is where the context-sensitive constraints for the arc are put. It may be thought of as the set of restrictions which must be satisfied for this arc to exist.

Changes is the (possibly empty) set of alterations that will be made to *state* if this arc is used. This is where requirements are provided. It may be thought of as a point of resolution for some set of restrictions.

Actions is the list of procedures or functions being applied on this arc, i.e., this is the user-opaque internal functionality of the dialogue, e.g., the generation of a list of filenames to be displayed. The other parts comprise the user-visible interaction points and their expected appearances and behaviours.

As an example we will show the analysis of a Dialogue Assistant using this context-dependent algebra. All real problems tend to be too big to conveniently describe in a book chapter such as this (i.e., the closure matrices are simply too large to print!). We will therefore take a rather simple problem to exemplify the approach.

The Assistant is a Save Assistant (mentioned earlier in section 3) which is called by users when they wish to save sets of data within a statistics application. The user provides a name and asks the save to proceed. The system then checks if a similarly named file of data exists. If it does not the save is carried out and the Assistant terminates. If it does exist the user is warned and can either proceed or cancel the operation, provide a new name and try again (or quit). The actual GRADIENT specification looks like this:

```
; Assistant           : save-assistant
; Written by          : John Mullin
; Part of system      : STATISTICS
; Described in document : P857-WP4-UST-032, P857-WP4-UST-033
; Parameters          : -
; Returns             : -
; Description         : allows the user to save the current set of data pairs

:assistant        save-assistant
:graphics         save-assistant

:slots
        save-message
                :valueclass    string
        file-name
                :valueclass    symbol
:end

:root-collection
    top-level-collection
                :events        cancel
                               doit
                :end
                :monitors      save-message-monitor
                               :shows              save-message
                :end
                :modifiers     file-name-modifier
                               :shows-and-alters   file-name
                :end
:end

:nodes
    :condition   start
                 :next    open-sub-images
                 :doing   (set-value
                          file-name
                          (get-value
```

```
                         (current-file of application-read-only-slots)))
                      (open (collection top-level-collection))
               :end
    :end

    :condition  open-sub-images
                :next    wait-for-event
                :doing   (open (event doit of top-level-collection))
                         (open (event cancel of top-level-collection))
                         (open (modifier
                                 file-name-modifier of top-level-collection))
                :end
    :end

    :event      wait-for-event
                :on      (event cancel of top-level-collection)
                :next    close-events
                :doing   (close (modifier
                                 file-name-modifier of top-level-collection))
                :end

                :on      (event doit of top-level-collection)
                :next    test-file-name
                :doing   (close (modifier
                                 file-name-modifier of top-level-collection))
                         (open (monitor
                                 save-message-monitor of top-level-collection))
                :end
    :end

    :condition  test-file-name
                :if      (member (get-value file-name)
                                 (get-value
                                   (all-files of application-read-only-slots)))
                :next    confirm-overwrite
                :doing   (set-value
                            save-message
                            (format nil "Overwrite ~A" (get-value file-name)))
                :end
                :next    save-file
    :end

    :event      confirm-overwrite
                :on      (event cancel of top-level-collection)
                :next    wait-for-event
                :doing   (close (monitor
                                   save-message-monitor of top-level-collection))
                         (open (modifier
                                 file-name-modifier of top-level-collection))
                :end
                :on      (event doit of top-level-collection)
                :next    save-file
    :end

    :condition  save-file
                :next    close-events
                :doing   (set-value
                            save-message
                            (format nil "Saving ~A" (get-value file-name)))
                         (set-value
                            (file-to-save of application-read-write-slots)
```

```
                        (get-value file-name))
                        (sleep 2)        ;;; nice delay
                        (close (monitor
                                save-message-monitor of top-level-collection))
                   :end
        :end

        :condition  close-events
                    :next     close-top-level-collection
                    :doing    (close (event doit of top-level-collection))
                              (close (event cancel of top-level-collection))
                    :end
        :end

        :condition  close-top-level-collection
                    :next     end
                    :doing    (close (collection top-level-collection))
                    :end
        :end
:end
:end
```

From this specification we generate (automatically) a labelled network
ready for a context-sensitive algebra analysis. Our analysis is interested in the
state (invisible, visible-passive or visible-active) of the objects in presentation
which the user sees. We are concerned lest we have inadvertently left open
objects or closed unopened objects, or expect input from disabled objects.
The possible states and the operations causing transition between them are
shown in Figure 14.

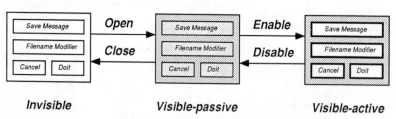

Figure 14: The possible states for a screen object

The resulting closure matrix is too large to display in full here. Its shape
is shown in Figure 15.

We shall examine some elements in detail.

This Assistant should have no net effect (so far as the resulting screen
appearance is concerned), so element $a_{1,9}$, abbreviated as $\{h\}$, should result
in no visible output. This is shown in Figure 16.

Each on-screen object is annotated with a list showing us what happened
to it in sequence (note that the sequence in the changes field is read right to
left, i.e., new entries are added to the tail of the list). There are four paths

$$\begin{pmatrix} \Phi & \{a\} & \{b\} & \{c\} & \{d\} & \{e\} & \{f\} & \{g\} & \{h\} \\ \Phi & \Phi & \{i\} & \{j\} & \{k\} & \{l\} & \{m\} & \{n\} & \{o\} \\ \Phi & \Phi & \{p\} & \{q\} & \{r\} & \{s\} & \{t\} & \{u\} & \{v\} \\ \Phi & \Phi & \Phi & \Phi & \Phi & \Phi & \Phi & \{w\} & \{x\} \\ \Phi & \Phi & \{y\} & \{z\} & \{A\} & \{B\} & \{C\} & \{D\} & \{E\} \\ \Phi & \Phi & \Phi & \{F\} & \Phi & \Phi & \Phi & \{G\} & \{H\} \\ \Phi & \Phi & \{I\} & \{J\} & \{K\} & \{L\} & \{M\} & \{N\} & \{O\} \\ \Phi & \Phi & \Phi & \Phi & \Phi & \Phi & \Phi & \Phi & \{P\} \\ \Phi & \Phi & \Phi & \Phi & \Phi & \Phi & \Phi & \Phi & \Phi \end{pmatrix}$$

Figure 15: The Save Assistant weak closure matrix

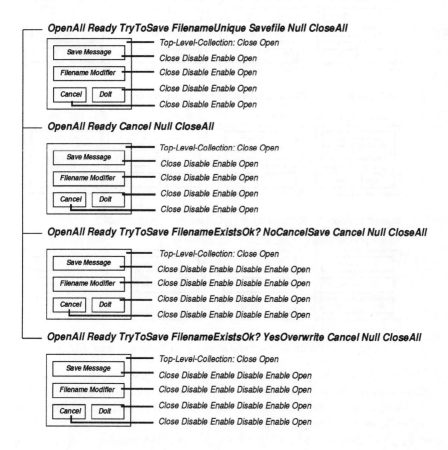

Figure 16: The four possible paths from node 1 to node 9

through the Assistant. All resulting states are clean, that is, all objects are always opened, disabled and enabled as appropriate and eventually closed. The actions field for each path shows us the actual sequence traversed. Each one is clearly correct.

Loops in the network can be found in the diagonal elements of the closure matrix. Since this algebra only finds simple paths (go through an arc once) loops will not show directly in the analysis. It is important therefore that loops are single valued (so looping many times has no effect). The only loop is $3 \rightarrow 5 \rightarrow 7$ shown by diagonal elements $a_{3,3}$, $a_{5,5}$ and $a_{7,7}$. These have the values shown in Figure 17.

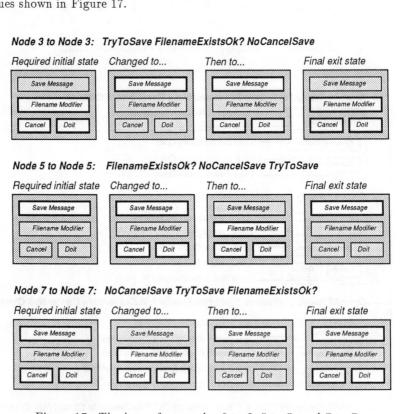

Figure 17: The loops from nodes 3 to 3, 5 to 5, and 7 to 7

In each case the overall effect is that the exit point of the loop has the same appearance and state as the entry point, so the design is acceptable.

Finally, we should examine the states reached at each node where interaction takes place between the user and the display objects (i.e., the values of $a_{1,3}$, $a_{1,5}$ and $a_{1,7}$). Firstly, we do not want the number of objects open or closed to depend upon the path to the node (this would confuse the user).

Secondly, we expect them to have the specific desired values. Their values are shown in Figure 18.

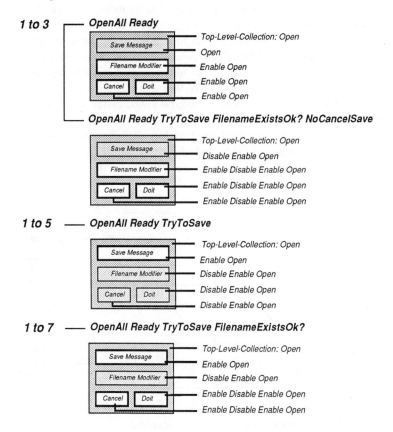

Figure 18 : The paths from node 1 to nodes 3, 5, and 7

Only $a_{1,3}$ has two alternative paths. However, it can be seen that the screen appearances and object states are the same.

Top-level-collection should always be open since it contains all the objects. At node 3, the user should be able to cancel, modify the filename (mod) or carry out the save (doit). A message here (mon) is not appropriate. At node 5, we must be able to display the overwrite message, hence mon should be open, but the user is not allowed to modify the name (only accept or reject). At node 7, the user can either cancel the operation or continue with the save. Thus, the network is acceptable.

There are many other analyses which could be carried out. Hopefully, this single example illustrates the power of the technique.

8   Other uses of the specification

The existence of the specification has proved to be most useful in other ways. For example, once an Assistant has been defined, the environmental specification may allow the dialogue designer to quickly design some simple presentation representations and try them out. A *minimal presentation* tool takes each definition in the specification, and offers a set of suitable representations to the designer from a standard set. Within a few minutes, a complete set of images can be created. Then the procedural specification is stepped through showing the actual operation of the Assistant. Of course, the images may not be the desired ones for the final product but will show the complete functionality of the interface, quickly and effectively, and can save much wasted design time in producing the more expensive presentation images. The tools form a complete set as shown in Figure 19.

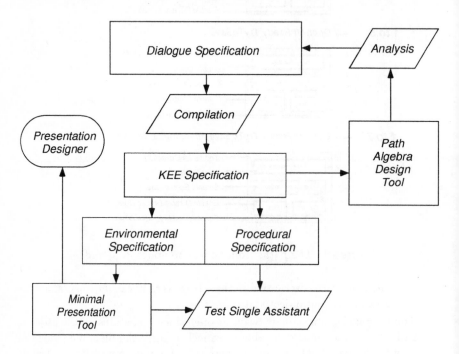

Figure 19: The overall tool concept in GRADIENT

The initial dialogue specification in the specification language is automatically converted into a KEE (Knowledge Engineering Environment) representation comprising the environmental and procedural specifications. The minimal presentation tool offers the designer possible pictures from the KEE picture library which match the specification. The designer then decides where these pictures should be placed on the screen. These are then stored for later use or modification. The procedural specification can then be run using the stored pictures to provide realistic prototype output for the Assistant. Alternatively, the minimal presentation tool can be used to give the presentation designer an overall view of what is required. The procedural specification can be transformed into a representation suitable for the path algebra tool PATHOGEN. Analyses can then take place to check properties of interest. This may result in changes to the specification. Note that the presentation designer has complete freedom within the limitation of the environment specification.

9 Conclusions

Many authors talk about dialogue specification but very little has actually been done to show the power of such a representation. Hopefully, these illustrations of the power of an algebraic approach will give some insight into what can be done.[2]

Acknowledgements

The authors acknowledge support from the CEC for ESPRIT project #857 (GRADIENT), and from the Science Research Council for research grant #GR/D 42368 which enabled the PATHOGEN system to be developed. Contributions from other members of the GRADIENT team are also acknowledged. In particular, John Mullin, who designed the dialogue specification technique used herein and implemented the dialogue specification tool, and Abdi Shahidi, who designed and implemented the 'channel handler' software.

---

[2]The PATHOGEN system runs on any Common LISP implementation vehicle, from PCs and Macintoshes to Cray X-MPs. Copies are available from the Scottish HCI Centre, George House, 36 N. Hanover St., Glasgow, UK.

Chapter 3

The Temporal Dimension of Man-Machine Interaction

F. Decortis, V. de Keyser,
P. C. Cacciabue and G. Volta

1   Introduction

1.1   Time in operator reasoning

A crucial aspect of man-machine interaction is its dynamicity, i.e., the tuning between the operator and the system. Complex systems are dynamic; they comprise numerous interacting variables that evolve in time [65, 224, 158, 251]. New information continuously changes the nature of the problem to be solved. Thus, in order to take decisions [228] a process plant operator needs to be able to reason about temporal information, to reason about changes, to predict the effects of his actions and of the changes he observes, to continuously make reference to what has happened, is happening and might possibly happen, to co-ordinate on the temporal axis the actions of several persons. From what can be observed in real situations, the cognitive processes of a plant operator aim at answering questions such as:

- One hour ago there was a rapid drop of flow in steam-generator-1, is this related to the pump-break?

- For five minutes the temperature of the steam-generator has been increasing very quickly, what does this mean?

- How does the operator choose the right moment to begin opening the turbine valves, taking into account the operational time and other constraints related to parallel events (elapsed and remaining time for a set of events)?

- How does the operator estimate the point at which to open the valve?

HUMAN–COMPUTER INTERACTION
AND COMPLEX SYSTEMS: ISBN 0-12-742660-4

- The operator has three hours to complete five tasks. He expects the first task to take 30 minutes instead of which it takes 1 hour. How does he recover the time lost in successive tasks?

- The operator cannot exceed an interval of 15 minutes between the end of one event and the beginning of the next. How does he estimate this time interval?

These few examples show that the present, past and future are involved in operator's reasoning.

1.2   Time and the role of the operator

The function of time in operator reasoning has been a matter of growing interest over the past few years. This correlates with the evolution of industrial technology and the corresponding evolution of the operator's role [72, 157]. Anticipation mechanisms and forecasting disturbances, linked with a good knowledge of the complex system's dynamicity, quickly emerged as essential aspects of the operator's reliability [110, 111, 59, 53]. These authors have studied temporal knowledge, acquired by practical experience in semi-automated plants, where manual control was still both possible and even necessary in case of disturbances.

Current automation of complex continuous processes integrates parts of the system which were previously isolated [47]. In this way, the physical system becomes more steady and reliable [217]. Most of the time, computers control the system and actions are directly controlled either by programmable automata in normal situations, or by specialised working teams who surround the production and intervene in case of emergency [58]. The operator rarely has access to all of the information coming from the process and loses direct control of the system [50]. Thereby, his operational knowledge, which represents the foundation for human reliability, is reduced. Implications of this loss of control on the safety of complex systems have been considered by Sheridan and Hennessy [209], Rasmussen [187] and by Moray [162].

Sometimes, a new operator role as system 'integrator' may compensate for the loss of reliability [58]. The specialised working teams that stand as satellites around the process grow in number with the increase in automation: engineers, maintenance staff, control specialists, computer scientists. All these persons interact with each other and with the control room operator. The latter has a central position in this cooperative network whereby he distributes information, plans the action and negotiates the goals of several people. He no longer directly controls the process but the global complex system and has to resolve conflicts between individuals and goals. His problem space and anticipation capabilities move towards a structural regulation [75].

Apparently, the control room operator attends less than before to anticipating incidents but rather aims for their quick reduction. Reducing system down-time, finding the appropriate person at the right moment, prediagnosing the incident and gathering the necessary information as required, become the main preoccupation.

Note, however, that this new tendency does not yet affect all sectors of continuous processes. Where the technological risk is high and public awareness is very sensitive to this risk, there is resistance to placing total trust in the computer for control of the process. Moreover, sectors such as fertiliser production, which have very unstable products, are resistant to complete automation because of the need for stable parameters. In other sectors, the continuous aspect of processes is illusive: they are in fact sequential processes in which the starting of sequences remains a manual operation. Such examples show the dangers in neglecting operator knowledge of the system dynamicity. A reasonable approach lies in trying to maintain this knowledge, whilst coupling it with a broader perspective on the system in terms of capacity, constraints, circulating flows of information, energy and material.

In this context of technological and organisational development, different surveys have emphasised the obstacles faced by the operator in controlling the dynamics of a complex system that both encompasses and extends beyond the production process [51, 56, 61, 225]. Furthermore, intelligent decision aids [105] have not yet reached the level of assisting the operator in coping with the system dynamicity. For support of such decisions by real aids rather than by prostheses [194], decision-support systems have to sustain the operator's reasoning and to follow his own logic, in particular his temporal reasoning and reasoning about changes in the domain.

1.3   Time in cognitive psychology and artificial intelligence

The function of time in reasoning processes has become a growing interest in cognitive psychology. Mechanisms of estimation of duration *per se* have been experimentally analysed [78, 156, 150]. Recent publications on artificial intelligence (AI) [4, 60, 213] have addressed the issue of reasoning about change. Recent work in qualitative reasoning has focussed on predicting the dynamic behaviour of continuous physical systems (i.e., predicting fluid flow, pressure stability, etc.) [236].

Planning models [148] which take time into account, have been proposed wherein the time required for each action and the relations of simultaneity among actions are given as input. The actions' sequence of the planning task are produced as output. Nevertheless, some critical features of the time experience are still being neglected. These include the interaction between subjective estimation of the time required by the various transitions within the system, and the choice of the time at which the intervention on the system has to be made.

Although the problem of time has been addressed in the context of scientific disciplines related to psychology, such as psychophysics, ontogenetics and psycholinguistics [143, 178], little is presently known about how man handles complex temporal situations. Little effort has so far been devoted to investigating how adults conceive time and how they react to it, especially in those situations where time is a central, critical, characteristic of the system being faced.

1.4   Two perspectives for the temporal dimension

The temporal dimension can be considered from two perspectives:

> **Time as an explicit variable.** The temporal variable is used and estimated for both reasoning and acting. Reasoning is dependent upon time estimation, i.e., how long an event takes or has taken. In addition, reasoning may be based on the order of events, e.g., in which sequence a set of events must occur. Acting is also based on time estimation, e.g., judging the right moment to take action.

> **Time as an implicit variable.** The dynamic aspect of the system in evolution is the organisational principle of the reasoning (a fact which is true now will or will not still be true at time $t + \delta t$). New events continuously change the nature of the problem to be solved. Reasoning is made about such change.

The distinction between these two perspectives is important since they correspond to the approach adopted by cognitive psychology and AI, respectively. Cognitive psychology privileges the estimation of duration *per se* as a dimension of the cognitive processes. In contrast, AI considers the duration as implicit in the causal relationships or in the consideration of changes as different states of the world. The two ways of considering the temporal dimension should fit with different needs and different problems related to planning and scheduling or diagnosis. For example, in planning tasks, it is easy to find problems of estimation of duration as they are linked to the action. Action implies generally precise estimation of times (when to act versus how to act). Diagnosis, on the other hand, involves prediction and evaluation of changes.

2   An integrated model

In this chapter we give particular attention to the most salient aspects of time in relation to man-machine interaction domains, field studies, cognitive psychology and AI. This leads us to analyse the theoretical modelling of the temporal dimension in human reasoning. Its relevance in the simulation of plant operators' cognitive activities is also discussed. We will concentrate on four aspects:

- Description of what operators do in a complex dynamic environment.
- Identification of mechanisms and processes by which operators apprehend the dynamicity of the complex system, i.e., how operators reason on the dynamic aspects of complex environment.
- Analysis of the temporal dimension of human error.
- Modelling of temporal reasoning.

2.1 Temporal structures in man-machine interaction

The consideration of time within an analysis of man-machine interaction in a complex environment has been the object of previous empirical studies [61, 56]. These studies are rich in data concerning how operators handle temporal reasoning, how temporal errors can be observed and factors which might facilitate temporal comprehension. These data are collected using different techniques:

- observations of operator behaviour;
- spontaneous and elicited verbalisations (direct interrogation of the operator on his goals and intentions, by an external observer);
- elicitation of experts and novices.

Three temporal structures are superimposed in man-machine interactions [63]. Each is characterised by its own scale and boundaries. The first concerns the temporal characteristics of the physical system being controlled, the second is that involving the entire control room team, and the third is the operator's time structure in relation to the complex system and the team. The integration of these temporal structures guarantees the operator's tuning to the complex system.

Events and actions related to man-machine interactions are organised in a temporal structure, and can be considered with respect to the system, the crew and satellite teams, and to the operator.

2.1.1 The physical system

So far as the physical system is concerned, the most important elements are:

- phases, sequences which govern the state transformation of a system component;
- machines, with their movement, their interactions and their reliability;
- mechanical accidents, which can affect the machines, the product, the work's organisation, and can propagate into the entire structure.

2.1.2   The team

For control room teamwork, including the satellite teams, the relevant elements are:

- actions which intersect, and which are concatenated with each other without directly affecting the process;
- actions on the process induced by the main operator acting as a relay;
- actions performed directly on the system.

2.1.3   The operator

The main operator can act directly on the process. He can also act as an integrator, linking system events with team's actions. He must then plan and co-ordinate the team actions in order to make them to take the proper action at the right moment. He carries out different activities:

- **Temporal planning:** He makes plans according to certain goals, taking into account the duration, order and simultaneity of events and actions, and future expected states on the basis of present and past ones.

- **Temporal evaluation:** He continuously estimates duration of events, actions, and their order on the temporal axis, using their temporal attributes.

- **Dynamic diagnosis:** He diagnoses possible disturbances by dynamically revising his interpretation according to the new information that continually arrives and to the temporal information brought by symptoms.

- **Plan execution and integration:** On the basis of his temporal evaluation and of his temporal planning, the operator acts in real time directly or indirectly on the state of the system. He integrates the different events' evolution of the physical system, corrects the course of events and, moreover, anticipates event evolution according to his expectations. Such anticipation allows him to have a direct influence on the future when the progressive evolution of the future (the one which is directly after his 'psychological present') does not fit his expectation.

- **Co-ordination:** The operator co-ordinates the activity of several people by conveying, in real time, information between operators and between the team and the system. This co-ordination induces him to get the system events and the team's actions to coincide.

2.2 Attributes of the structure

2.2.1 Structure links

In analysing these temporal structures it is useful to relate events and actions. Events and actions can occur both independently, organised in a pattern (the pattern being either rigid or loose), in a sequence (before, after) whose boundaries are (sharply or loosely) fixed, and simultaneously.

These possible relationships between events and actions are applicable to their initial occurrence as well as to their terminal instant. For example, events and actions can initiate simultaneously and terminate sequentially. As far as the event's intrinsic duration is concerned, this can be either irrelevant or bounded within loose or rigid boundaries.

More particularly, the intrinsic time duration of a physical system is linked to response times such as the time required for a phase transformation, the attainment of the operational temperature of a component, the tank's capacity and refilling times, etc. These constitute 'histories' of the system which have significance for the operator.

In the physical system, as well as in the teams, it is possible to identify operations which are implemented independently of each other. The sequence of these actions is irrelevant. Some patterns allow structural flexibility, in that the boundaries and/or the sequences are loose, sequence inversions are allowed, and actions can be omitted. Other patterns do not allow structural flexibility but do allow loose boundaries for durations. For example, actions must take place in a fixed order, yet their durations need not be fixed. For certain operations, the time duration can vary within given boundaries. This is the case for the phase transformation of a product which take place under certain constraints. An unexpected interference can slightly modify the action's duration, but only within precise limits. The operator has a fundamental concern to appreciate the general configuration of structural links between objects in the system, and to understand where flexibility is permissible, or is not.

2.2.2 Occurrence of events

Event occurrence can be:

- **regular/irregular**: Wherein, the problem is related to the rhythm and the possible anticipation of events. The machines and their components have life cycles which are known to the operator. He can forecast, for example, engine failures due to wear. Certain actions are repeated every day, at precise times.

- **frequent/infrequent**: When an event takes place frequently it can be easily identified, thanks to familiar cues. In this case, the event, especially when undesirable, can be anticipated thanks to its precursor signs.

2.2.3   Observability of events

Events related to objects which evolve dynamically may be more or less observable by the operator, either directly or through the instrumentation. In continuous processes, where the product is visible and moving, the spatio-kinematic effect appears to assist the operator in mastering the temporal dimension more so than with non-visible products. Chemical transformations in tanks or even fluid transportation through pipes make the temporal estimation impossible if indications are not displayed to the operator in a dynamic form. The distance between the worker and the product is growing with automation and installations are often covered in order to avoid nuisance, e.g., heat, gas emissions. This hindrance to direct observability of the product being controlled should be remedied by providing equivalent information through visual displays.

2.2.4   Accidental events

Accidental events also have particular temporal characteristics. These are linked to their time of occurrence within the sequence, their possible repetition, and their speed of propagation.

2.3   Key-points in the temporal control of the system

We can sum up the preceding discussion, deriving key points of the temporal control of the whole system. Up to a certain point, the system and the team evolve in time in a similar but independent way. The operator acts as a mediator between the system and the team through direct actions on the system, information gathering and transfer, or by way of orders relayed to the satellite teams.

Key-point events are those for which there is no flexibility in the system, either because there is precise temporal boundary, or because the possibility to complete two actions in any order at a given time have finally been exhausted.

2.3.1   Nodes in the process development

These are transitions from one stage to another, or from one state to another, which require either an action of the operator, or several combined actions of the operator and another member of the team. This transition can be more or less delicate and a source of accidents. The moment when actions must take place may be more or less precise.

2.3.2 Stages in the team's actions development

There are inevitable bottle-necks with series of actions which have to be done before the next stage. Before this bottle-neck, preceding actions may have been taken either sequentially or without regard to order. Their sequence is not important with respect to the fact that they have been carried out before the bottle-neck as if they were preconditions for the next stage. The crucial aspect of this critical stage depends strongly on the strictness of the moment when it must take place. This can relate to a precise moment or to a change, a node or to the process. When dispersed actions need to be carried out in several locations of the plant, it is up to the control room operator to judge whether transition conditions to the next stage are fulfilled, or whether a possible articulation in process nodes can be done.

2.3.3 Machines' life cycles

The irregular wear of the equipment and of the machines implies that a whole maintenance system moves around the production system. Though generally well programmed, this is a source of increased circulation and disturbances. The operator has to know the life cycles of the machines in order to plan and anticipate the intervention of specialised teams. This additional knowledge (knowing the machines' life cycles, how and when they have been repaired) is necessary for avoiding misinterpretation of disturbances.

2.3.4 Accidents

Accidents that generally take place in the operator's direct area of control and those which appear out of his direct area of control require urgent responses to change the process development, to minimise consequences, to co-ordinate the actions of several persons, and diagnose the accident. 'Dilatory actions' [59] allow the operator to reduce the propagation of the accident in order to find time for reasoning. The occurrence of an accident requires the operator to have an instantaneous view of the global state of the system. This is difficult when the accident takes place out of the operator's direct area of control. His appreciation of the accident and his efforts to recover pass through the exchanges with operators close to the machines.

3 Mechanisms for time apprehension

A crucial problem is to explain time in terms of mechanisms and processes that provide adequate tuning of the organism to its environment, and in our case of the operator facing a complex system. Hypotheses on the mechanisms can be made on the basis of empirical studies (e.g., [61, 63]) and experiments in cognitive psychology (e.g., [178, 143, 150, 156]). The mechanisms inferred are:

- internalisation;

- logical estimation;

- physical estimation;

- synecdochal prediction;

- extended prediction;

- explanation revision.

These can be used simultaneously or separately depending upon the context.

3.1   Explicit use of time

3.1.1   Internalisation

If events are regular, the time duration can be internalised. Time is directly estimated without attention control. Man has the ability to learn rhythms and to estimate durations that appear regularly. This estimation relies on a direct knowledge of durations. As operators have limited resources, this internalisation economically allows for reduced information gathering and facilitates the anticipation of events. Regular events can be related to the process or to the satellite teams.

Empirical studies show that the operator trusts this internalisation and the available rhythms, whereas he is dubious about the reliability of the information displays. De Keyser [54] relates the case of a nuclear power plant operator who for several hours ignored alarms concerning a tank refill while trusting his own estimation of the event's duration. Unfortunately, the refill time duration had changed due to a modification of flow which was ignored by the operator.

Such time estimation is exposed to possible distortions since it employs no external or objective confirmation and has to be made while coping with urgency, risk and uncertainty. Furthermore, this internalisation can be completely upset under situations of stress, as when an accident is announced. Severe temporal distortions can be produced which affect time perception and estimation of duration. The persistence of internalisation is not well understood. Is it reinforced by repetition, does it disappear once the reactivation is removed or is it definitely settled even if it no longer fits the environment constraints? Field studies have shown adaptations in operator behaviour to subtle deviations of the rhythmical aspect of the environment as well as fixations that lead to error once a change in the regularity of events appears [58].

3.1.2   Logical estimation

Estimates of time duration can be attained on the basis of temporal intervals characterised by initial and terminal events. Thus, operators work out their representation of the time duration by the relationship among the set of time intervals involved. For this estimate, everything works by means of comparison. The estimation of an event duration is done by comparison with other events. In comparing temporal intervals, certain factors, such as the time boundary events, play a crucial role. For instance, in the context of the operator's apprehension of the temporal dynamics of the system, well-defined (identifiable) initial and terminal events facilitate the operator's task.

3.1.3   Physical estimation

The content of the elapsed events is used to evaluate time duration. The relationship established by the operator between velocity, space and time corresponds to the covariation of the physical system. For example, given a fixed velocity, an increase in the travelled distance yields an estimation of the time passed. The time duration is derived and estimated when knowing the velocity of a body and its travelled distance. This estimation mode is based on causality. During the start-up of a thermo-electrical plant the estimation of time duration relies on information on the parameters' speed of evolution. This is the case with the use of gradients. Estimation is based on the gradient of several parameters (gradients of the temperature of the steam-generator, of the temperature of the turbine, etc.).

The difficulty here seems to be related to the fact that the variation velocity has different values in different portions of the complex system and these different gradients need to be compared by the operator in order to estimate the duration of the integrated evolution. This mechanism is easily used by the operator when he has a good knowledge of the system, i.e., when he is able to understand links of cause and effect. The observability of the process is a condition *sine qua non* for the physical estimation. Observability can be direct for processes with a spatio-kinematic movement (for example, the steel defiling in a steel and iron factory), or indirect through an informational display. Such displays should restore the dynamic evolution of physical objects which are otherwise concealed through geographical constraints and of physical functions such as the evolution of a variable over time.

3.2   Implicit use of time

3.2.1   Synecdochal prediction

Prediction of the future is done using a partial representation of the world, i.e., of the past events that should influence an event's change in the future and of the future events that should modify the course of the prediction made. The hope is that factors which have been ignored will not have significant influence. For example, the operator can make a prediction on the evolution of a variable over time taking into account a reduced model of the past (not all parameters that possibly influence the evolution of the variable are considered) and of the future events (a sudden failure of a key component) that would modify the expected evolution of the variable. In making these predictions, the operator uses a reduced representation of the complex system on the basis of the functional relation of both the target and the source problem. One difficulty is to know which events are taken into account by the operator, i.e., which events are judged significant for the prediction.

3.2.2   Extended prediction

The prediction is extended over a certain period of time which is estimated by the operator according to his believe of how long this evolution will keep the same trajectory before being changed by a new event.

3.2.3   Explanation revision

The 'psychological present' is the time interval during which the operator revises his explanation of the world according to the new information that continuously arrives. New information perceived by the operator may be integrated into his set of hypotheses because it fits the current representation of the problem and thus helps to refine his hypotheses. Alternatively, new information can be rejected because it contradicts his current set of hypotheses and is judged irrelevant. On the other hand, contradictory information can change the current hypothesis because its degree of incoherency is such that it completely shifts the original hypothesis. This mechanism of explanation revision can be viewed as a variety of matching along the time axis between new events and the current representation mentally built by the operator.

4   Temporal errors

Difficulties met by operators in planning, evaluation, diagnosis, integration and co-ordination, and their related errors, should give some guidance on solving problems in the lack of display support. Several temporal errors have been identified which are related to different types of discrepancies between the temporal structures. A classification of temporal errors was constructed in order to map the several temporal modes of failures.

- **Misestimation of sequences of actions and events**: inversion (reversals) of actions within a sequence, omissions of actions (cf. Hollnagel,

Chapter 4). Operators do not succeed in organising event and actions in a sequence whose boundaries are precise. This type of error is probably due to a lack of knowledge of physical response times and of operational times.

- **Mis-estimation of time duration of events which have precise boundaries**: because they use wrong indices or due to the appearance of some temporal distortions. Temporal distortions are related to over-estimation of 'full' time durations and underestimation of 'empty' time durations. This type of error is probably due to failure of one of the estimation mechanisms (internalisation, logical estimation or physical estimation).

- **Failure in estimating the right moment to take action**: the action is taken at the wrong moment due to an operator's mistake in estimating a time duration or because he does not recognise the precise moment, within a global evolution, at which to intervene. Here, too, there is a failure of the mechanisms on which the judgement for taking action relies.

- **Failure in anticipating some events**: the operator does not succeed in predicting the possible evolution of actions and events in the future and thus misses the moment to take action or to co-ordinate actions taken by other people. A mistake of prediction and anticipation is probably due to a failure of the synecdochal mechanism, i.e., an error in the estimation of past, present or future events that can influence a prediction. This can also be due to a mistake in estimation of the temporal horizon during which an event will be changed or remain unchanged.

- **Failure in synchronisation of collective actions**: misestimation of the right moment to decide collectively to take several actions. Such errors are generally linked to problems in verbal communication exchanges. They are also related to a lack of knowledge of the operational times of the component under consideration and of the displacement times (time required to reach and localise different points of the plant).

5   Time in the operator's model

A first attempt to introduce the temporal dimension within the framework model of operator behaviour during accident situations was made [62]. This framework model consists of: a physical system, which represents the complex world; a model of recognition and diagnosis (ARCC); a model of planning; and a cognitive filter. (This model is described in detail elsewhere [23, 36].)

The approach taken in this modelling project was to build a structure for the different kinds of cognitive activities that operators perform in complex environments and more especially when an accident occurs, i.e., recognising, diagnosing, planning and acting on the control system in order to restore a stable state. This modelling approach has two major goals: to understand the mechanisms that produce human errors, thereby predicting the human contribution to risk, and to contribute to the development of decision-support systems [35].

A conceptual framework has been developed whereby the models of the physical system and of the operator act as interactive components in the man-machine system simulation. A distributed implementation allows for dynamic interaction between the physical system model and the operator model. The model of the physical system runs on a SUN3 and continuously sends data to the operator model which runs on a Symbolics, using KEE (Knowledge Engineering Environment). The mechanisms of matching such information with the operator's knowledge, i.e., Abstract Reasoning on the bases of Concrete Cues (ARCC), and of performing a selected strategy of actions by FUzzy Goal-Oriented Script (FUGOS), are the parts of the model which interact directly with the physical system.

In this part of the model, human cognition is presumed to possess two distinct structural components: a limited, serial but computationally powerful working memory and a virtually limitless knowledge-base [195]. The model has different mechanisms for bringing stored knowledge units into working memory. Two such mechanisms are the heuristics of similarity matching (SM), and frequency gambling (FG).

Similarity matching matches the symptoms on the basis of the correspondence between states of the world and the characteristics of the stored knowledge structures. More explicitly, this matching confronts symptoms that are perceived (i.e., after having been treated by the cognitive filter) with symptoms that are known at different levels of abstraction. Frequency gambling is able to resolve conflicts (between schema candidates) in favour of contextually appropriate, high frequency knowledge structures.

5.1 ARCC

In the diagnosis model, explanations are sought on the basis of observed symptoms. This explanation search process needs to be dynamic and revised according to information which continuously changes the nature of the problem to be solved. The diagnosis process in ARCC proceeds in two directions. A data-driven strategy treats information coming from the complex world with their temporal attributes and yields a provisional diagnosis. This is then affirmed in the schema-driven processing by a collection of further information.

5.1.1 Data-driven processing

The human model continuously receives data from the physical system model. These data, after having been treated by several filters, constitute the set of perceived symptoms on which the operator bases his diagnosis. Symptoms are described in specific terms (e.g., the temperature of steam-generator-1 is decreasing rapidly). and will activate a search for an explanation on the basis of abstract knowledge related with several Virtual Types of Accidents (VTA).

Virtual types of accidents and their specific sets of Virtual Accidents (VA) contain descriptions of symptoms peculiar to them. This global set of information constitutes the operator's knowledge. The operator model compares one (or several) specific detailed cues with similar ones encoded under type of accidents (VTA). A first matching is done between specific cues perceived and abstract symptoms of the typology. One or several typologies are generally activated if at least one symptom of the perceived world matches one symptom of the typology.

5.1.2 Schema-driven processing

When an accident has been identified (CIF, Currently Instantiated Frame) through a matching of symptoms with a typology, the operator model begins the confirmation of the known complementary symptoms of this specific accident. Symptoms checked first are those which have the greatest diagnosticity. Confirmed and unconfirmed symptoms are progressively added to the initial set of perceived symptoms until the operator is convinced about his diagnosis.

Incoherence between symptoms checked in the environment and symptoms characteristic of a specific accident provokes the reinitiation of the diagnosis process, i.e., a matching between the set of the symptoms perceived (the symptoms known after the schema-driven processing are added to the initial ones), and the symptoms known at the typology level. The problem of explanation revision in function of time is achieved by matching between new and old symptoms and knowledge structures.

5.2 Time experience model

Temporal knowledge and temporal reasoning have to be modelled as higher processes which are inherited by the differents parts of the operator's model. Temporal knowledge can thus be defined as metaknowledge which comes into play when needed. Modelling the temporal dimension of reasoning and knowledge has implications on how to represent making the plan valuable in the future; reasoning about order and duration; estimating event duration with the internalisation, physical and logical modes; predicting the future on the basis of partial information of the past; and evaluating changes that occur in the present.

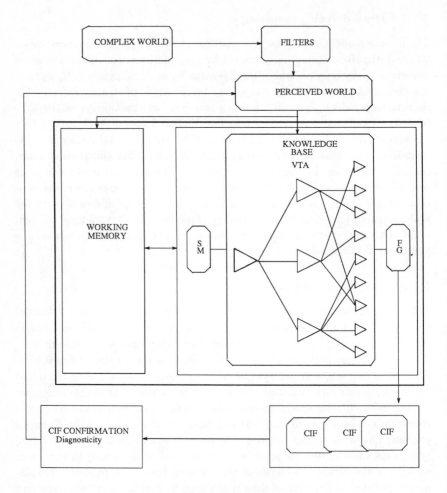

Figure 1 : Structure of the abstract reasoning module (ARCC)

5.2.1 Temporal knowledge-base

The models consideration of the time dimension employs AI formalisms and tools, e.g., the concepts of 'histories' and 'episodes' [100, 236] which define the conceptual roots of the knowledge-base. Events and actions are related to each other using various relationships [4]. Inferential mechanisms based on those relationships derive new temporal assertions and incorporate them into the knowledge-base. In this way, it is possible to access them later by a query.

The physical system is described in terms of the behaviour of each state variable and the relevant temporal relations between events. State variable behaviour over time is referred to as history. A single history is a sequence of intervals called episodes. Thereby, a temporal map is constructed which contains knowledge related to episodes and histories.

An episode is an interval during which a fact (action/event) is true. A time interval is associated with each episode e, which is referred to as the episode's temporal extent, and is bounded by the beginning and end points $t_{begin(e)}$ and $t_{end(e)}$. A fact which is true during an episode can be defined with regard to the past, present and future; its duration is known in the past and can be precisely defined. It is then possible to estimate this duration retrospectively. In the present, a fact could have begun in the past (then the beginning of the interval is known), continued in the present and could finish in the future (the duration and the interval end are unknown). Episodes can be contiguous, distantiated, or overlapped. They are related one to another according to the relations shown below (cf. Figure 2):

Before (e_1, e_2): e_1 is before e_2 and they do not overlap;

After (e_1, e_2): e_1 is after e_2 and they do not overlap;

During (e_1, e_2): e_1 is included in e_2, e_1 begins after e_2 begins and ends before e_2 ends;

Meets (e_1, e_2): e_1 is before e_2 and there is no interval between them, i.e., e_1 ends where e_2 starts;

Overlaps (e_1, e_2): e_1 starts before e_2 and they overlap;

Equal (e_1, e_2): e_1 and e_2 have the same interval;

Starts (e_1, e_2): e_1 shares the same beginning as e_2 but ends before e_2 ends;

Finishes (e_1, e_2): e_1 shares the same end as e_2 but begins after e_2 begins.

Histories are sequences of episodes in which two attributes are considered: the concatenation of episodes $(e_1 \ldots e_n)$, and history duration for a set of episodes. Several histories may evolve in parallel as they concern descriptions of state variables' behaviour over time.

The temporal map, based upon characteristics of the physical system, is used by operators in the past, present and future. Episodes and histories are applicable, for instance the duration of system components can be described using the temporal extent of an episode within a history.

5.2.2 Temporal evaluation

The estimation of order and duration can be modelled as detailed below.

Before	(e_1, e_2)	e_1 end	$\leq e_2$ begin			
After	(e_1, e_2)	e_1 begin	$\geq e_2$ end			
During	(e_1, e_2)	e_2 begin	$\leq e_1$ begin	*and* e_2 end	$\geq e_1$ end	
Meets	(e_1, e_2)	e_1 end	$= e_2$ begin	*or* e_2 end	$= e_1$ begin	
Overlaps	(e_1, e_2)	e_1 begin	$< e_2$ begin	$< e_1$ end	$< e_2$ end	*or*
		e_2 begin	$< e_1$ begin	$< e_2$ end	$< e_1$ end	
Equal	(e_1, e_2)	e_1 begin	$= e_2$ begin	*and* e_1 end	$= e_2$ end	
Starts	(e_1, e_2)	e_1 begin	$= e_2$ begin			
Finishes	(e_1, e_2)	e_1 end	$= e_2$ end			

Figure 2: Relationships between events and actions

(a) Order judgements

Judging the order of two elements should be done using a psychological mechanism for extracting linear order information, for example, using the ordinal relations of events and actions like 'before', 'after', 'meet', 'overlaps'. The problem here concerns the human flexibility in directly extracting information on linear ordering. Research on linear ordering [181, 223] suggests that order information is directly available and that one does not have to chain through the intermediate terms in a series to determine their order. In Anderson's ACT* [11] judging the order of two elements is accomplished by means of a special match predicate, for order in which order judgements are not implemented as a series of nexts. For example, the production would directly retrieve the answer to the question whether A is before D in the string ABCDEF. A distance effect is observed in which even though subjects memorise only adjacent pairs (A before B, B before C, C before D), judgements become easier with elements that are farther apart.

(b) Time estimation mechanisms

Several co-interacting mechanisms by which the operator estimates times are considered. These could be divided into two main types of processing, the first concerned with automatic processing, others related to control processing in which attention intervenes (cf. Figure 3):

- Internalisation (I): the internalisation of certain events is dependent upon the regularity of their occurrence. An episode duration is directly estimated if this episode is regular.

- Logical estimation (LE): the operator works out his representation of the time duration by the relationship among the set of time intervals involved. Estimation of an episode duration is achieved by comparison

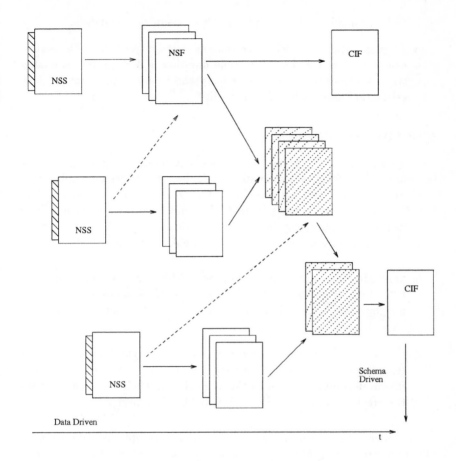

Figure 3: The CIF problem

with other episodes (in the same history or between different parallel ones). The first heuristic is a search within the known episodes for those which have evolved during the one to be estimated. If some of the parallel episodes are internalised, the result of the internalisation is used for the comparison and yields an inferior boundary. Of course, two episodes may meet, i.e., they evolved in sequence during the episode to be estimated. In this case, they are 'summed', i.e., e_1 and e_2 are summed, the result of the sum being used for the comparison. A second heuristic is a search of episodes which start or finish with the episode to be estimated. This heuristic yields to a superior boundary.

- Physical estimation (PE): the content of the elapsed events is used to evaluate time duration. The time duration is derived and estimated when knowing the velocity of a body and its travelled distance. This estimation mode is based on causality.

5.2.3 Dynamic diagnosis

During data-driven processing salient cues may interrupt on-going processing and shift the focussed explanation, shift the virtual accident explanation (VA) or, at a more abstract level, shift the typologies of accident explanation (VTA). The shift from CIF to CIF should be processed by matching symptoms and frames along the time axis, the matching making obsolete the original set of symptoms or frames (see Figure 3). For example, at :

t_0 an original set of perceived symptoms (NSS = new set of symptoms) activates in memory an original set of frames (NSF = new set of frames), making them OSS (old set of symptoms) and OSF (old set of frames), respectively ;

t_1 a new set of perceived symptoms (with some symptoms in common regarding the original set), activates a new set of frames (with some frames in common regarding the original set). Their occurrence change the previous NSS and NSF to OSS and OSF, respectively.

A matching is performed between the new set of symptoms and the old set of frames in order to confirm or disconfirm some of the frames which no longer have any symptoms in common with the NSS. At this point, there are two solutions. Either the new symptoms are incorporated and reduce the number of virtual frames inside the NSF because they make precise explanation or the symptoms are contradictory with regard to the current set of frames. In the latter case, these symptoms are declared suspect and are the object of a confirmation attempt, or they are ignored. The confirmed frames are added to the more recent set of frames and the NSF is then formed from the late NSF plus frames from the OSF which have been confirmed. The NSS is always formed from perceived symptoms, i.e., those which have come through the cognitive filter. Dynamic reasoning continues as long as symptoms pass the filter.

As in the framework model, reasoning proceeds in two directions. The first direction treats data coming from the world with their temporal attributes and results in the formulation of a number of hypotheses. The second direction tries to confirm the hypothesis by collection of further information.

5.2.4 Data-driven processing

As facts change in time, the cognitive model considers temporal attributes and relationships of histories and episodes (temporal extent, duration, sequence). Duration can be processed when beginning and ends are known. The operator model processes the temporal information to generate hypotheses for explanation. For instance, an hypothesis can be generated on the basis of past histories, their order (concatenation) and their own duration, or on the basis of an interval between a past event and a present one (e.g., 15 minutes ago I had a sudden drop of flow, now a pump is broken). A hypothesis may be formulated on the basis of the length of time for which an event remains true. The choice between two episodes which have differing durations will orientate the diagnosis because it is this duration that is important to the operator's diagnosis and allows for differentiation of two possible explanations. This differentiation relies, in turn, on the retrospective estimation of duration.

5.2.5 Schema-driven processing

The operator model confirms hypotheses using temporal information. After formulating a diagnosis, further changes, i.e., changes that have appeared between the diagnosis and the current evaluation, may confirm a hypothesis. The hypothesis formulation has then been anticipated with regard to the following changes. The time separating the diagnosis and the evaluation can be more or less spread, depending on cognitive strategy. The order of events which appear between the 'past' diagnosis and the current evaluation can also serve as information for diagnosis evaluation.

5.3 Temporal error factors

The factors responsible for temporal misestimation are divided into two mains categories depending on whether they belong to 'subjective' or 'objective' factors. Subjective factors are related to the cognitive state of the operator, whereas objective factors rely on the characteristics of the task. These factors influence an overestimation or underestimation of the times and thus lead to temporal errors.

Subjective factors include attention, motivation, knowledge and stress and fatigue. Objective factors include number and complexity of stimulations, repetitive activity, familiarity with the task, short or long interval, empty, full or divided interval.

6 Conclusions

A first attempt has been made to introduce the temporal dimension of human reasoning into the operator's model. Temporal reasoning and temporal knowledge are defined as higher processes inherited downwards by the model as part of the Time Experience Model. This approach tries to integrate AI approaches with psychological aspects. The present system uses AI formalisms and makes assertions on a temporal map. In taking into account histories and episodes, the model bases its reasoning on past events and projects the evolution of possible future events.

For this, the approach is definitely cognitive. Temporal mechanisms are modelled and allow the estimation and comparison of time duration. In this approach, time is not only considered as an external variable imposed on the operator. Rather, he plays an active role on the temporal dimension. Indeed one of the most interesting features of the control of complex systems is that the operator is active, in the sense that his strategy modifies the temporal dimension of the system and the rate of its transformations.

With respect to previous psychological studies on time, one further feature is added. The man-world circle is closed by considering the operator's active role on the physical time of the system. The operator builds his temporal strategy on times imposed by external constraints. He can thus make these events extremely variable. The operator compares time durations. He fixes temporal boundaries using the temporal references available to him. He puts plans into action, anticipates certain events, co-ordinates others and ensures the required simultaneities in order to avoid mismatches among event sequences, and so avoid 'temporal losses'.

The time handled by the model fits with human behaviour. By modelling temporal reasoning, temporal estimation mechanisms and temporal distortions, the model does not limit itself at a physical, objective, external time. As experience of time and subjective estimation are not uniform, temporal errors are easily observed. When estimating durations temporal distortions are possible. The process control environment also facilitates temporal errors as there may be hours of inactivity followed by periods of intense activity with lots of new information arriving at the same time.

From a human reliability point of view, it is very important to be able to predict temporal errors. Such prediction is one of the goals of the model. Future research focussed on human error modelling might open itself to such a dimension. Errors which are clearly time related could then be more extensively investigated. As it is, the model has potential for extension to cover the group activities. In fact, the temporal dimension of human reasoning and of co-ordination appears to be the core problem on which the model of the group should be based.

Chapter 4

The Phenotype of Erroneous Actions: Implications for HCI Design

Erik Hollnagel

1 Introduction

1.1 System complexity and 'human error'

> An ant, viewed as a behaving system, is quite simple. The apparent com-
> plexity of its behavior over time is largely a reflection of the complexity
> of the environment in which it finds itself [215, p. 24].

One of the classical 'truths' of Human-Computer Interaction (HCI), normally
attributed to the preceding quote from H. A. Simon, is that the complexity of
a system's behaviour may as well be a function of the system's environment
as a function of its internal complexity. In relation to HCI this means that the
complexity of user behaviour in the interaction with the computer to a very
large extent is determined by the complexity of the local environment, i.e.,
the structural and functional characteristics of the human-computer interface.

   User behaviour is, of course, a very broad term which covers many different aspects. The concern with HCI may be directed towards efficiency, safety,
general workload, comprehensibility, speed, etc., and each aspect may require
its own class of solutions. Efficiency may, for instance, be enhanced by using
an interface based on icons and symbolic manipulation, which seems to be
a strong trend in the development of operating systems for micro-computers
and workstations (e.g., the Macintosh, the Presentation Manager, X, NeWS,
etc.). Comprehensibility, and thereby the general ability to use the system's
resources adequately, may be enhanced by including various types of intelligent help in the system, as demonstrated by the ESPRIT P280 Eurohelp

HUMAN–COMPUTER INTERACTION
AND COMPLEX SYSTEMS: ISBN 0-12-742660-4

project [97]. In this chapter I will look at the aspect of erroneous actions (sometimes also referred to as 'human error'), both because it is a growing concern in most systems and because it has an effect on many of the aspects mentioned above. I will make the assumption that the **number** of erroneous actions (rather than the **types** of erroneous actions) will increase as the complexity of the system increases, i.e., as the complexity of the HCI increases. Knowing more about what the erroneous actions are is accordingly useful, and probably even necessary, in order to improve the design of the HCI. This chapter will provide a conceptual analysis of erroneous actions, establish a classification scheme or taxonomy, and suggest some implications for the design of HCI.

1.2   A definition of HCI

With the risk of labouring the obvious I would like to provide a working definition of what is to be understood by human-computer interaction. Taken at face value the term simply means the interaction between a user and a computer with the implied purpose of carrying out a certain task or achieving a certain goal. We may show this as in Figure 1a.

The computer is, however, rarely itself the target of the interaction but rather a tool or a mechanism, by means of which the goal can be reached. The user therefore interacts with an application (or the world) through the computer, and the latter serves as an intermediary in some sense.

The computer as an intermediary can have two completely different roles. In one case it can serve in an embodiment relation, i.e., 'relations in which the machine displays some kind of partial transparency in that it itself does not become objectified or thematic, but is taken into my experiencing of what is other in the World' [109, p. 8]. The embodiment relation can be established with all types of machines and not just computers. A classical example is the way in which one can 'feel' the surface of the road when driving a car. The machine somehow transforms the experience and mediates it to the user. More than that, it also amplifies the experience, e.g., by highlighting those aspects of it that are germane to the task while simultaneously reducing or excluding others. The embodiment relation may therefore also be characterised as an amplificatory relation. We can show this as in Figure 1b.

In the second role, the computer serves in a hermeneutic relation to the user. Here the user's 'experiential terminus is with the machine... There is a partial opacity between the machine and the World and thus the machine is something like a text' [109, p. 11]. Put differently, the user has moved from an experience **through** the machine to an experience **of** the machine. It is thus the state of the world as represented by the machine which in itself becomes important. In the extreme case there actually is no experience of the world except that provided by the machine. The hermeneutical relation

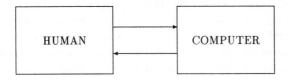

(a) The simple relation

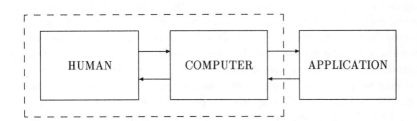

(b) The embodiment (amplificatory) relation

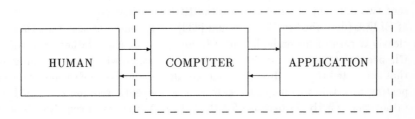

(c) The hermeneutical (interpretative) relation

Figure 1: Relations in HCI

may therefore also be characterised as an interpretative relation. This can be shown as in Figure 1c.

In terms of HCI, the embodiment (amplifying) relation and the hermeneutic (interpreting) relation are clearly distinguishable. Computer-Aided Design (CAD), or even a simple drawing program, is a clear example of the embodiment relation. Here the computer is transparent and the interest is focussed on the application (although it in a sense only exists in the computer). Other examples could be the development of a semantic network (a knowledge-base), the manipulation of mathematical models (e.g., computational fluid dynamics), computer-enhanced pictures, computerised fund transfer (automated tellers, banking), etc. The hermeneutic relation is exemplified by most cases of computerised industrial process control, computer games, fractal geometry, etc. In industrial process control in particular, the user is often removed from the process and may even have no previous experience with it outside the control room. Thereby, the way the process is represented in the control room, i.e., by the computer system, easily becomes the real process. The user's understanding may accordingly become dependent on the surface presentation of the process and the user's experience may be representation-dependent shallow knowledge. Less extreme, but more frequent, is the relation that may be developed through casual interaction with a networked computer (e.g., a workstation). This suggests the possibility that the more 'advanced' is the HCI, the more likely we are to depend upon it, hence to be governed by an interpretive (hermeneutical) rather than an amplificatory (embodiment) relation.

The two relations are, of course, not mutually exclusive but rather represent two different ways of viewing the HCI. Consider, for instance, the case of ELIZA (described in Weizenbaum [233]). For computer scientists this was clearly a case of an embodiment relation (i.e., an HC-I rather than an H-CI) because they were interested in the application, which was the program that simulated the non-directive therapeutic session. For the casual or unsuspecting user this was instead a case of a hermeneutic relation (i.e., an H-CI rather than an HC-I) because for them ELIZA was real, even though some of them actually knew that it was a computer program. What the computer represented to them was the application (literally, the text) itself. To take another example, a word processor formerly represented the embodiment relation when formatting was carried out by the use of format codes (e.g., early versions of WordStar) but is now more likely to represent the hermeneutical relation, where the concept is What-You-See-Is-What-You-Get (e.g., the various forms of Desk Top Publishing).

This distinction between the two relations serves to clarify the nature of HCI and is particularly interesting in the case of assessing the impact of artificial intelligence (AI) on HCI. AI clearly provides the possibility of amplifying the cognitive functions of the user, hence to permit new kinds of embodiment relations. But at the same time AI may be used to enhance the computer's functional repertoire and its interpretative powers, thereby strengthening its hermeneutical role. This may happen as a simple consequence of the increasing complexity of the applications and of the perceived need to increase the access to expert knowledge and expert skills. Thus the very development of expert systems may unknowingly favour the dominance of the interpretative role of computers, hence the fragmented view on HCI described in the following. The development of user support systems and advanced HCI functions, such as the action-monitoring system described in this chapter, should, however, rather aim at amplifying the capacities of the user.

1.3   HCI design and complexity

In the field of HCI, reference is sometimes made to the design of complex systems. While systems that require HCI clearly may be complex, it is quite misleading to think that they are designed to be so; on the contrary, systems should be designed to be simple rather than complex. The problem for HCI design is rather that we, as users and researchers, often are faced with systems which are complex because they have been badly designed. The challenge is therefore to produce an HCI design which can reduce the complexity so that users are actually able to manage the system.

HCI design can, somewhat polemically, be seen from either a holistic or a fragmented point of view. In the holistic (or monist) view the system is seen as a whole or a unit, which cannot and should not be broken into smaller parts. In the fragmented (or dualist) view the focus is on one out of a number of aspects of the system, either the functional aspects (grouped together as the User-System Interaction, e.g., application, command structure, resilience to errors) or the structural aspects (grouped together as the Man-Machine System, e.g., interface media, channel capacity, control requirements, response time).

While it is a reasonable aspiration to use a holistic rather than a fragmented approach, the hard facts are that we (as cognitive system engineers) are often forced to adopt the fragmented approach because we are allowed to deal only with a part of the system. Firstly, any reasonably sized Man-Machine System will be so large that the design activity is split among several teams or people. Secondly, the HCI expertise is often brought in at too late a stage or only allowed for the specific User-System Interaction aspects. Thirdly, there is a lack of methods and techniques which support a holistic approach. Thus even if one could, in the best of all possible worlds, adopt a holistic approach from the very start of a project it would represent a formidable problem due to the lack of established solutions or even recognised guidelines. Currently, the two main approaches are the use of generic interfaces and the use of a generic analysis principle. While both are useful, neither is adequate as a complete solution.

1.3.1   Generic interfaces

One approach to a holistic HCI design is the use of so-called generic interfaces. In this approach the representation of information is standardised by
means of symbols, icons, command facilities, display methods, etc. (and a
similar solution is normally sought for the presentation technology). This is,
however, not adequate because it looks at the interface side only. The idea
of a generic interface is based on the fact that the user never should see the
system except as it is being presented through the interface (cf. the interpretative relation described above). In consequence, the goal of the interface
designer is to provide a system image which is sufficiently simple that the
user is able to use and understand it. In a sense, the whole system is being designed by designing the interface. The practical problem is that the
generic interface can only be approached but never fully attained. Pieces of
the 'engineering' system or application still pop up, e.g., because of regulatory
or company requirements or because the HCI design is introduced too late
in the development. Even so, the generic interface approach is a major step
forward from conventional human factors engineering because it considers the
semantics of the interface, rather than just the syntax and the morphology.
The creation of an 'artificial' world through the interface, however, requires
that one has a sufficiently adequate basis for doing this, e.g., a conceptual
basis like Cognitive Task Analysis [248].

1.3.2   Generic analysis principles

A second approach to HCI design is to use a systematic analytical principle
such as Multilevel Flow Modelling [139]. While this has proven to be very
valuable for many aspects of the system design, the weakness is the assumption that the user is able to understand the functional structure of the system
as it comes out of the analytical principle (e.g., Yoshimura *et al.* [253]). If that
assumption does not hold, then the approach will eventually fail. Furthermore, one must recognise the possibility that the actual construction of the
display may obscure the elementary principles used by the analysis, e.g., the
goals-means relations provided by Multilevel Flow Modelling, so that the functional (de)composition is not adequately represented by the interface. Again,
the ideal circumstances are that the system can be consistently designed from
the start through application of the analytical principle. The more realistic
case is that the analytical principle can be applied *post hoc* to improve the
design or to develop support systems ('crutches'). The advantage of using
systematic analytical principles or formal methods (such as Multilevel Flow
Modelling or Path Algebras) is that one can insure (or even prove) that the

user has got all the information that he needs, or that he has been brought through all the steps that are required in a given path.

From a dichotomous point of view the weakness of the generic interface approach is that it is biased towards the User-System Interaction, while the weakness of the analytical approach is that it is biased towards the formal requirements (goals and needs) of the task. What is needed is a more unified approach which, so to speak, is able to maintain and balance both biases at the same time. One example of this can be found in cognitive systems engineering [107], e.g., in its combination with dialogue specification (e.g., [106], although this only represents an initial attempt). The dialogue is a goal directed development, where the end might be reaching a diagnosis, specifying a plan for a contingency, specifying a maintenance plan, specifying a procedure, etc. The dialogue specification can be seen as a way of guiding the user through the goals-means structure of the decision process, hence as an analogue to the Multilevel Flow Modelling approach—although it clearly is not so ambitious. Cognitive system engineering and cognitive task analysis are intended to guard against either bias precisely by looking at the interaction and the requirements in relation to the goals and needs of the task.

A different way of characterising the two ways of considering HCI design is via the terms user centred versus system centred. In a user-centred design the emphasis is on the user's tasks and needs because this is assumed to constitute the 'real' bottle-neck for a safe and efficient operation of the system. The user-centred design is thus close to the holistic point of view, although it tends to favour one part of the system. In a system-centred design the emphasis is more on the technological and engineering requirements for safe and efficient operation with the user being regarded as no more than a part of the system. This view has its roots in Taylorism and classical human factors engineering, and is represented by the so-called Procrustean approach [221]. System-centred design is a clear example of the fragmented point of view.

System-centred, fragmented design has dominated HCI until recently. There are many reasons for this: ignorance about the impact of human performance (and human errors) on system performance, a lack of relevant psychological knowledge (cognitive systems engineering and cognitive science) and scientists who could use it, limitations of computer hardware (dumb terminals, character-based graphics), the absence of suitable software technology (e.g., knowledge-based systems) to implement HCI functionality, the 'naive' assumptions about user abilities (essentially that they have the same knowledge and skills as the designer), and last, but not least, the adaptability of users. All of these factors have been undergoing change, starting slowly in the late 1970s and gaining speed during the 1980s. This has challenged the traditional basis for man-machine systems design, unfortunately without providing a clear alternative. In consequence, the field has been left in a state of turmoil and confusion, not least on the part of the users and customers. Although there seems to be a growing consensus about certain aspects, e.g., the use of a WIMP-based presentation surface, a closer investigation reveals that these are more often based on available technology than on proven scientific facts. While there need not be a conflict between the two, it would be nice if they played a more equal role.

1.4   HCI and erroneous actions

Erroneous actions pervade HCI in all fields of application: from personal computing and administrative functions to process control and transportation. Erroneous actions are usually regarded as inevitable in the sense that there is some minimal level of occurrence below which they cannot be reduced, no matter what is done. Yet there may be different views on erroneous actions and therefore also on the remedies for dealing with them. These views are very closely related to the view on HCI and, in a sense, the philosophy of HCI that implicitly is behind the design.

One view is that erroneous actions are unavoidable consequences of the imperfection of the human information processing system, a snake in the garden of Eden, and that they will occur even under the best conditions. Erroneous actions are by their nature unpredictable in form and frequency, although some patterns can be found. According to this view the best remedy is to eliminate the deficient parts of HCI by having the computer take over. This is compatible with the interpretative human-computer relation and the fragmented approach to HCI. In this case it is important to know the statistics of erroneous actions and to find the areas that are most vulnerable, but it is less necessary to elaborate the analysis and understand erroneous actions on a deeper level.

Another view is that erroneous actions are the results of unfavourable (working) conditions or an unforgiving environment. Erroneous actions are predictable both in form and frequency and it is therefore possible—in principle as well as in practice—significantly to reduce their number. According to this view the best remedy is to improve the working conditions (the information environment) by providing the human with the appropriate tools and by amplifying human strengths rather than reducing human weaknesses. This is compatible with the embodiment relation between human and computer as well as with the holistic approach. In this case it becomes important to know more about the nature of erroneous actions, both with regard to the conditions under which they occur and with regard to the causal 'mechanisms' that lie behind their overt manifestation. In other words, it is necessary to develop a detailed theory of erroneous actions that can be used to analyse events and guide the development of solutions.

The remaining part of this chapter describes an approach to develop a more detailed theory of erroneous actions. The approach starts with the observable phenomena rather than cognitive theories. At the present state of development it has only taken the first step, but it has already served as the basis for developing a specific tool, which is described towards the end.

2 The genotype and phenotype of erroneous action

Actions carried out by a user of a computer system, or more generally by human operators of complex systems, can logically fail to achieve their goal in two different ways. The actions can go as planned, but the plan can be inadequate. Or the plan can be satisfactory, but the actions still do not go as planned. It is the latter situation (also known as 'Actions Not As Planned') which is of interest here. Such incorrectly performed actions are often referred to as human errors, although this term is misleading in its connotations. It would be more correct to say that the actions are erroneous *vis-à-vis* the current plan and goals, because they make them more difficult or even impossible to achieve. The term 'erroneous actions' will therefore be used here.

The two ways in which actions can fail are commonly referred to by the concepts of mistake and slip. A mistake is defined, following Norman [168] and Reason [190], as a planning failure, i.e., an error of judgment or inference where the actions go as planned but where the plan was incorrect. A slip is correspondingly defined as an action that is not in accord with the actor's intention, i.e., the result of a good plan poorly executed (cf. the discussion in Moray and Senders [164]). A slip is clearly a case of 'action not as planned', but the concept must be further refined to be of practical use.

There are two fundamentally different ways to consider erroneous actions. One is with regard to their phenotype, i.e., how they appear in overt action, how they can be observed, hence the empirical basis for their classification. The other is with regard to their genotype, i.e., the functional characteristics of the human cognitive system that are assumed to be a contributing cause of the erroneous actions. (In some cases they may even be assumed to be the complete cause of the erroneous actions!)

One way to improve HCI and partly compensate for the increasing complexity will be actually to design and implement a system which can recognise possible erroneous actions and alert the user of their occurrence. Such an example can be found in ESPRIT P857 - GRADIENT [104, 234], which is summarised towards the end of this chapter. From this point of view it is, in principle, sufficient to be concerned only with the phenotype of erroneous actions. That is, provided patterns of plans and rules for deviations are given, it is a relatively simple matter to construct a plan recognition system. Erroneous actions are, however, not completely random events but depend on the context and the specifics of the current task. Thereby, knowledge of the genotype may be of advantage in the recognition of erroneous actions, since this may be combined with context information to improve the speed and correctness (hit rate) of classification and recognition. Nevertheless, a proper operational definition of the phenotype is required as the foundation for an action-monitoring system which should automatically detect an erroneous action.

3   The genotype of erroneous actions

There are relatively few models or theories of human error/malfunction, which is surprising considering the frequency of erroneous actions. The two models which we shall consider here are commonly recognised in the field. One theory is implied by the CSNI taxonomy [189], wherein the group of mechanisms of human malfunction (cf. Figure 2) contains the following elements:

- **Discrimination:**

    o Stereotype fixation
    o Familiar shortcut
    o Stereotype take-over
    o Familiar pattern not recognised

- **Input information processing:**

    o Information not received
    o Misinterpretation
    o Assumption.

- **Recall:**

    o Forget isolated act
    o Mistake alternatives
    o Other slip of memory

- **Inference:**

    o Condition or side-effect not considered

- **Physical co-ordination:**

    o Motor variability
    o Spatial Misorientation

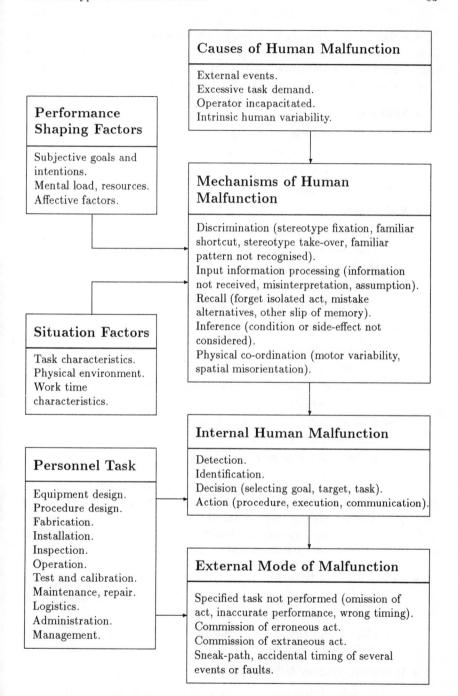

Figure 2: The CSNI taxonomy of human malfunction

Another model, proposed by Reason [192], tries to relate the error-shaping factors with typical error types, using a combination of established theories of cognitive human performance (skill-based, rule-based, and knowledge-based [184]). The error-shaping factors are the following:

- **Skill-based:**
    - o Recency and frequency of previous use
    - o Environmental control signals
    - o Shared schema properties
    - o Concurrent plans

- **Rule-based:**
    - o Mind set ('it has always worked before')
    - o Availability ('first come, first preferred')
    - o Matching bias ('like relates to like')
    - o Over-simplification (e.g., 'halo' effect)
    - o Over-confidence ('I am sure that I am right')

- **Knowledge-based:**
    - o Selectivity (bounded rationality)
    - o Working memory overload (bounded rationality)
    - o Out of sight - out of mind (bounded rationality)
    - o Thematic vagabonding and 'encysting'
    - o Memory cuing / reasoning by analogy
    - o Matching bias revisited
    - o Incomplete / incorrect mental model

These error-shaping factors are, however, of limited interest unless they can be related to a classification of error types (phenotypes). The proposed classification is not strictly operational but includes a mixture of genotypes and phenotypes. More important, therefore, is an account of the varieties of cognitive failures given by Reason [191], which reads as follows:

- **Control mode failure:**
    - o Double-capture slip (attention is captured and, as a result, a dominant plan takes over).
    - o Place-losing and place-mistaking errors (not knowing one's place in the action sequence).

- **Intention system failure:**
    - o Detached intentions (incorrect action sequence carried out, not related to goal).

> o Lost intentions (forgetting intention with current action, not attaining goal).

- **Action system failures:**
  > o Blends (confusion between action sequences, reversal of actions).
  > o External activation of action schemata (automatic triggering of incorrect action sequence).
  > o Program counter failure.
- **Input function failures:**
  > o Perceptual confusion (confusing objects or functions).
  > o Local unawareness (not really knowing what one is doing).

There are clearly many common elements in the two theories of erroneous actions. This is by no means surprising, since they have a common background in cognitive psychology and aim to account for the same set of phenomena. The aim of the work reported here is not to develop or select a theory of human malfunction in the execution of actions, but rather to find a coherent description of the phenotypes, both in the sense of relating genotypes to phenotypes and in the sense of improving the speed and efficiency of a classification. For that purpose the theories presented here are useful in providing a list of the phenomena that must be taken into account. As such they outline the set of events that must be recognisable by a system which purports to detect erroneous actions. The next step is to find some way of ordering this set.

4 Simple phenotypes of erroneous actions

Purposeful action is guided by goals and carried out according to plans. A plan can be defined as:

> a ...representation of both a goal (together with its intermediate subgoals) and the possible actions required to achieve it; where both are related to some time period which may be stated either very precisely or only in the vaguest terms, but which must be specified in some degree [190, p. 69].

In order to produce an initial characterisation of the simple phenotypes of erroneous actions, we shall consider a plan as a single sequence of actions leading to a goal. The actions will be denoted (A, B, C, D, E). We shall further assume that this sequence of actions is necessary and sufficient to reach the goal G. Two additional simplifying assumptions are that the actions take place in an ordinal sequence, i.e., that neither the time of their occurrence

nor their duration is of importance, and that the actions are single actions
that can be executed one at a time, i.e., the success or failure of an action
can be determined immediately.

Of course, these assumptions are not tenable when we consider more realistic cases of erroneous actions. Even in this simple case we can, nevertheless,
distinguish several basic phenotypes of erroneous actions. The basic phenotypes are derived partly from an analysis of the finite number of ways in which
a set of actions can be permuted, and partly from the concepts provided by
the classifications mentioned above.

4.1   Intrusion

If the correct sequence of actions is

(A   B   C   D   E)

and the actual sequence of actions is

(A   B   C   **X**   D   E)

then, clearly, a new action has entered in the sequence as an intrusion (cf.
Figure 3). The intruding action may be totally unrelated to the on-going
sequence, and may have serious negative effects. It may, however, also be
neutral, hence not have any effects. We shall later make a distinction between
intrusions and insertions.

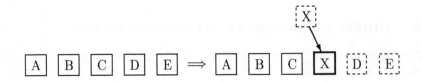

Figure 3: Intrusion

Note that intrusion must be the first or default hypothesis for any erroneous action. The detection that something is wrong is triggered by the
occurrence of an unexpected event. Since we, for the moment, are disre-
garding time the only possible triggering condition is the **occurrence** of an
unexpected event. (When time is included, the **absence** of an event may
also be a triggering condition.) Even an omission cannot be ascertained with
certainty before it has been determined that the following action is in the
sequence. The same goes for repetition which can be seen as a special kind
of intrusion.

4.2 Replacement

If the correct sequence of actions is

(A   B   C   D   E)

and the actual sequence of actions is

(A   B   C′   D   E)

then, clearly, one of the actions has been replaced by another (cf. Figure 4). The replacement is, however, not fatal to attaining the goal since the new action somehow achieves the same as the old one—although this can only be determined when the following action D has been carried out. Replacement may be seen as a special type of intrusion combined with omission, where the intruding action is benign rather than malign. It is, however, reasonable to consider this as a separate category.

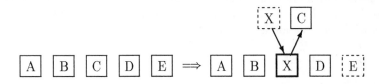

Figure 4 : Replacement

4.3 Omission

If the correct sequence of action is

(A   B   C   D   E)

and the actual sequence of actions is

(A   B   nil D   E)

then, clearly, one action has been omitted from the sequence (cf. Figure 5a). The sequence is incomplete and the goal cannot be reached unless the omitted action is reinserted or reproduced, provided that this is still possible. If the correct sequence of actions is

(A   B   C   D   E)

and the actual sequence of actions is

(A   B   C   D   nil)

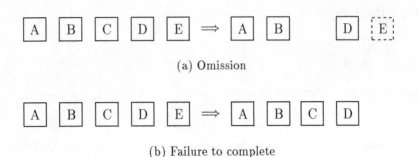

(a) Omission

(b) Failure to complete

Figure 5: Types of omission

we have a special type of omission of the last action, which is a *failure to complete* the sequence (cf. Figure 5b). Experience has shown that this may be a frequent contribution to erroneous actions, particularly when more than one plan is carried out simultaneously. A symmetrical case would be the omission of the first action in a sequence, i.e., the correct sequence:

(A   B   C   D   E)

would be replaced by

(**nil** B   C   D   E)

This is assumed not to be nearly as serious as omitting the last action since it only means that the action sequence is not started (or that the first action is missed; but if the actions can continue then, clearly, the first action was not crucial for attaining the goal, i.e., it was optional rather than required (see below).

4.4   Repetition

If the correct sequence of actions is

(A   B   C   D   E)

and the actual sequence of actions is

(A   B   C   C   D   E)

then, clearly, one of the actions has been carried out twice, i.e., it has been repeated (cf. Figure 6). Depending on the situation this may or may not be crucial for whether the goal can be attained.

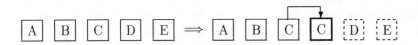

Figure 6: Repetition

4.5 Reversal

If the correct sequence of actions is

(A   B   C   D   E)

and the actual sequence of actions is

(A   B   **D**   **C**   E)

then, clearly, two of the actions have been reversed in the sequence (cf. Figure 7). This may have serious consequences for attaining the goal. The detection of the reversal of two actions C and D is a slightly more complicated affair and requires that a record or log of previous events is kept. Reversal can actually be seen as an omission of an action C, followed by an intrusion of action C (after action D, which is needed to detect the omission anyway). We shall restrict the meaning of reversal to cover only the cases where two neighbouring actions replace each other.

Figure 7: Reversal

4.6 Simple erroneous actions and time

This defines five simple phenotypes of erroneous actions, as illustrated in Figures 3–8. Note that so far we have not made any assumptions about the possible underlying causes, i.e., the genotype. The five simple types are, however, incomplete. In order to extend them we must introduce the dimension of time. Even in the cases we have considered so far, where the timing of actions is not used explicitly, some kind of chronological order or event record is still required to make the final identification.

The introduction of time means that each step in the action sequence describes both *what* the action is and *when* it should occur. Without going into the specifics of how time is represented, and assuming that time is given as a point rather than an interval, we can define two additional phenotypes of erroneous actions.

4.6.1   Absence of action

If the correctly timed sequence of actions is

$$(A \quad B \quad C \quad D \quad E)$$
$$(t_1 \quad t_2 \quad t_3 \quad t_4 \quad t_5)$$

and the actual sequence of actions is

$$(A \quad B \quad nil \quad \ldots)$$
$$(t_1 \quad t_2 \quad t_3 \quad \ldots)$$

then, clearly, the action **C** did not occur when it was expected to, i.e., there was a delay in its execution.

What is detected is actually the absence of an action or the intrusion of the action **nil**. We must therefore distinguish between the following subsidiary cases (cf. Figure 8):

$$(A \quad B \quad nil \quad C \quad D \quad E)$$
$$(t_1 \quad t_2 \quad t_3 \quad t_3' \quad t_4 \quad t_5)$$

If action C occurs later than it should have but still before action D occurs, thus maintaining the correct sequence, then there was a *genuine delay*. (Action D may, of course, also be disturbed and occur at t_4' rather than at t_4.)

$$(A \quad B \quad nil \quad D \quad E)$$
$$(t_1 \quad t_2 \quad t_3 \quad t_4 \quad t_5)$$

If action C did not occur but action D did, then the delay can be regarded simply as a *genuine omission*.

$$(A \quad B \quad nil \quad X \quad E)$$
$$(t_1 \quad t_2 \quad t_3 \quad t_4 \quad t_5)$$

If the action at time t_4 is X rather than D or C, then it must be further analysed to determine the precise phenotype.

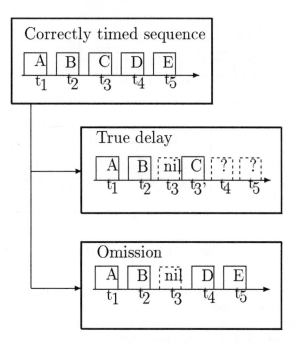

Figure 8: True delay and omission

4.6.2 Unexpected action

If the correctly timed sequence of actions is

$$(A \quad B \quad C \quad D \quad E)$$
$$(t_1 \quad t_2 \quad t_3 \quad t_4 \quad t_5)$$

and the actual sequence of actions is

$$(A \quad B \quad \mathbf{X} \quad \ldots)$$
$$(t_1 \quad t_2 \quad t'_2 \quad t_3)$$

then, clearly, an action occurred *before* it was expected. Corresponding to the case of a delay, we can define the case of a *premature action* as

$$(A \quad B \quad \mathbf{C} \quad \mathbf{nil} \quad D \quad E)$$
$$(t_1 \quad t_2 \quad t'_2 \quad t_3 \quad t_4 \quad t_5)$$

In this case the action occurred earlier than expected (cf. Figure 9). In all other cases the action X at t'_2 must be further analysed, and the erroneous

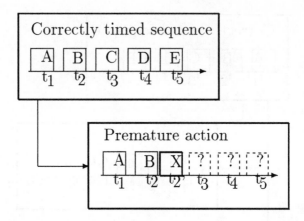

Figure 9: Premature action

action may belong to any of the simple phenotypes of repetition, intrusion, replacement, and reversal.

The common point in these cases is that a measurement of time is important for the detection of the erroneous action. The detection is, in a sense, active rather than passive because it looks for an event at time t_2 rather than waiting for something to happen. Considerations of time can in principle be combined with all the detection criteria described in this section.

5   Complex phenotypes of erroneous actions

The simple phenotypes described above were mostly derived from an analytical basis, considering single actions in relation to an abstract sequence of actions. In order to get a more realistic set of phenotypes for erroneous actions we should consider more complex cases involving longer segments of (two or more) actions, as well as cases where action sequences occur in parallel to each other and where they possibly interact and interfere. Since the analytical procedure we used above quickly will produce too many combinations, a better approach is to consider the existing taxonomies and classifications schemes based on empirical data.

5.1   The CSNI taxonomy

One source for defining the complex phenotypes of erroneous actions is the classification system or taxonomy for event reports developed by Rasmussen *et al.* [189]. The purpose of this taxonomy was to support the reporting of abnormal events in nuclear power plants. It contains the following seven main groups:

- Cause of human malfunction.
- Performance-shaping factors.
- Situation factors.
- Mechanisms of human malfunction.
- Internal human malfunction.
- Personnel task.
- External mode of malfunction.

The details of these seven groups are shown in Figure 2. With regard to the development of the phenotypes, only the last group is directly relevant. This contains the following elements:

- **External mode of malfunction:**
  - Specified task not performed.
  - Omission of act.
  - Inaccurate performance.
  - Wrong timing.
- Commission of erroneous act.
- Commission of extraneous act.
- Sneak-path, accidental timing of several events or faults.

Even a cursory look reveals that the types of human malfunction listed here correspond rather well with the simple phenotypes defined above, partly because the malfunctions refer to single or isolated actions. Thus:

- **Omission of act** obviously is the same as the phenotype 'omission'.
- **Inaccurate performance** means that the action was performed but in an unsatisfactory way. This is not a unique characterisation and is not included in the simple phenotypes. It could, however, be seen as a form of inadequate replacement. A further reason for not including inaccurate performance among the phenotypes is that it, usually, cannot be detected at the time of occurrence but only when the consequences become clear.
- **Wrong timing** can be seen as being either of the phenotypes 'true delay' or 'premature action'.

- **Commission of erroneous act** can be further specified as either of the phenotypes 'repetition', 'reversal' or 'replacement'.

- **Commission of extraneous act** corresponds to the phenotype 'intrusion'.

- **Sneak-path** refers to composite actions or events, hence does not belong to the simple phenotypes.

5.2 The classification of 'Action Not As Planned'

A different classification can be found in the study made by James Reason of everyday cases of 'Action Not As Planned' [190]. The classifications were based on diaries from thirty-five volunteers who over a period of 2 weeks recorded their cases of 'actions not as planned'. In this study the following categories were applied:

- Discrimination failure:
  - Perceptual confusion (physically similar objects are confused).
  - Functional confusion (functionally similar objects are confused).
  - Spatial confusion (objects in close proximity are confused).
  - Temporal confusion (time is misperceived leading to inappropriate actions).

- Program assembly failure:
  - **Reversal of program elements.**
  - Confusion between currently active programs.
  - Confusion between on-going and stored program.

- Test failure:
  - Stop-rule overshoot (actions proceed beyond intended end point).
  - Stop-rule undershoot (actions are terminated prior to end point).
  - Branching error (common initial sequence results in wrong route taken).
  - **Multiple side-tracking** (temporary diversion by side-steps).

- Sub-routine failure:
  - **Insertions** (unwanted actions added to a sequence).
  - **Omissions** (necessary actions are left out of a sequence).
  - **Misordering** (correct actions are carried out in the wrong order).

- Storage failure:

    o Forgetting previous actions (losing one's place in the sequence).
    o Forgetting discrete times in a plan (forgetting single actions).
    o Reverting to earlier plans (with incorrect starting conditions).
    o Forgetting the substance of a plan (forgetting goal or purpose).

The number of categories here is larger than in the CSNI taxonomy, probably because this classification refers to sequences (combinations) of actions rather than actions in isolation. Note, however, that only a few of these categories (written in **boldface**) refer to proper phenotypes. Instead, most of the categories describe either causes or reasons for the erroneous action, i.e., they refer to the genotypes. For instance, a branching error will show itself as an insertion (or intrusion) and only an extended analysis will reveal that the intrusion was of a whole sequence rather than of a single action (hence the branching error) and reveal what the cause of this was. The reason for this mixture of phenotypes and genotypes is probably that the data material was subjective or introspective reports from the people who committed the 'actions not as planned'. They therefore had inside or privileged knowledge of the conditions that existed in each event. Accordingly, they could provide descriptions that went beyond those of pure phenotypes.

5.3 The need to operationalise the phenotypes

The problem of describing the complex phenotypes of erroneous actions is to constrain oneself to use only what can be observed or recorded. Since we know about erroneous actions from ourselves, it is difficult not to include 'state descriptions' of the cognitive system such as 'confusion' and 'forgetting'. We all know how the loss of attention can lead to unexpected developments in our actions, such as making the wrong turn while driving or losing track of what we are doing. Loss of attention, however, cannot be observed directly but must be inferred from the pattern of actions. (Although it is conceivable that loss of attention, directly or indirectly, may be measured physiologically we will in this context assume that this is not a practical solution.) It does, accordingly, not belong to the phenotypes. The same is the case for many of the other types in the classification developed by James Reason. While this mixture of phenotypes and genotypes may be quite proper for the psychological analysis of erroneous actions it is, unfortunately, not permissible in the approach we take here. In order to design a system that can actually detect erroneous actions, we must remain strict empiricists (or even positivists!) whether we like it or not. The study of both phenotypes and genotypes is, however, a very useful element in the analyses leading to the design of such a system.

6   A taxonomy of phenotypes of erroneous actions

One conclusion that can be made on basis of the theories and models presented so far is that a classification cannot be limited to single or isolated
actions. Many of the concepts used in the theories and taxonomies relate to
longer segments of an action sequence. Branching, for instance, means that a
common initial sequence is continued along the wrong branch. If only a single action was considered, the situation would be classified as, e.g., intrusion.
But if the larger segments of action sequences are included in the analysis,
the end result may be different. The same goes for most of the other simple
phenotypes.

This has an obvious impact on the design of an automatic classification
system. If we limit the system to work with single actions or short segments
of actions, corresponding, e.g., to a short time span, then it will only be able
to classify the relatively simple erroneous actions. If we extend the length of
the action sequences or the time span that the system can work with, then it
will be able to detect the more complicated types of erroneous actions. It will,
however, also be far more complex, among other things because it will need to
maintain a larger set of possible classifications, i.e., a larger set of hypotheses
of erroneous actions for a given situation. The system will slowly change
from making a classification of erroneous actions to recognising hypothetical
actions sequences or plans. The difference may seem subtle, but it will play
a decisive role for how a system is constructed.

An implementation of an action-monitoring system necessarily represents
a trade-off between the level of analysis of the actions and the precision of the
outcome. If the analysis is focussed on the simple phenotypes, the outcome
will be a very precise classification but it will be expressed in terms of single
actions rather than events or plans, hence have little bearing on higher-order
concepts such as goals or purposes. If the analysis is focussed on the complex
phenotypes, the outcome will be a less precise classification of longer action
sequences which, however, will be more directly relevant for a description in
terms of plans and goals. The analysis will also be 'delayed', because the
system has to consider each action in the context of those which follow it,
and because the results may be subject to revisions. The balance between
the level of analysis and the precision of the outcome is something which must
be determined for each particular case.

With that in mind, we will go on to combine the models and classifications
presented so far, as shown in Figure 10. This is a proposal for a taxonomy of
the phenotypes of erroneous actions which includes simple as well as complex
phenotypes. Reading from top to bottom, the following comments can be
made:

• **Action in wrong place.** Here the action belongs to the current se-

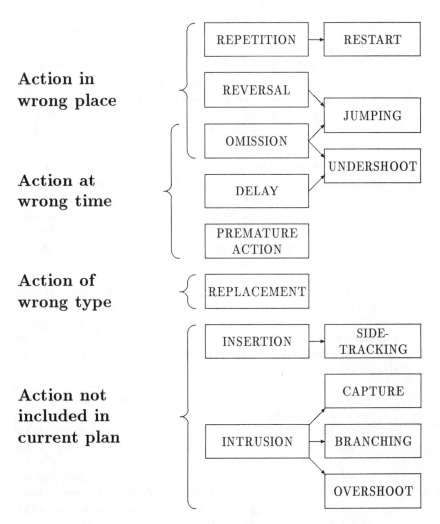

Figure 10 : A taxonomy of phenotypes of erroneous action

quence, but is placed incorrectly.

  o One simple phenotype is **repetition**, i.e., an action is a repetition of the previous action. (Note that this can only occur when the actions are contiguous. Otherwise the erroneous action will be considered as a case of forwards or backwards jumping, cf. below.) The corresponding complex phenotype is **restart**, i.e., that an already completed segment of the action sequence is repeated, possibly from the very beginning, starting with a jump backwards.

  o A second simple phenotype is **reversal**, i.e., the next two actions in the expected sequence are reversed. The corresponding complex phenotype is **jumping**, i.e., segments longer than one action are reversed or more than one action is skipped (hence jumping ahead in the sequence, cf. below).

  o A third simple phenotype is **omission**, i.e., that the expected action is missing. There are two complex phenotypes that correspond to this. If more than one action is omitted we effectively have a case of **jumping forwards**, cf. above. If the rest of the action sequence is omitted, we have a case of **undershoot**, i.e., that an action sequence is not completed as planned. A special case of this is the omission of the last action of an action sequence.

• **Action at wrong time.** The simple phenotype omission could also occur if the action was not carried out when it was required. In fact, the classification of actions that occur at the wrong time can in principle be combined with any of the other classifications (wrong place, wrong type, wrong action sequence). There is, however, good reason to consider this classification in its own right. There are two additional cases.

  o One simple phenotype is **delay**, i.e., that an action does not occur when it is required. A true delay means that the sequence of the following actions is maintained (although it may become subject to temporal contraction [63]). Otherwise the absence of an action (i.e., the intrusion of the action **nil**) may be followed by any of the other phenotypes. If the delayed actions conclude the action sequence the corresponding complex phenotype will be **undershoot**, because the remaining actions in effect are omitted - at least within the time span of the observation.

  o A second simple phenotype is **premature action**, i.e., that an action occurs when no action was expected. The action may be either correct or of any of the known simple phenotypes. (Premature action may, in particular, occur during compression of actions to compensate for an earlier delay.)

- **Action of wrong type.** This category means that the action was incorrect although not so wrong that it disrupted the on-going plan.

  o The simple phenotype is **replacement**, i.e., that the action is a proper substitute for the expected action. The two actions are functionally equivalent in the sense that the replacement does not invalidate the conditions that must remain for the continuation of the action sequence. The exact criteria for this will depend on the domain and the task. There is no corresponding complex phenotype, but replacement may be of a single action or a segment of actions. (Determining that an action is a replacement may require either additional input from the user or await an evaluation of the consequences.)

- **Action not included in current plan.** Here the action does not belong to the current action sequence.

  o One simple phenotype is **insertion**, which occurs if the action does not belong to the action sequence and if it does not disrupt it. This is the case when a single, unrelated action occurs in the middle of an action sequence (spurious insertion). The corresponding complex phenotype is side-tracking, where a segment or sequence of unrelated actions is carried out before the current action sequence is resumed. Note that this is not the same as a subroutine, which is not an erroneous action. It also differs from branching (and capture) because the original plan eventually will be resumed.

  o A second simple phenotype is **intrusion**, which occurs if the action does not belong to the action sequence, and if it disrupts it. There are three complex phenotypes that correspond to this. The first is **capture**, which means that the action sequence is effectively disrupted and replaced by a rivalling (and probably more dominant) action sequence. The second is **branching**, which means than an action segment, which is common to two or more action sequences, is continued along the wrong action sequence (i.e., effectively taking the wrong branch at a decision point). The third complex phenotype is **overshoot**, which means that an action sequence is continued beyond its end point, i.e., after the goal criteria have been satisfied.

Note that the distinction between insertion and intrusion cannot be made at the time of the event, but only later when longer action segments have been analysed and the consequences ascertained. To be more precise, if the action sequence is successfully resumed, then the event was an insertion or side-tracking; otherwise it was an intrusion or one of the corresponding complex phenotypes.

A symbolic representation of the complex phenotypes is given in Figures 11 and 12.

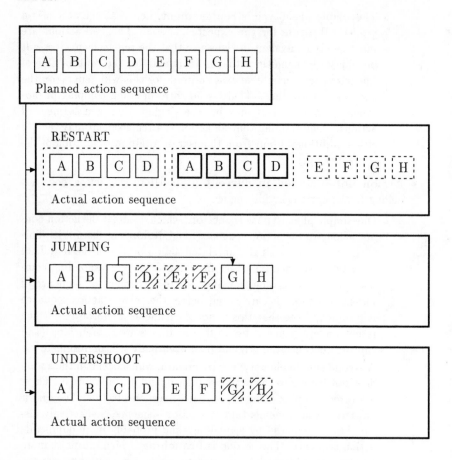

Figure 11: Complex phenotypes of erroneous actions

The purpose of this taxonomy of phenotypes of erroneous actions is to establish a basis for a working action classification system, i.e., a computer program. The taxonomy makes no pretensions of explaining erroneous actions and does not include any assumptions about the genotype. From the practical point of view one difficulty with this taxonomy, and I suspect of all other taxonomies as well, is that it cannot be implemented as a purely data-driven (bottom-up) system. Even the simple phenotypes require some kind of event record and back tracking, and the complex phenotypes certainly depend on the maintenance and gradual refinement of multiple hypotheses (classification). Current software methods, particularly the use of object-oriented

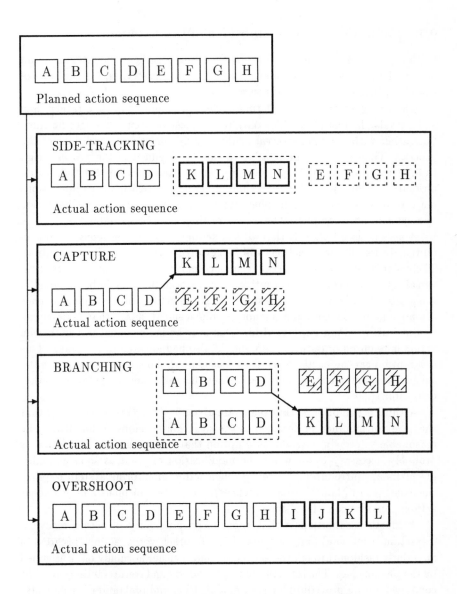

Figure 12: Complex phenotypes (continued)

programming languages and rule-based systems, may, however, overcome this problem.

6.1   Limitations and assumptions of the taxonomy

With the possible design of an automatic action classification system in mind it should be noted that the above taxonomy of phenotypes, for the sake of simplicity, makes a number of assumptions.

The first assumption is that time is defined as points in time rather than as intervals. In real life actions only rarely need to occur at a specific time, but rather within a time interval defined by dynamics and conditions of the process. Time may also be relative to the development of the process (e.g., **before** the pressure of X becomes Y) rather than refer to real time as an absolute indication. Considering time intervals and relative time indications may not require changes of the phenotypes, but does make the implementation of a system more complex. The aspect of time is discussed later.

A second assumption is that all the actions in an action sequence are required. In real life some actions will be **required** and some will be **optional**. The order of actions in an action sequence may also be optional, so that reversals are not necessarily disruptive. Such information should be included in the plans. It is, however, **not** assumed that the actions in an action sequence are all unique. In fact, the phenotype replacement shows that actions can be both **unique** and **replaceable**. This may be independent of whether an action is required or optional, but should also be indicated in the plan. (This assumption can be partly relaxed by considering plans in terms of goals and subgoals, i.e., states to be achieved, rather than as actions, cf. also the earlier definition.)

A third assumption is that plans are given *a priori* (predefined) and that they are not modified or changed as the situation develops. While it may be reasonable to remain with the assumption that plans are given *a priori*, it is probably necessary to allow for the modification of plans as soon as multiple plans are introduced. Since a proper action-monitoring system requires the existence of plans (action sequences), recognition of plans and erroneous actions must be considered together.

A fourth assumption is that there is no possibility of action recovery, retractions (undoing) and counteractions. In other words, actions progress in an orderly fashion through the action sequence, either normally or as assumed by the phenotypes. The introduction of retraction and counteractions must be combined with a procedure for plan modification and replanning. It may also require an adequate state identification system and, probably, a simulation-based consequence propagation mechanism.

A fifth assumption is that there is only one current action sequence, i.e., the observed action is compared against a single plan. The extension to cover multiple plans will, however, not require additional phenotypes, as the same comparison can be made for multiple plans. In fact, multiple plans are required for some of the complex phenotypes, such as branching, although one can still assume that only one action sequence is active. Problems may nevertheless arise with regard to the order of comparison (assuming it will be sequential rather than parallel) and the priority or weight given to different matches, corresponding to the effect of endorsement for correct plans/actions. This assumption is, however, the easiest to eliminate.

The taxonomy, by definition, only considers erroneous actions. In order to be really useful it may have to be extended with the phenotypes of correct actions, in particular the phenomena of nesting and suspended actions. This could, for instance, be useful for the design of an advanced plan-recognition system.

7 Erroneous actions and time

The consideration of time is important for the analysis and description of human error (and human action more generally). Surprisingly, few of the existing action and error taxonomies include the aspect of time, but rather describe and classify human error on an atemporal (static) basis, i.e., a classification of past and observed events. Time may enter in a few cases as one of the possible causes (i.e., incorrect timing of actions), but the focus is predominantly on the consequences of the actions (which led them to be classified as human errors).

In many domains it is, however, necessary to include time in a much more conspicuous way, as, perhaps, one of the principal 'mechanisms' or 'error areas' of human action. In addition to the well-known mistakes and confusions in a physical space (mistaking control buttons, places, etc.) there may also be similar mistakes and confusions in a temporal space. This is particularly important with respect to planning and scheduling. In error taxonomies the actual planning of actions occurs only under the guise of intended actions. The top-down goal analysis may recognise the breakdown of an act into separate actions related to subgoals, but this is seen as a set of discrete events, i.e., moving through the state-space in a step-by-step fashion. In addition one must also consider the aspects of temporal planning (scheduling) and the position of action steps *vis-à-vis* one another.

Time was introduced in the presentation of the simple phenotypes to compensate for some obvious shortcomings in the proposed categories, and time will obviously also be important for the complex phenotypes. In order fully to assess the impact of time on the recognition of erroneous actions, we must consider both how time can play a role in the erroneous actions (as a causal factor in the genotype and as a performance trait in the phenotype) and how time can be represented in plans and actions and thereby be used in the recognition process.

7.1 The phenotype of temporal errors

Despite the obvious importance of time for human action there is a surprising lack of analyses of the role of time in how actions are carried out [63]. For instance, the error taxonomies mentioned above either fail to address that aspect or only treat it cursorily. One of the few descriptions of temporal errors can be found in Decortis and Cacciabue [62], who presented the following classification of time-related erroneous actions:

- **Misestimation of sequences of actions.** Inversions (reversals) of actions, omissions of actions. Here users fail to organise actions in a sequence with precise boundaries.

- **Misestimation of time duration.** Temporal distortions either as overestimation of subjectively filled time intervals or underestimation of subjectively empty time intervals.

- **Failure in estimating the right moment to take action.** This may be due either to incorrect estimation of duration or to a failure to identify the correct moment (conditions) when an action should occur.

- **Failure in anticipating an event.** The user makes a prediction of future events which is temporally imprecise.

- **Failure in the synchronisation of collective actions.** This is an extension of one or more of the previous temporal errors which specifically covers the scheduling of collective action.

This classification is obviously aimed at the genotypes rather than the phenotypes. It may, however, be set in relation to the previously defined phenotypes in the following way.

- Misestimation of sequences of actions and events are clearly related to the simple phenotypes of **reversal, repetition** and **omission**.

- Misestimation of time duration may be classified as either **undershoot** (concluding the actions too early) or **overshoot** (continuing the actions beyond the expected stopping point).

- Failure in estimating the right moment to take action can be classified as either **premature action** or **delayed action**.

- Failure to anticipate an event is clearly a genotype rather than a phenotype, because the failure only shows itself indirectly, i.e., through an erroneous action.

- Failure in the synchronisation of collective actions is also a genotype rather than a phenotype. Furthermore, the action-monitoring system we are discussing here does not yet include the monitoring of collective actions (although the system as such is unable to determine whether an action has been carried out by one user or by many).

The conclusion from this short discussion of temporal errors is that the set of phenotypes already developed can be used to classify temporal errors as well. The knowledge that temporal factors play a role can be used to suggest additional causes for the phenotypes, i.e., to enhance the diagnosis. The knowledge may also be used to introduce additional criteria for detecting an erroneous action, i.e., an active (goal-driven) detection based on expectations of action occurrences, as opposed to a passive (data-driven) detection triggered by the occurrence of an action.

7.2 The representation of time

Since time is clearly important for action monitoring and the recognition of erroneous actions, we must consider the possibilities for temporal relations between two actions, and how these can be represented in a plan. The proper representation of time is an important issue for any action monitoring system. On the one hand there is the time identification of the actions as they occur. This will most naturally be given as some kind of time stamp, either in real time or a suitable derivation thereof. On the other hand there is the time indications for the individual actions in the plan. This will only rarely be in real time, because the actions seldom need to be carried out at a precisely defined moment. (Obvious exceptions are launching of satellites, celebrations of the new year, and bank robberies—at least according to the myth of many films.)

A good starting point for this analysis is a proposal by Allen [3] on how to classify the temporal relations between two events. (The distinction between actions and events will be made clear below.) If the events are called $Event_i$ and $Event_j$, respectively, the following relations are possible:

- **Before** $(Event_i, Event_j)$: $Event_i$ is before $Event_j$ and they do not overlap.

- **After** $(Event_j, Event_i)$: $Event_j$ is after $Event_i$ and they do not overlap. This is equivalent to **Before** $(Event_i, Event_j)$.

- **During** $(Event_i, Event_j)$: $Event_i$ is included in $Event_j$, i.e., $Event_i$ begins after $Event_j$ has begun and ends before $Event_j$ is ended.

- **Meets** $(Event_i, Event_j)$: $Event_i$ is before $Event_j$ and there is no interval between them, i.e., $Event_j$ starts when $Event_i$ ends.

- **Overlaps** ($Event_i, Event_j$) : $Event_i$ starts before $Event_j$ ends and continues after $Event_j$ has started but stops before $Event_j$ does.

- **Equal** ($Event_i, Event_j$) : $Event_i$ and $Event_j$ occupy the same time interval.

- **Starts** ($Event_i, Event_j$) : $Event_i$ starts at the same time as $Event_j$, but ends before $Event_j$ does.

- **Finishes** ($Event_i, Event_j$) : $Event_i$ ends at the same time as $Event_j$, but starts after $Event_j$ begins.

The relations described above can be shown graphically as in Figure 13: Allen's classification is clearly a pure phenotype which specifies correct or proper temporal relationships. For each of these an incorrect relationships can be defined as a violation of the specific condition. For instance, if the relation **Before** ($Event_i, Event_j$) has been prescribed any other relation between the events, as they occur, will constitute an error. In that sense using any other category to describe the observed relation between the events will mean that an erroneous action has occurred. This, nevertheless, does not mean that Allen's classification constitute a phenotype of erroneous actions.

Allen's classification refers to events rather than actions. Events can be defined as segments of behaviour which have a duration as well as clear criteria for initiation and termination (also often referred to as start rules and stop rules, respectively). Actions can be defined as segments of behaviour that do not have a duration, but which may have clear initiating conditions. An event is essentially a sequence of actions, and it is often initiated (and terminated) by a specific action. For instance, baking bread is initiated by putting the unbaked bread in an oven and terminated by removing the baked bread from the oven.

It is obvious from this classification that the times when an event starts and ends are important. We may, however, improve the precision of the characterisation by using four different time indications:

- **Earliest Starting Time (EST).** This is the earliest time at which an event can be started, or the time before which an event must not be begun. It can also be used to refer to the earliest starting time for an action.

- **Latest Starting Time (LST).** This the latest time at which an event can be started, or the time after which an event must not be begun. It can also be used to refer to the latest starting time for an action.

- **Earliest Finishing Time (EFT).** This is the earliest time at which an event can be stopped, or the time until which an event must continue. The minimum duration of an event is thus EFT - LST.

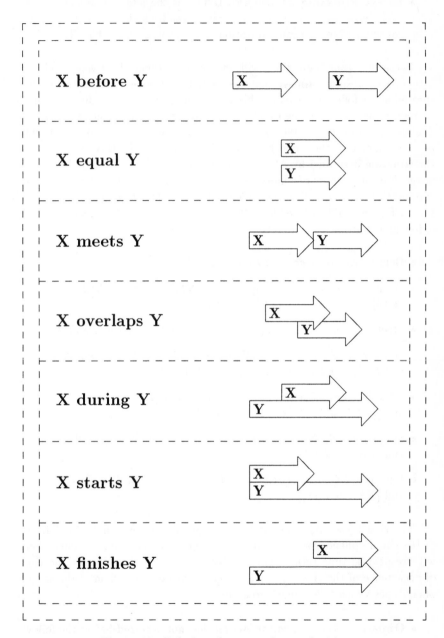

Figure 13: Relations between time and action

- **Latest Finishing Time (LFT).** This is the latest time at which an event may be stopped, or the time beyond which an event must not continue. The maximum duration of an event is thus LFT - EST.

These four time indications will, of course, normally be given as relative rather than absolute times, i.e., they will be given in relation to another (preceding or following) event. This will at the same time specify the logical temporal conditions for the events, e.g., that $Event_j$ should not start before $Event_i$ has been completed ($EST_j > LFT_i$). Clearly, EST and LST may be the same, and the same goes for EFT and LFT. In this case we have the situation described by Allen's analysis where only one time indication is given. For the purpose of a more complete analysis it is, however, necessary to employ all four time indications. We shall use the four time indications EST, LST, EFT and LFT indexed for either $Event_i$ or $Event_j$, thus producing the following definitions:

- Before $(Event_i, Event_j) : LFT_i < EST_j$.

- During $(Event_i, Event_j) : [[EST_i > EST_j]$ or $[LST_i > LST_j]]$ and $[[LFT_i < LFT_j]$ or $[EFT_i < EFT_j]]$.

- Meets $(Event_i, Event_j) : (x, x \in [EFT_i, LFT_i]$ and $x \in [EST_j, LST_j])$.

- Overlaps $(Event_i, Event_j) : [[LST_i < EST_j]$ and $[EFT_i > LST_j]]$ or $[[LST_j < EFT_i]$ and $[EFT_j > LFT_i]]$.

- Equal $(Event_i, Event_j) : [[EST_i = EST_j]$ or $[LST_i = LST_j]]$ and $[[EFT_i = EFT_j]$ or $[LFT_i = LFT_j]]$.

- Starts $(Event_i, Event_j) : [[EST_i = EST_j]$ or $[LST_i = LST_j]]$ and $[LFT_i < EFT_j]$.

- Finishes $(Event_i, Event_j) : [[EFT_i = EFT_j]$ or $[LFT_i = LFT_j]]$ and $[EST_i > LST_j]$.

By using these definitions it becomes possible to extend the definitions of the simple phenotypes to include the aspect of time, i.e., to define them with respect to time rather than as abstract events. If we denote the time of occurrence of the $Action_j$ as T_j, we can provide a definition of the simple phenotypes which takes time into account.

- **Omission** occurs when the $Action_j$ has not occurred before the following $Action_k$ occurs, i.e., $T_j > LST_k$. This is the same as saying that when the $Action_k$ occurs at $T_k (T_k \geq LST_k)$ then $Action_j$ has not yet taken place, hence T_j is unknown.

- A **repetition** can in principle take place both as a Before and Meets condition. (It could, in principle, also be During, Overlap, Equal, Starts and Finishes although the simultaneity of the two occurrences of the same action probably would cancel any effects—apart from the possible interlocks in the system which may prevent it from happening. In a psychological sense it is also impossible to do the same thing twice at the same time.)

- **Replacement** can be qualified by requiring that the substitute $action_k$ takes place when the original $action_j$ should have happened, i.e., $EST_k \geq EST_j$ and $LFT_k \leq LFT_j$.

- **Reversal** can be specified as the case when the 'reversed' action takes place before its predecessor, i.e., $LFT_k \leq EST_j$ or the conditions Before and Meet.

Finally, the two time-related simple phenotypes premature action and true delay can be defines as follows:

- Premature action: $T_j < EST_j$
- True delay: $T_j > LST_j$.

The initiating condition for an action or an event can be a temporal relationship ('start X when Y has finished', 'start X 90 seconds after Y has started', etc.) but may also be a state condition. Similarly, the termination of an event may be defined temporally or as a state condition (or a combination). A temporal relation is thus just a special case of the conditions that can be used to describe initiating and terminating criteria. In that sense Allen's classification somewhat overemphasises the importance of time.

The important issue is that the relations between actions and events must be defined in the plans which serve as the reference for the action monitoring. By specifying the initiating and terminating conditions for events and the initiating conditions for actions, either in terms of temporal relations or process states, it becomes possible to specify precisely the sequence or order that the actions must maintain. This can be done once and for all or revised during the execution of the actions, whenever plans are revised. It is important for the action monitoring to be able to make this assumption, since without that the identification of erroneous actions becomes hypothetical. While this may be a feasible solution, it does call for entirely different measures, and will therefore not be considered here.

7.3 The operationalisation of the phenotypes

In order to design a plan-recognition system, the simple phenotypes described in the preceding chapter must be formalised and specified in an operational form, i.e., in a way which can be used by an information-processing artifact. Only this will determine if they are pure phenotypes, or whether they combine phenotypes and genotypes. Given the assumptions made so far, a tentative set of operational definitions can be given. In the first four cases, where time is not included, the identification of the phenotype is triggered by the occurrence of an unexpected event. The principles of the operational specifications are shown schematically in Figure 14.

The fifth simple phenotype, reversal, is more difficult to detect. Unlike the other four simple phenotypes, the detection of a reversal requires that a log or recording has been made of the actions that have occurred, as well as of the erroneous actions that have been identified. As mentioned earlier, a reversal can be seen as the omission of an action followed by the omitted action. Assuming that the identifications of the simple phenotypes are expressed as facts which may be interpreted by rules, the reversal can very simply be expressed as a conjunction of the two facts 'omission' and 'intrusion'.

A system which performs a detection of erroneous actions based on these principles can easily be implemented but this only constitutes the first step in building an error recognition mechanism. Note that the operational definitions only include the simple phenotypes. The reason is that an identification of a complex phenotype, e.g., jumping, must be based on a previous identification of a simple phenotype. As a matter of fact, the recognition of erroneous actions must logically start from a very simple basis and augment that by introducing a reasoning mechanism that knows about the simple and complex phenotypes.

8   The Response Evaluation System (RESQ)

8.1   GRADIENT system overview

The objectives of the ESPRIT project P857 on Graphics and Knowledge-based Dialogue for Dynamic Processes (also known as the GRAphical DIalogue ENvironmenT or GRADIENT) are to investigate the use of knowledge-based systems to support the operator of industrial supervision and control systems, specifically:

> to enhance the monitoring of dynamic processes;

> to enable the operator to conduct an intelligent graphical dialogue (supported by graphical expert systems) with the process;

> to support the designers of such systems by means of specific tools.

These objectives are achieved by building a set of cooperating knowledge processing systems which supports a dynamic dialogue. The GRADIENT system architecture is shown in Figure 15.

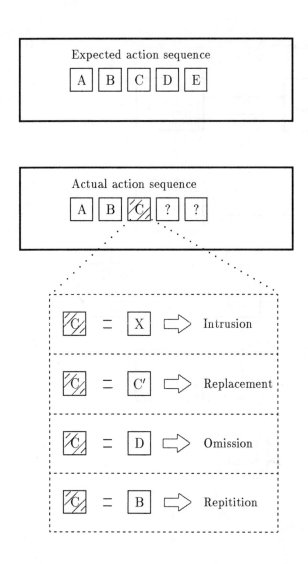

Figure 14: Basic phenotypes of erroneous actions: detection principles

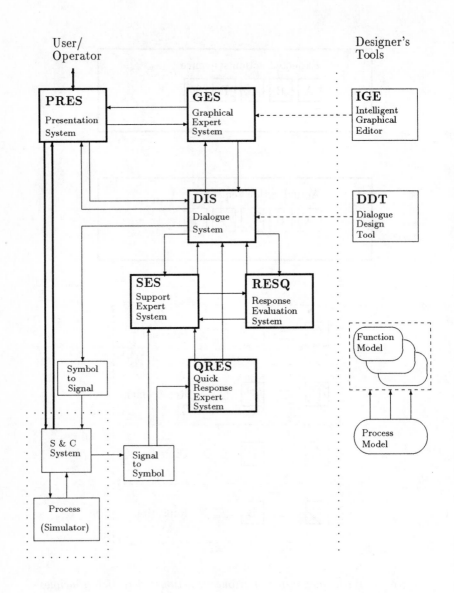

Figure 15 : Overall functional architecture of the GRADIENT system

Operator support is provided by three knowledge-based GRADIENT modules:

- The **Quick Response Expert System** (QRES) monitors key values from the process though the Supervisory and Control (S&C) system and handles alarms generated by the existing S&C system. Using a set of small knowledge-bases, QRES responds quickly to error syndromes, advises the operator of the most important condition and recommends possible restorative action.

- The **Support Expert System** (SES) acts as an intelligent consultant to both the operator and the other modules of the GRADIENT system, focussing on procedural support, consequence propagation and state-based diagnosis.

- The **Response Evaluation System** (RESQ) combines knowledge of the system status from SES with knowledge of the operator's actions from the Dialogue System to recognise and evaluate the goals of the operator. RESQ is described in detail below.

Interaction with the operator is supported by the following GRADIENT modules:

- The **Dialogue System** (DIS) is a knowledge-based module which channels communications between SES, QRES and RESQ and the operator(s), handles operator queries to SES, and provides content to such exchanges from the dialogue specification contained in its Dialogue Assistants.

- The **Dialogue Design Tool** (DDT) affords a means of composing dialogue for any GRADIENT application, via an interactive design environment, which allows the designer to describe his desired dialogue in high-level (presentation independent) terms.

- The **Presentation System** (PRES) allows the operator to get the information he requires, acting as a delivery system for the mainstream of measurement and control information from the S&C system, and for graphical specifications generated via the **Intelligent Graphical Editor** (IGE) or via the **Graphical Expert System** (GES). The PRES also allows the operator to make changes in the process states. It consists of one or more displays and uses function keyboard and mouse as input devices.

- The **Graphical Expert System** (GES) supports the DIS by handling the dynamic graphical pictures presented by PRES. GES includes results from several phases of **Intelligent Graphical Editors** (IGE):

designer support for engineering-oriented tasks and semi-automatic picture generation from the underlying process-related knowledge representations, design and prototyping of graphical operator dialogues, and ergonomic and user modelling aspects.

8.2   The purpose of RESQ

RESQ is a subsystem of the GRADIENT system designed to use plan recognition techniques to support the operator of an industrial process control system. Whereas the QRES subsystem monitors information from the S&C system and generates messages for the DIS, RESQ monitors information from DIS and returns the appropriate responses. RESQ is an advisory system that is triggered as a result of actions of the operator, thus being asynchronous with the process. It monitors the operator's actions to detect situations where the action pattern is inconsistent or incorrect *vis-à-vis* the assumed goal(s) of the operator. Such situations may occur, for instance:

- when operators forget actions that were taken some time ago;

- when the execution of actions has been delayed;

- when several lines of action are executed simultaneously;

- when the operator misunderstands the situation or loses track of what he is doing;

- when two or more operators share a task between them;

- in the transition between work shifts.

RESQ analyses the actions of the S&C system operator, attempts to recognise what plans and goals the operator is trying to achieve and evaluates these in terms of the current system status. If the operator's actions are found to be faulty, RESQ attempts to diagnose the erroneous action and support the operator in correcting it. When RESQ has identified the plan that the operator is engaged in, the system may offer the operator a shortcut to complete the remaining steps of the plan. RESQ is expected to recognise an inconsistent action and make an appropriate response before the process deteriorates. The required response time is therefore domain dependent, but is usually in the order of minutes. Note that RESQ serves as an advisory system only. Thus, if the operator persists, RESQ cannot overrule his actions.

The RESQ system consists of three main modules (cf. Figure 16). The **Plan Recogniser** determines which plans the operator may be following given the current action. The **Plan Evaluator** determines the operator's most likely goal given this set of possible plans and the **Error Handler** diagnoses and supports the operator in correcting any errors which may occur.

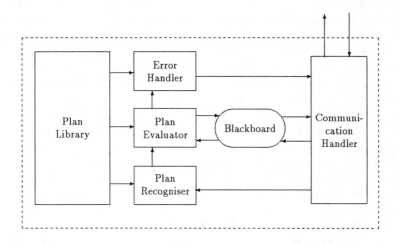

Figure 16: Structure of the RESQ system

Information about plans is stored in the **Plan Library** and the results of RESQ's analysis are posted to the **Blackboard**.

The **Plan Library** is the only domain dependent module in RESQ. The library stores all plans known in the system and is RESQ's sole basis for plan recognition. A plan is defined to consist of a goal and a set of actions with constraints which when met achieve that goal. A complex plan may consist of a number of subgoals as well as actions which may be optional or replaceable. Actions may have time, fact, and equality constraints. The knowledge in the Plan Library is provided in advance by the system designer using design knowledge or extensive knowledge elicitation. All modules in RESQ may access the Plan Library. Plans are stored in frames and are written in an abbreviated logical form.

The **Plan Recogniser** uses the Plan Library to determine which plans the operator's action may be part of. The plans that each action may be part of are predetermined before being stored in the plan library in order to reduce search time. That is, stored with each action are links to all plans that the action may contribute to. These plans also contain links to higher-level plans and abstractions of these plans. These chains are traced upward until a highest-level goal is reached. If no path from the action to a high-level goal is found, then the action must be erroneous. In this case, the action is passed on to the Error Handler.

This methodology uses graphs to represent the upward inference from the action level to the highest plan level and the means to match these graphs to combine actions that contribute towards the same goals, cf. Kautz [124]. The Plan Recogniser processes input from the operator, creates an entry in the action log, and produces a plan graph representing this action. The Plan Recogniser then controls the matching of this graph to graphs representing currently incomplete plans. When all matches of this action are found, the set of possible explanations of the actions are passed to the Plan Evaluator.

Actions which contribute positively to the state of the process either start a new plan or continue an existing plan. The graph representing the new action is matched with graphs representing previous actions. A match with these graphs indicates that the action continues an earlier plan. If there is no match or if the action starts a new plan, then the graph representing this action is maintained separately from earlier graphs. After the matching process, the Plan Recogniser provides the Plan Evaluator with a structure containing all possible interpretations of the current action in light of previous actions.

The Plan Evaluator uses meta-plan rules and the current system status to narrow down and order the likelihood of plans that the action may be part of. Meta-plan rules include rules like:

> H : An action is more likely to continue an existing plan than start a new plan. This could be called a *recency* heuristic.

> H : Plan X is executed more often than Plan Y. Therefore an action which is a step in both plans is more likely part of Plan X. This could be called a *frequency* heuristic.

Meta-plans are stored in sets. The value of the results obtained from these heuristic sets may be dynamically allocated according to the system status. Therefore, different heuristics may be used for different phases of operation. Information from the Blackboard may further reduce the number of interpretations of the action. For example, a plan which is recommended by the system through the Support Expert System may be considered very likely.

When multiple interpretations of the operator's actions are equally likely, the Plan Evaluator halts and waits for further actions to disambiguate these interpretations.

When the significance of the operator's action(s) has been determined as nearly as possible, the Blackboard is updated with the new plan information. If the action completes a high level plan, the actions which contributed towards this plan are considered explained. This explanation is placed in the action log and these actions are no longer considered in further matching. If the operator's plan is identified, RESQ may offer the operator the option of completing the remaining plan steps automatically.

The **Blackboard** contains RESQ's current best guess of what the operator is doing. Specifically, the Blackboard stores the name of the current plan, its goal, the actions completed so far in this plan and the next expected plan steps. This information is used by the rest of the RESQ modules to refine further the interpretation as more actions are taken into account and may be accessed by other modules of the GRADIENT system. The results are posted to the Blackboard incrementally, i.e., as they are discovered, and may come from a variety of sources. Most results on the Blackboard are determined by the plan evaluator but other sources may contribute knowledge opportunistically as well. The Blackboard also contains the set of actions and plans considered error-free by the Plan Evaluator.

The **Error Handler** assesses the severity of the error and determines whether or not to inform the operator or demand operator intervention to correct the error. In addition, the Error Handler uses a knowledge-base of common human error syndromes to diagnose the error. This knowledge-base is based on error phenotypes, as presented above, and includes such common mistakes as forgetting a step in a plan, reversing the order of two steps, and substituting an incorrect action for the correct one. Using this diagnosis of the error RESQ can not only warn the operator of the error but also explain why the error occurred. Where the determination of a remedy for the error does not require deep domain knowledge, the Error Handler should present this remedy to the operator through the Dialogue System.

Errors may be divided into two types: *action errors* and *plan errors*. Action errors are discovered by the Plan Recogniser and have three particular instances:

- **no-match-found**: the action is not part of any high-level plan known by the system at this time. No path from the action to a high level goal has been found. Either the action is incorrect or the Plan Library is not complete. This corresponds to the basic phenotype *intrusion*. RESQ determines whether or not the action type is known in the plan library. If the action type is not known, RESQ generates an error message indicating that the Library should be updated. If the action type is known, RESQ checks the action against expected actions determined by the Plan Evaluator. If there is a match, then RESQ generates a message indicating that the action was correct, but the parameters were wrong and provides these parameters if known. Where the action is known by RESQ but was not expected, RESQ merely identifies the error and waits for further actions.

- **goal-not-as-specified**: the goal of the action does not match the goal specified by the operator. The action is incorrect and RESQ can suggest the correct action.

- **goal-not-as-preferred**: the system has recommended a goal to the operator, but the operator's action does not contribute towards this goal. The action is probably incorrect and RESQ can suggest the correct action.

Plan errors are discovered by the Plan Evaluator when there are no continuous hypotheses. The error `no-continuous-hypoths` may be further broken down into three particular instances:

- **repeated-action**: the last two actions are of the same type. This matches the basic phenotype *repetition*. RESQ merely generates a message warning the operator about the error.

- **missed-a-step**: one step in a current plan has been skipped. RESQ warns the operator and recommends the intervening action. This matches the basic phenotype *omission*.

- **missed-several-steps**: more than one step in a current plan has been skipped. RESQ warns the operator and recommends the intervening actions. This matches the *jumping* phenotype.

The error handler has a routine which removes actions from its current list of actions to explain. Until more actions are input for processing, the most recent action can be easily removed from consideration. After that, succeeding actions must be re-matched and evaluated in order to re-examine the current situation.

9   The recognition of erroneous actions

The detection and recognition of an erroneous action under realistic working conditions is far from simple. In an artificial action-monitoring system the detection must be completely made by the system itself, whereas in real life the detection can take place in a number of ways.

In many cases the user who carries out the action will himself detect that it was erroneous. This may happen quite soon after the action was taken or even at the moment it is done. That people do make these detections is obvious from, e.g., Reason's data material which consisted exclusively of self-detected erroneous actions, as well as from general experience. The negative consequences of such erroneous actions can in many cases be controlled or avoided because counteractions may be taken before the system has deteriorated. It is, in fact, generally assumed that such erroneous actions rarely, if ever, are reported, hence that their frequency is grossly underestimated.

Even if the user himself does not detect the erroneous action, other users may. These may be other members of the working crew, (coincidental) observers, supervisors, etc. This detection may also occur within a short time after the action has taken place, hence allow a successful recovery. In many cases the system (the computer or the process) may also contribute to the detection. Almost all industrial process systems continuously monitor themselves and test the condition of predefined critical parameters (e.g., limit checking and alarm analysis). Whenever one or more of these parameters pass predefined limits, the system will annunciate that to the user.

If this strategy does not work (and the problems of limit violation and alarm annunciation are extremely complex in most realistic process domains) the user may detect the erroneous action when the system goes into an unexpected state. This event may be benign or malign. The last belongs to the class of accidents where it is very obvious that something is wrong. In most cases, unfortunately, there is very little that can be done about that, i.e., it is too late to make a recovery. In these cases it is the consequence of the erroneous action, rather than the erroneous action itself, which is detected. Analysing the events that led to the detection may point to the erroneous action as a causal factor.

Consequently, the detection of erroneous actions in real life takes place in a number of ways. In many cases the basis is the detection of a deviation in the state of the system from what it was supposed to be, e.g., by a limit-checking alarm system. It is, however, reasonable to exclude the erroneous actions that lead to major system breakdowns or failures, since the latter will be detected by the system anyway. (The occurrence of an alarm is not necessarily the result of an erroneous action of the user—or of an erroneous action at all. Similarly, an erroneous action does not necessarily result in a recognisable alarm condition. An alarm may occur because there has been a failure of a physical system, or because some other spurious event has happened. This can, in many cases, be traced back to an erroneous action on a different level, i.e., during design, construction, quality control or maintenance. But that is of little importance here, since we are considering the erroneous actions during operation.) The remaining set of erroneous actions nevertheless constitutes an important category, since they may occur in daily situations as well as situations of stress. The value of including action monitoring as part of the HCI becomes particularly important in abnormal situations, where it is vital that the user carries out a sequence of rather well-defined actions (e.g., emergency procedures) in order to restore the system and contain the accident. Since such procedure following is prone to error, an action-monitoring system may be a useful safeguard and lead to an improvement in the speed and correctness of such actions.

To summarise, the function of an action-monitoring system cannot be to detect all cases of erroneous actions. It should limit itself to those erroneous actions that may occur during the execution of predefined procedures— whether in an accident situation or not. The conditions for its function is that there are clear patterns in the user's actions, i.e., that the user does indeed follow a plan (or several plans), and that these plans can be made known to the system in advance. This may limit the actual uses in real-time situations, but it also means that the same procedure can be applied as an analytical tool for the investigation of event records, i.e., a 'post-mortem' analysis. This may be particularly important for research, hence for the development of guidelines for HCI design and operating procedures.

9.1 Limitations of action monitoring in HCI

One problem with simple action taxonomies, such as the description of the phenotypes, is that they do not include an underlying model of behaviour, i.e., they can be used to detect the individual cases but do not necessarily help to identify the underlying causes. A system which could make the actions transparent and allow the user to see the causes would clearly be an example of an embodiment relation. This goal may at present be beyond the powers of a formalised approach (i.e., artificial reasoning) but instead require human intelligence. The goal of the phenotypes is restricted to be operational, but it is very important to realise the further problem, i.e., the risk in stopping at the operational level. The phenotype is useful for detection but, since it does not provide any explanation, it cannot be used for correction and improvement. For that purpose a genotype (i.e., a theory) is needed. This amounts more or less to a model description of human erroneous behaviour, which can be useful in clarifying how the User-System Interaction takes place, hence how it can be improved when necessary.

Another problem is the rate of alerts, in particular the false-alarm rate. In any concrete situation it is important that a proper balance is attained, which neither tires the user nor misses clearly serious events. The precise level will depend on the context as well as on the system demands (e.g., the difference between aircraft and word processors), and may also be determined by the needs of the user. The more serious concern is, however, that this may lead to a fragmented approach as in the creation of adaptive interfaces, i.e., the action monitoring as an adaptive system in its own right. An adaptive interface is really no solution to the complexity problem, because it only increases the complexity by extending the hermeneutical relation. The user, ideally, should be able to understand the functioning of the error recognition mechanism, i.e., it should amplify his cognition rather than interpret the information. The point is that designing an error tolerant system may be a step on the way towards more effective HCI (as well as a much sought after technical solution), but it is not the end. The real value of the taxonomy, and possibly of the empirical data from an application, will be to identify problem areas in User-System Interaction which can then be used to improve the design, not by introducing additional systems, but by reducing the complexity of the User-System Interaction to avoid the erroneous actions from occurring.

Acknowledgements

The work described in this report has partly taken place within the ESPRIT Project #857 - GRADIENT. The project is carried out by a consortium consisting of Axion A/S, Birkerød, Denmark (prime contractor; formerly the AIP Division of Computer Resources International); Asea Brown Boveri, Heidelberg, Federal Republic of Germany; Technical University of Kassel, Federal Republic of Germany; Scottish HCI Centre, Glasgow, Scotland; and Catholic University of Leuven, Leuven, Belgium. The support of the CEC and the contribution from the other partners in the consortium is gratefully acknowledged. Thanks are also due to Dave Woods for insightful comments to an earlier version of this work.

Chapter 5

Modelling the User: User-System Errors and Predictive Grammars

Paul A. Booth

1   Introduction

It is now generally accepted that present systems analysis and design methodologies do not adequately account for the user's (or operator's) needs, and that
many system-usability problems are a consequence of these inadequacies. Yet,
such inadequate systems analysis techniques are being used to design systems
for control of chemical process plants and the like. Information technology
provides an opportunity to lessen the conceptual gap between operators and
the process plants they monitor and control. However, if the techniques employed during the design and development of information systems do not
adequately account for the user, then there is a danger that the introduction
of computers into complex systems might increase rather than reduce the
gap between the process plant and its operators (or users of the information
system), whose job it is to understand, monitor and control these sometimes
hazardous processes and procedures.

The issue addressed in this chapter is how we might best augment present
systems analysis and design methods to ensure that the user is adequately
and accurately represented. One proposed solution to this problem has been
to provide predictive grammars (also called analytic techniques) for analysing
the user's tasks. Consequently, the development of such methods has been
the focus of much research within the Human-Computer Interaction (HCI)
community. But what do we mean by the term *grammar*?

In its most straightforward sense a grammar is a notation for describing
an aspect of a task, a system, or user behaviour. The purpose of a grammar

HUMAN–COMPUTER INTERACTION
AND COMPLEX SYSTEMS: ISBN 0-12-742660-4

is to break down a task or system into manageable units, as well as show-ing the relationships between these units. In this way, inconsistencies and complexities can be exposed. These methods are predictive in the sense that they are used to analyse a task and predict some aspect of user behaviour. This approach has been characterised by the development of grammars that rely less upon design principles, than upon particular models of one or other aspect of cognition. That is to say, a model of the user and of cognition is implicit within the constructs and conventions of the notation. Moran's Com-mand Language Grammar (CLG) [159] and Payne and Green's Task-Action Grammar (TAG) [175] are both examples of notations that fall within this category. In essence, this sort of grammar is a form of user modelling; these methods address the question of how the user represents the task and system.

The aim of CLG is to describe the user's mental model of a system, while TAG is concerned with the cognitive complexity of performing a task. In other words, when a task or interface is described using the symbols and conventions of a grammar such as TAG, the output (the number of rules describing the task) is considered representative of the cognitive complexity of task performance. At this point, it may be useful to understand how these grammars work in a little more detail. We will look more closely at Payne and Green's Task-Action Grammar (op. cit.) as it is one of the more appealing grammars and addresses the area of task-action mapping, which is viewed as being of theoretical importance.

2   The use of a modelling technique

Payne and Green's TAG is concerned with the question of how we map our conceptual model of a system onto our actions towards that system. In short, it is a model of how we relate what we understand to what we can do. Payne and Green describe the purposes of the model in the following way:

> The central aim of TAG is to formalize [the mapping from the task level to the action level] in such a way that simple metrics over the grammar, such as the number of rules, will predict aspects of the psychological complexity of the mapping.

They go on to say:

> A secondary aim of TAG is to help the analyst appreciate the structure of a task language.

2.1   The model underlying TAG

Within TAG, the task language is described in terms of *simple tasks* and *rule schemata*. *Simple tasks*, according to Payne and Green, are tasks that are cognitively automated. That is to say, they are tasks that do not require conscious control. An example might be the actions that are required to drive a car. Changing gear, where the clutch is depressed, the gear lever moved, the clutch released and the accelerator (throttle) applied, is clearly complex, yet it is possible for the driver to engage in other activities simultaneously, such as conversation with a passenger. Within Payne and Green's model, it is as if we have a great library of these automated tasks to draw upon in any given context.

The *simple tasks* are selected from this library according to their features. This selection occurs according to the *rule schemata*. The rule schemata are memory structures in which the *simple tasks* are represented according to their features. Hence, Payne and Green's term *feature-tagged rule schemata*. These structures enable task descriptions to be mapped onto action specifications. In other words, *simple tasks* (represented in the rule schemata) are selected and ordered according to their features to provide an action specification. A simple example will illustrate this point.

Imagine that we have decided to make a cup of coffee. There is a vast array of actions or *simple tasks* that we can choose from. However, only one set of actions is likely to succeed. There are many related actions we might inadvertently choose, such as taking a tea-bag from the cupboard. Other simple tasks, such as selecting fourth gear in the car are clearly a long way from the making-a-cup-of-coffee set of actions. Indeed, one of the arguments that Payne and Green advance for this model is that they can show that making a cup of coffee is similar to making a cup of tea, and far-removed from driving a car. Choosing the correct set of actions to make a cup of coffee, in an appropriate order, is the responsibility of the *rule schemata*, and Payne and Green suggest that the actions of these *rule schemata* can be modelled according to certain rules which relate to the grammar of TAG.

2.2 The grammar of TAG

A description of one aspect of the MacDraw^{TM} system on the Apple Macintosh can be seen in Figure 2. However, if we are to understand this description then we need to know a little about the MacDraw system.

To draw an ellipse on this system we must select the 'ellipse' tool from the side of the window (see Figure 1). We must then use the mouse to position the cursor on the screen, press the mouse button, and move the mouse to another position to create the ellipse. The size and shape of the ellipse is determined by the position to which the mouse is moved.

We might, however, decide to draw a circle. The MacDraw system treats a circle as a special-case ellipse. To draw a circle we must follow the same series of actions as before, but the 'shift' key must be held down while the operation is executed. The series of actions for drawing a rectangle are the same as those

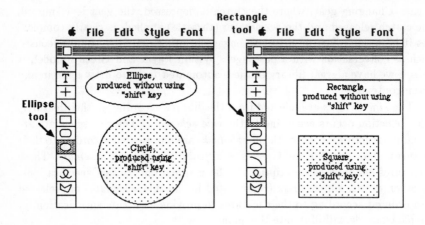

Figure 1: Two partial screens from the MacDraw system

for drawing an ellipse, except that the 'rectangle' tool is selected instead of the 'ellipse' tool. Again, to draw a square, which is treated as a special-case rectangle, the shift key must be held down as the operation is performed. Intuitively, it appears as though there is a consistency between these two operations, as drawing a square or a circle requires the use of the 'shift' key. These actions are represented in the single rule of the TAG grammar shown in Figure 2 (original source, Green [91]).

task [effect = insert, type of entity = ANY, special-case = ANY]
$\Rightarrow$ special action [special-case] + draw-object [type of entity]

draw object [type of entity] $\Rightarrow$ select tool [type of entity] + move mouse...

Figure 2: A rule from a TAG description of the MacDraw package for the Apple Macintosh

The 'effect = insert' means that entities (rectangles or ellipses) are being added to the picture, not moved or deleted. The 'type of entity = ANY' means that the rule stands for any entity, whether it is a rectangle, ellipse, or whatever else. The 'special-action [special-case]' means that if it is a special-case (i.e., a square or circle) the special action is performed, which means holding down the 'shift' key.

As Green [91] points out, the compact representation, shown in Figure 2, is only possible when the interface language is structured consistently and this structure fits the user's own representation, according to Payne and Green's model. In short, the number of rules that are required to describe a system is a guide to the cognitive complexity of that system, and the extent to which the system is likely to match the user's mental representation of the system. This, of course, assumes that Payne and Green's model accurately reflects the structure of cognition.

Overall, Payne and Green's TAG has a number of particularly attractive features. It appears to take account of a number of factors when assessing cognitive complexity, rather than just considering goals and subgoals (cf. Kieras and Polson, [125]). Furthermore, the model addresses an area that is seen as being of theoretical importance; that of task-action mapping (see Young [254]). The strong theoretical base of TAG is undoubtedly one of its greatest assets, and the uses and advantages of user modelling techniques in general have been presented positively within the literature.

2.3   What do user modelling techniques offer?

A number of uses of user modelling have been identified. These include:

- Matching the facilities that a system provides to the needs of the user.

- Suggesting metaphors to improve user learning.

- Guiding design decisions and making design choices and assumptions explicit.

- Guiding the design of experiments and helping in the interpretation of the results.

- As a predictive evaluation tool for proposed designs.

- As a means by which variations in the user population can be identified.

Some of the above claims might be better viewed as goals rather than achievements. For example, it is not clear how any of the existing grammars might be used to expose differences and variations in the user population. Nor do present techniques show us how to structure a system so that it appears simple and straightforward to some users, and progressively more complex for those who wish to exploit the system to its fullest capabilities.

Nevertheless, the advantage of using a formal notation is that a prototype does not have to be developed in order to evaluate the proposed system. Perhaps the most helpful aspect of any grammar is that it can show a design in a new and revealing light. Sufrin, although writing about Z notation, which is not based upon any cognitive model, makes just this point:

> ... it is only by understanding the essence of the purpose of an information system — abstracting from the details of any proposed implementation — that one can begin to judge the validity of design choices concerning the user-system interface [219].

In other words, grammars can reduce a system to its basic elements, as well as exposing the logical relationships between these different elements. In essence, the advantage of using grammars is that they increase the amount, type and quality of information that is available when making a design decision. A grammar that has, as its basis, a cognitive model of some aspect of the user's cognition (a user modelling technique), supposedly has the further advantage that its results should reflect more accurately the cognitive complexity of performing a particular task in a particular way on a particular system, because the way in which its measurements (the number of rules) are constructed should more accurately mirror the user's representation.

2.4   The disadvantages of predictive grammars

Despite the advantages of grammars, particularly those that attempt to model the user, there have been criticisms of their proposed use within the design and development process. For the purposes of the argument here, eight drawbacks to employing predictive grammars have been identified. The intention, in presenting these criticisms, is not to develop any single damning argument that might lead to the abandonment of research into the further development of such grammars; it is doubtful whether such an argument exists. Moreover, the perceived strength and importance of an argument is dependent, at least in part, upon the general consensus of opinion within the field rather than upon the validity of the argument itself. The purpose is rather an attempt to further expose the limitations of cognitive grammars, following the leads given by a number of other authors. The basic tenet is that cognitive grammars do not quite deserve the attention they presently receive within the HCI field. There are other areas of concern that deserve as much, if not more, consideration.

2.4.1   The grain of analysis

Firstly, there is the ever-present problem of the grain-of-analysis of a technique. For example, how, in practical terms, do we decide what is and what is not a *simple task* when using TAG? Is a *simple task* a single action such as unscrewing the lid to the coffee jar, or is it the whole sequence of actions from opening the cupboard door through to replacing the jar after the coffee has been placed in a cup? Clearly the answer is that it depends upon the extent to which sequences of actions have become automated, but how can we know what is and what is not automated?

Knowles [127] makes essentially the same point, while criticising Cognitive Complexity Theory (CCT) [125]. She points to CCT's unjustified assumption that the different production rules used to represent tasks are equivalent to one another in terms of short-term memory load.

This problem does not just have theoretical implications for the use of TAG, but also practical repercussions. For example, it appears quite possible that we might analyse one task assuming simple tasks of a particular size and then analyse another task and divide the simple tasks up in a different way. In other words, we cannot be consistent without knowing exactly what is and what is not cognitively automated, and there appears to be no practical way in which this information might be obtained. In essence, the argument is that these techniques measure a sort of formal consistency, where the result depends upon how the modeller broke the task down; they are not measures of cognitive complexity, as we do not know what is and what is not cognitively automated.

One argument [88] might be that an analysis that reflects formal rather than cognitive complexity can still be of some use. However, this depends on whether the tasks are broken down in a consistent manner. Imagine we have to compare the alternatives of replacing an engine in a car and repairing the engine from underneath the car. When we divide up the tasks for these alternatives, if we divide up the tasks into slightly smaller chunks than we do for the replacement procedure, then there is a danger that the repair procedure will appear more complex than the replacement procedure, when this is not actually the case. This is because, in general, the more a task is broken down into subtasks, the greater the number of rules that are needed to describe the activities required to perform the task as a whole. Consequently, comparisons of complexity may more strongly reflect the way in which the modeller analysed the tasks than any true complexity of task performance.

Inconsistency in the grain-of-analysis is an acute problem for grammars such as GOMS (Goals, Operators, Methods and Selection rules; Card *et al.* [39, 41]) and CCT (Cognitive Complexity Theory, Kieras and Polson, [125]). Kieras and Polson's CCT is a production system model based on the GOMS model. One response to the 'grain-of-analysis' problem might be to provide guidelines as to how grain size should be determined during analysis. However, one of the arguments that has previously been used in favour of cognitive grammars is that guidelines are difficult to interpret and apply, and are often disregarded during design. Consequently, given that these grammars were developed, at least in part, as alternatives to guidelines, using guidelines to steer the analysis of a task using a grammar might be viewed as inefficient, as well as being something of an *own goal*.

In essence, then, there are two arguments; one theoretical and one practical. The first is that grammars measure some sort of formal complexity, not cognitive complexity, as we do not know what procedures are and are not cognitively automated. The second is that the results from applying cognitive grammars may reflect the way in which the task has been broken down more readily than the true complexity of performing the task, and that inconsistencies in breaking down alternative tasks may lead to incorrect and invalid comparisons.

2.4.2   User consistency

A second problem with predictive grammars is that they assume that the user is consistent from one situation, one task and one action to another. Yet much of the evidence from research into reasoning has demonstrated that our behaviour does not always conform to the rules of formal logic, but is based rather upon our knowledge of the domain in which our problem lies. Johnson-Laird [119, 120], for example, has demonstrated that if logically identical problems are presented in different knowledge domains then people produce different answers, according to the domain. Johnson-Laird found that, when Wason's [229] four-card problem was presented in one domain people generally chose one card as a solution to the problem they were set. However, when a logically identical problem was set in another domain, people tended to produce a different answer. Behaviour, then, is based upon the knowledge the user possesses and brings to bear upon the task; it is not necessarily consistent from one task to the next. Consequently, techniques such as CCT (Kieras and Polson [125]) appear to be based upon a false assumption. For example, Polson states that:

> It is assumed that rules common to two tasks represent common elements
> and that these common rules can be incorporated in the representation
> of the second task in a training sequence at little or no extra cost in
> training time [179].

This, then, is one of the problems of using a predictive grammar. Such methods rely upon formal consistency in behaviour, yet we are not always consistent from one task to the next, but base our behaviour upon knowledge we already possess about a particular problem area. As a consequence, models such as CCT can only be considered, at best, as approximate, and, at worst, as inaccurate. We can, however, only make rough guesses about the knowledge that any one individual or user group might possess. Even if we could chart all of the knowledge a user possesses, we cannot always know which areas of knowledge an individual will use in dealing with a new situation or task.

For example, if we return to the MacDraw system that was discussed earlier, then we might remember that both a circle and a square were treated as special-case ellipses or rectangles respectively. To obtain these special-cases (either a circle or a square) then the user had to hold down the 'shift' key as the drawing operation was performed. As the 'shift' key is held down for both special-case operations, this appears to be intuitively consistent. However, imagine that we have a user group which has previously used a different drawing system. They can draw squares without difficulty, by holding down the 'shift' key. When these individuals try to draw a circle then they complain that the system is not consistent. They expect to have to hold down the 'control' key to draw a circle, not the 'shift' key. This, they claim, is quite consistent; 'S' stands for 'square' and 'C' (or control) stands for 'circle'.

Consistency, then, depends upon our perspective and our knowledge of previous tasks and situations. With respect to formal logic, we are not consistent from one situation to the next. However, a system that requires the user to depress 'shift' for a square and 'control' for a circle might be viewed as consistent by some users, yet would not be considered so using a predictive grammar. In short, by trying to ensure that systems are presented to the user in a consistent fashion we may, for some of the time, be pursuing an inappropriate goal. This issue is not a question of inconsistencies between users, but about the fact that any single user may be formally inconsistent from one situation to the next. By making an interface consistent we are not necessarily matching it to the needs of the user.

At this point an analogy may be useful. Imagine that we have been employed to design a new car for the year 2000. We decide that the interface between the user (the driver) and the machine must be as consistent as possible. For much of the time such an approach might be helpful. However, as the clutch, throttle, brake, horn, etc., are all operated by pressure, with drivers pushing a button or lever away from themselves with varying degrees of force, our interface would be more consistent if other controls worked in a similar manner. Consequently, we could introduce a gear lever for a *shift* or *manual* car that, instead of being moved forwards and backwards and from side to side, moved up and down, or in and out to different positions. This would mean that fewer rules would be required to describe our new car interface and it could be declared to be more consistent.

However, in this case we know, as most of us drive a car, that such an arrangement would not be popular and might confuse many users (drivers). The fact is that we are not consistent in the way in which we want our tasks presented to us, and the way in which we perform our tasks. Consequently, designing a consistent system may, at times, be at odds with the aim of designing a task that matches the needs of the user. Sometimes, of course, we might wish to impose consistency on the user, but it might be argued that there are many cases where this is not appropriate.

2.4.3   Predicting behaviour without 'world knowledge'

Although there is a mathematical argument for the belief that we cannot consistently predict the detail of behaviour (see Chapter 12), there is, nevertheless, an argument to support the statement that we can predict behaviour for some of the time. Consider behaviour at a bank for instance, we write a cheque and the cashier hands over money. Thus, we can predict a great deal of behaviour for much of the time when it is related to routine tasks. But to do this we use our knowledge of the tasks involved, and of previous similar situations. In essence, we use our knowledge of past events to predict future ones. Such knowledge, however, is not embodied within cognitive grammars (see [127], with respect to GOMS and CCT), and it appears doubtful whether such world knowledge could be usefully embedded within any grammar.

Essentially, the argument is this: we cannot predict user behaviour in a consistent and reliable way using grammars or tests because we require world knowledge to make such predictions. Even when we have this world knowledge there is no guarantee that our predictions will be correct. Consider, for example, the way in which a designer might make predictions about user behaviour, where his or her use of world knowledge is skewed by a mechanistic view of the user's tasks. An alternative way to view this mismatch between the user and the designer is to say that they do not have *mutual knowledge* [95] of the tasks in question. That is to say, the designer and the user may share knowledge of how to cash a cheque at a bank, and so can predict each other's behaviour in this circumstance, but they do not always have shared knowledge of the user's tasks, where the user's work activities are outside an everyday context.

It appears as though a user's behaviour at a new system is determined according to the knowledge that is possessed and which portions of that knowledge are applied. To successfully predict the user we might need to know much more about the way in which human knowledge retrieval occurs. Which cues at an interface provoke what sort of retrieval pattern? Moreover, there is a danger, given the evidence that human knowledge retrieval is very complex [121, 196], that even if we fully understood this process we still could not accurately predict its outcome.

An interesting illustration of the way in which people sometimes use their knowledge was provided by a middle-aged gentleman who had been asked to attempt a number of tasks using a system that employed a desk-top metaphor. After some time on the system the man became both agitated and excited. His attention was directed mainly at the icon shown in Figure 3. He repeatedly selected the icon using the mouse and, instead of opening it, would type in combinations of letters and numbers on the keyboard. Eventually, the man explained that it was obvious to him that this icon was something to do with the security of the system, and that he had been attempting to enter passwords that he thought might allow him access. The gentleman was particularly disappointed when it was explained to him that it was a mailbox icon and could be opened in the normal way.

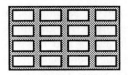

Figure 3: An icon from a system employing a desktop metaphor

It is only when we stop to consider which elements of knowledge the user was applying that we begin to appreciate how he arrived at his conclusion. The mailbox icon is intended to represent a set of pigeon holes, but the man perceived these to be iron bars. The gentleman also stated that he had read about security problems in computer systems in the press and, seeing as he had been told that he could not break the system and was free to do as he saw fit, assumed that this icon represented some window to the security system that he ought to try.

From the user's explanation we can see that he used his knowledge about prisons/iron bars, and the scant knowledge of computers he had picked up from the press, to draw a quite sensible conclusion about an icon on the screen. It seems impossible to imagine that we might predict such a deduction on the part of a user. However, by examining the behaviour of users at systems, and questioning them, there is no reason to believe that we cannot gain some understanding of the areas of knowledge that users are likely to recruit when attempting to understand a system. Once we know which areas of knowledge are likely to be applied in understanding a new system we can then make some predictions regarding user behaviour towards that system. More specifically, we can pinpoint those areas where confusions are likely to occur and where mismatches in the user's model may develop. How to use such information, as an alternative to grammars, is addressed later in this chapter.

2.4.4   User involvement

A fourth problem with predictive grammars is that these techniques might show the designer what the user should need, working from a logical basis, but they do not inform the designer of what the user *actually* wants or needs from a system [31]. Because the user is not involved they do not show where the user has a conceptualisation of the task which is markedly different to that held by the designer. For example, if the user viewed ellipses as 'special-case' circles (the opposite way around to how the MacDraw system is presently constructed) then, as Green [91] points out, the use of 'shift' to mean 'special-case' breaks down.

Our earlier example against consistency in task design might also be taken as an illustration of this related issue. However, these are separate points. The former is concerned with the assumption of consistency in behaviour, while here, the point is that predictive grammars do not necessarily expose the mismatches between the user's and the designer's models of the task. In other words, a grammar might demonstrate that an interface is formally consistent, but will not show where the user has a view of the task that is different to that held by the designer.

2.4.5   Compatibility with the design process

The extent to which predictive grammars might be of use within the design and development process has been the focus for the majority of the criticism of these techniques. The character of the design and development process has been summed up by Carroll and Rosson [45]:

1. Design is a *process*, it is not a state and cannot be adequately represented statically.

2. The design process is *non-hierarchical*, neither strictly bottom-up nor top-down.

3. The process is *radically transformational*, involving the development of partial and interim solutions which may ultimately play no role in the final design.

4. Design intrinsically involves the *discovery of new goals*.

Design is not merely a simple process in which a specification is agreed and then implemented. A system evolves throughout the design and development process *via* compromises and trade-offs, and only gradually does a more complete and coherent picture emerge. Carroll and Rosson [45] use this picture of design, as a semi-organised race against time and budget, to argue that current grammars do not fit easily into present design and development practice. They argue that:

> ... the formal evaluation of a given set of design specifications does not provide the kind of detailed qualitative information about learnability, usability, or acceptance that designers need in order to iteratively refine specifications, rather it assigns a figure... of merit to the design [i.e., the number of rules needed to describe part of the system]. This could be used to order a set of alternative designs, but contrasting alternative designs is an extremely inefficient means of converging on the best solution [op. cit.].

Carroll and Rosson go on to say:

> In a word, analytic approaches [modelling techniques/grammars] do not support the process of design... The initial definition of design specifications can often rely on analytic methods. But this initial definition is only the beginning of the design process. Unfortunately, this is where the analytic approaches stall [ibid.].

The doubts expressed by Carroll and Rosson as to the usefulness of predictive grammars (or analytic techniques) appears to be supported by some recent research. Bellotti [22] reports a study into the use of such techniques within commercial environments and concludes that some constraints upon design teams, such as their lack of autonomy, their poor access to user and task information and market pressures, are unavoidable. Furthermore, she suggests that:

> ...HCI DETs [Design and Evaluation Techniques, such as TAG and CLG], although potentially valuable to commercial design, are not applied in practice. The design environment conditions required for the successful application of current HCI DETs do not appear to be satisfied by commercial design projects. The reason for this is the existence of unavoidable constraints in commercial design which future HCI DETs should try to cater for [op. cit.].

2.4.6 Understanding the task

Not only is it apparent that predictive grammars may not easily fit into the design and development process, but furthermore, the information that is required to use such a technique might not be available in the early stages of design, when their use might be of most benefit. Using a predictive grammar requires a clear view of the task that is to be analysed. However, because of the way in which a design evolves, a clear view of how a task might be performed may not emerge until the system is beginning to be implemented. In an ideal world this should not be the case. However, in reality, with the pressures placed upon many design and development teams, this form of development is viewed by many as inevitable [22].

2.4.7 Practical complexity

Although the conventions and meanings of many notations are abundantly clear to those who invent them, almost all predictive grammars have been criticised as too complex and time consuming to use. Moran [160] has answered the criticism regarding the time and effort required to use a grammar by suggesting that such models should only be applied to small aspects of the design. However, this leaves the question of how to select those small parts of a design that require attention. Furthermore, the complexity of these methods remains an unanswered criticism, with Bellotti reporting that designers found such methods '...intimidating in their complexity. [op. cit.].'

It appears as though present predictive grammars are too complex to understand and use on an everyday basis. Using these methods to describe even the interface to a cash dispenser at a bank or building society has often proved too difficult for those new to such grammars. Given these problems, there would be some doubts as to whether even the authors of these grammars might be able to describe a complex system using some of the notations currently offered as design tools.

2.4.8   The areas addressed by a method

One argument in defence of any one predictive grammar might be that, despite its evident complexity, the information it provides justifies the time and effort required to learn and use it. This might imply that only one method will be needed during design. However, most grammars address only one area of concern. For example, the GOMS model and CCT are essentially performance models, while Payne and Green's [175] TAG deals with only one aspect of cognition; that of task-action mapping. Although TAG may deal with an important aspect of HCI, it addresses, nevertheless, only one of the gulfs of interaction described by Norman [170]. Moreover, it addresses only *one aspect* of this gulf; it does not address the identification of goals, planning issues, etc. In essence, the argument is this: if even one grammar is intimidating in its complexity how can we expect members of a design team to learn and use several complex formalisms? Furthermore, a sound theoretical knowledge of these techniques might also be required in order that the design team may be able to choose the formalism that best suits their needs at any particular time.

2.5   The major and minor points

Several points have been urged in each of the two preceding sections. Consequently, it may be useful to review our arguments in terms of the theoretical and practical points. The theoretical points are:

1. Cognitive grammars do not measure cognitive complexity, they measure a formal complexity that is (at best) an approximation to cognitive complexity.

2. Users are not consistent, and so designing totally consistent systems may not always be appropriate.

3. Knowledge is required to predict behaviour, and such knowledge is not embedded within current grammars.

The practical points are:

1. Inconsistencies in analysing alternative routes through tasks can significantly affect the outcome of an analysis.

2. Users are not involved; grammars might expose formal inconsistencies in the system without identifying those points where the user's and the designer's model of the system and task do not match.

3. Incompatibility with the design process.

4. Cognitive grammars require a clear view of the task that is not always present during the early stages of design.

5. Cognitive grammars appear too complex to understand and use on an everyday basis.

6. No grammar accounts for all aspects of interaction, and each only accounts for a limited aspect of interaction.

7. Designers need theoretical knowledge to know which grammars to apply in any given situation.

A less obvious, and probably less significant point, is that using cognitive grammars in design and development may focus attention upon cognitive complexity to the detriment of other possibly more important issues. For example, replacing some types of sealed-unit bearing by using the new bearing to hammer out the old is much quicker and less complex than first removing the old bearing and then inserting the new. Yet, this quicker and less complex method carries with it a 15 % chance of damage to the new bearing as it is inserted. Clearly, when choosing between these alternative methods of bearing replacement, this risk needs to be borne in mind and weighed against issues such as the cost of the bearing and the consequences of its failure in a hazardous environment. Similarly, the issues addressed by cognitive grammars are only a small part of a wider set of factors that need to be considered when making design decisions. Sometimes this appears to be forgotten.

2.6   The role of predictive grammars

The eight drawbacks to using predictive grammars within the design and development process might imply that predictive grammars have no place within HCI. However, these are criticisms of present methods, and need to be considered against their suggested uses and advantages (see Grant [88], for a broad review that places these arguments in a wider context). Some of the criticisms might be viewed as serious problems, while others are best viewed as drawbacks, likely to weigh less heavily in the cost-benefit analysis of the usefulness of cognitive grammars. This has not been an argument for the abandonment of research into such grammars, rather it is suggested that, given the theoretical and practical problems inherent in such methods, they do not deserve to be the primary focus of research within HCI, as they have been to date.

As the design and development process changes in character over the coming years, and more sophisticated, but usable, grammars are developed with accompanying software support, it is possible that such methods may have a permanent place in the design itinerary. Certainly, approximate predictive techniques may have a place if used judiciously. Although such techniques might not be able to predict all aspects of user behaviour, they might, nevertheless, make a contribution in steering the early stages of design in an appropriate direction. Their shortcomings might be mitigated in the later stages of an iterative design process. Nevertheless, it is difficult to accept that such grammars can replace testing systems with users, as some have claimed [179]. For the present, however, these techniques do not appear to have a practical place within design and development. But what is their current role within HCI?

Firstly, they are the possible forerunners of methods that will be of practical use within design (as has just been suggested). Secondly, they can be considered as research tools [25]; they are a means by which we can test cognitive models of the various aspects of interaction, such as task-action mapping. In short, the empirical validation of the predictions of a formalism can be used as an indicator of the advantages and disadvantages of the model of interaction embedded within the notation. In this second respect, grammars such as TAG are clearly advances on techniques such as CCT, in that TAG provides a model (simple tasks and rule schemata) around which we can base our thinking about interaction and the performance of a task. CCT, for example, cannot tell us anything about errors, and assumes error-free performance. Although some might claim that errors cannot be modelled, this is clearly not the case. TAG provides some idea of how errors occur (i.e., inserting an incorrect simple task into a sequence of actions, or omitting a correct simple task), while Marsden [146] has developed a computational model of human decision making, based upon Reason's [196] Underspecification Theory of knowledge retrieval. This model exhibits error forms that correlate highly with those exhibited by human subjects.

Models such as GOMS, Command Language Grammar (CLG) [159] and CCT have been used as stepping stones *en route* to grammars that more accurately reflect cognition. TAG might be viewed as one of these developments. Nevertheless, TAG has its faults, as Payne and Green [175] will admit. It would be wrong, therefore, to view any of the present grammars as end points, or as new paradigms, as some have claimed. They may only be vehicles for the development of more accurate, useful and usable grammars. The development of future grammars, however, may depend, to a large extent, on the way in which the problems of current grammars are addressed. Successful grammars might need to demonstrate that:

1. Cognitive complexity predictions match user opinions of complexity and more quantitative measures of complexity, in complex environments as well as the laboratory.

2. They can be applied consistently, with the same grain of analysis across tasks and subtasks.

3. Design changes instigated as a result of using a grammar are viewed positively by users.

4. Users want formal consistency in a task, and that where consistency is imposed it is helpful.

5. Designers can readily understand the grammar and view its everyday use within the design and development process positively.

3   Analysing user-system errors

Having decided that predictive grammars are unlikely to be presently suitable for use within the design and development process, particularly with respect to complex systems, this raises the question: *how can we model the user in design?* One possible answer is to concentrate upon the errors that occur during HCI. An analysis of such errors may expose the underlying and fundamental mismatches that often exist between the designer's and the user's understanding of the task.

3.1   What are user-system errors?

There are a number of possible terms which may apply to user-system errors. Indeed, it is questionable whether the term 'error' is really the most appropriate in this context. A better term might be 'misunderstanding'. Even this might not be as precise as we would like, for it appears to imply that such occurrences are trivial. Consequently, it is suggested that events where the user's actions and the system's responses are not wholly compatible should be considered as *dialogue failures.* A dialogue failure is a breakdown in communication between the system and the user; it is where either the computer or the user do not understand one another, or some information about the nature and structure of the task is not properly communicated.

A dialogue failure can be seen as evidence of a mismatch between the user's and the designer's model of the task and system. In other words, that dialogue failures can reveal model mismatches. While present grammars attempt to predict potential model mismatches, dialogue failures directly reveal actual mismatches between the user and the designer. Although the general notion of a dialogue failure may prove to be of use in a formal sense, in practice an operational definition may be of use. Here, a dialogue failure is considered to have occurred if:

- the user reports any degree of misunderstanding during the interaction (i.e., the system does not do what he or she wants it to do);
- the user asks for help in any form;
- the user enters an illegal command that is not purely the result of a keystroke error, mental slip or lapse.

Clearly, this definition needs to be interpreted carefully, but it has already been used to identify the dialogue failures that occurred during the use of a small word-processing system. It may be useful to describe one or two aspects of this limited study as a means of illustrating the nature of the dialogue failures that occurred.

3.2   The Memomaker study

The Memomaker word-processing system is a limited application produced some years ago by Hewlett Packard that runs on an HP 150 PC with touch-screen. The design of the study is not of direct relevance here. The twelve subjects, however, were a mixture of staff and students at Huddersfield Polytechnic. Subjects were required to perform twelve tasks on the Memomaker package. With the exception of the first, all of the tasks related to a short piece of text comprising three paragraphs. During the evaluative sessions, any signs of dialogue failure were noted by the evaluator. Users were asked to explain their intentions as well as how the system differed in any way from what they wanted or expected. Any misconception of the system that was revealed by the user's explanation was noted as a dialogue failure. Following this, the part of the system that had been misconstrued was explained to the subject. They were then asked for further comments. At the end of the experimental session, the subjects were asked to comment upon the system, the tasks and anything else they considered relevant. Following this, subjects were debriefed. The length of sessions varied between 45 and 90 minutes.

In total, seventy-five different dialogue failures were identified for the twelve tasks with the twelve subjects. Interestingly, a number of dialogue failures were peculiar to each subject, as though each subject's knowledge and expectations gave rise to some dialogue failures that occurred to no other subject. More importantly, however, there was an evident *common core* of dialogue failures that almost all subjects experienced. A chart of the number of dialogue failures against the number of subjects who experienced the failure can be seen in Figure 4. This figure shows each mismatch (numbered from 1 to 75) against the number of subjects who experienced the mismatch. Towards the end of the experimental sessions, subjects exhibited mismatches that had occurred earlier, and so the frequencies of these earlier mismatches would rise. However, new mismatches were more likely to be unique to an individual (as the common ones had already shown up), which accounts for the trailing-off in the chart towards the later (higher-number) mismatches. Apparently, dialogue failures experienced by most or all of the subjects were also those that were most serious. That is to say, these were the failures that prevented continuing further with the task.

An example of a dialogue failure experienced by almost all of the subjects was that the 'backspace' key did not delete the text, it only moved the cursor backwards, and acting as a further cursor key. All of the subjects who experienced this dialogue failure were unable to proceed until they had been informed of the correct way in which text might be deleted. An example of a dialogue failure experienced by only one subject was where the subject complained that the 'CAPS' mode indicator was not obvious. The first example, we suggest, is a serious dialogue failure and model mismatch, while the second is trivial to the extent that it did not prevent the user proceeding through the task.

It is evident that, although a large number of dialogue failures were peculiar to each individual, there was, nevertheless, a common core of problems that might be addressed fruitfully by a design and development team. Furthermore, this common core of failures was evident, despite the differences between the subjects in terms of their ages, backgrounds and experience.

3.3 The advantages of considering user-system errors

The advantages of considering user system errors, or dialogue failures, is that they directly expose actual model mismatches between the user and the designer. Freud described human errors as: '...windows to the mind' [79]. Within HCI, user-system errors may be viewed in a similar light; as a means of exposing clashes between conflicting models of a task. A central aim of predictive grammars is to expose potential model mismatches that might or should arise. The problem with this approach is that the detail of user behaviour is difficult to predict. By concentrating upon user-system errors, however, this problem is avoided, and it appears as though such an approach may allow more accurate modelling of the user. Furthermore, such an approach might also allow us to model just those aspects of a task that require analysis; those parts where the user and the designer disagree. In essence, a consideration of user-system errors can help to highlight those parts of a design that require attention.

A further advantage is that such an approach might fit readily into present

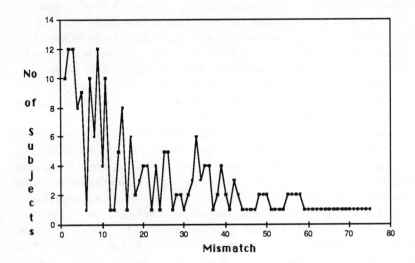

Figure 4: Chart of mismatches

design and development practice. Most systems are now developed in an iterative manner, even if these systems are not always tested systematically with users. Moreover, the trend within the major information technology companies is towards more rigorous usability testing of systems as they are iteratively refined. In many cases, user-system errors are already considered, but often in a manner that lacks formal analysis. Consequently, a formal technique for the analysis of such errors may fit easily into both current and future design practice.

3.4   How might we analyse user-system errors?

While we may be clear about the place of a formal user-system error analysis tool within the design and development process, the form that such a tool might take is not immediately obvious. One possible approach, adapted from approaches to human error, might be to employ classification techniques. Thereby, classifying user-system errors according to their origin and so progressing toward a greater understanding of the root cause of any model mismatch. Directly using human error frameworks, however, does not appear to be a viable proposition. For example, consider Rasmussen's distinction between skill-based slips, rule-based mistakes and knowledge-based mistakes [183, 184]. How might we apply this to the examples given earlier? Subjects using the Memomaker system complained that the 'backspace' key did not delete the text, it only moved the cursor backwards; acting as a further cursor key. It does not appear as though classifying such a user-system error as either skill-based, rule-based or knowledge-based would help in better understanding the model mismatch. The reasons for this are two-fold.

Firstly, models of human error and their associated techniques are aimed at analysing errors within cognition While a user-system error is a mismatch between two models, it is not necessarily an error within either of these models. In other words, a user-system error is a mismatch between systems, not an error within just one. Secondly, although the terminology used within the human error field might reflect human cognition in a useful fashion, such terminology may not translate to the design and architecture of computer systems. Any classification scheme might require a set of concepts and terms that have currency both within the computing and cognitive domains. Such an elementary scheme has been developed (an Evaluative Classification of Mismatch (ECM) [26]) although it is not further described here.

We suggest that two basic types of error occur during interaction: human errors and user-system errors. A human error is an error within one cognitive system. This may be a mistake where the user inadvertently selects the wrong intention; such as making a cup of tea when the correct task would have been to make a cup of coffee. Alternatively, it may be a slip, where the person accidentally slips from one routine or plan into another; such as making a cup of tea and accidentally putting instant coffee in the teapot [187, 196].

On the other hand, a user-system error is an error between two cognitive systems, it is not an error within one. In essence, user-system errors are mismatches between the user's and the designer's or system's model of the task at hand. These mismatches can be of two sorts; either mapping mismatches or incongruity mismatches.

An abstract representation of a user's model and a system's/designer's model, illustrating these different types of user-system error, can be seen in Figure 5.[1] Here, parts of the two models are identical, and correctly map onto one another (see area A in Figure 5). Other parts are identical, but have been incorrectly mapped onto one another (see area B). These are mapping mismatches; where the problem is with the mapping between the two models. Finally, some parts are not identical, but are incongruous to one another (see area C). These are incongruity mismatches, where the models cannot be

---

[1] Area A shows where the models are identical and the mappings between the models are correct. Area B shows where the models are identical, but the mapping between the models is incorrect (the incorrect mapping is shown with a thick arrow). Area C shows where the models are incongruous, and cannot be mapped onto one another (a thick arrow shows the mapping that cannot be achieved).

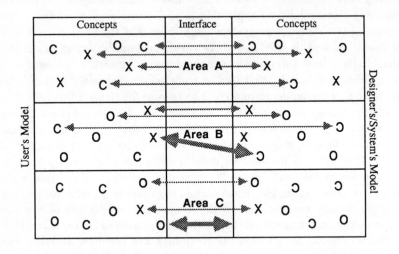

*Figure 5: An abstract representation of a user's and a designer's/system's
model of a task*

mapped onto each other because the model elements are not the same, or are
in different positions in relation to other elements.

3.5 The pitfalls of considering user-system errors

Despite the potential advantages of analytic techniques aimed at addressing
user-system errors, there are, nevertheless, a number of drawbacks to such an
approach. Although these problems by no means preclude a consideration of
user-system errors, they need to be borne in mind.

Firstly, although a consideration of user-system errors may prove fruitful
in a number of respects, it would be a mistake to consider such an approach
as the only means by which useful information can be obtained regarding
HCI. Yet there is a danger, with the wealth of qualitative and quantitative
information that errors provide, of some design teams regarding the analysis
of user-system errors as the only analysis they need apply. Furthermore, the
insights into HCI sanctioned by a consideration of errors, provide a seductive
and potentially misleading appeal that may lead some to neglect the wider
evaluative context of such information.

Secondly, if user-system errors are considered in an isolated fashion, and
not pieced together to form a wider picture, there is a possibility that an

analysis that focussed upon errors might become piecemeal. In other words, unless a theoretical basis underpins any analysis technique, in such a way so as to provide a wider framework for considering different but related user-system errors, there would be no possibility of modelling the user. Such an analysis might be prone to personal biases, as greater degrees of judgement regarding the importance and context of errors would be required. Consequently, any analysis method that is not based upon a theory or framework might prove both inconsistent and inferior.

4 Conclusion

Present predictive grammars appear ill-suited for use within the design and development process. The application of such techniques to information technology systems that are to become integral parts of complex systems, such as nuclear or chemical plants, may be viewed as even less desirable. This is because there are problems using these methods consistently from one task to another (i.e., grain of analysis), they: assume a formal consistency in user behaviour; attempt to predict behaviour in a context-independent fashion; may not expose actual model mismatches between the user and designer; are not presently compatible with current design practice; require an unambiguous view of the task (which is not always available); are too complex to use on an everyday basis; and many such notations would be required to address each aspect of a design. Consequently, it would be better to view present predictive grammars either as research tools or prototypes for later, more usable tools.

An alternative, but potentially complimentary approach, focusses analysis upon user-system errors; developing techniques for modelling the user by analysing the results of interaction. Such an approach appears to offer a means of user modelling that is both theoretically appealing and practical. This approach is theoretically attractive since it focusses attention upon actual mismatches between the user's and the designer's model of the task and system, rather than predicted mismatches that might be present. The approach has the practical appeal of fitting easily into present design and development practice. Furthermore, it should help by focussing attention upon those parts of a system that require change.

Acknowledgements

This chapter has been much improved as a result of the comments I received on earlier drafts from Simon Davis, Thomas Green, George Weir, Gill Brown, and the feedback from Erik Hollnagel, Dave Woods, Ernest Edmonds, Jim Alty, Terry Mayes, and all of those at the workshop meeting in Scotland. I am particularly grateful to Simon Grant, whose well-thought out replies to the criticisms of cognitive grammars presented in this chapter were invaluable in helping to elucidate and refine my arguments.

Chapter 6

Cognitive Task Analysis ?

Simon Grant and Terry Mayes

1 Introduction

Task analysis is the breaking down of a task into component subtasks and elementary actions. In general, there are many possible ways of doing this, and, unlike the case in some branches of the longer-established sciences, there is no established canonical method for analysis of tasks, nor any widely agreed set of primitive elements which the analysis would give as end points. The more complex the task, the more potential choice there is of different analyses or styles of analysis, just as there is more potential choice of methods of performing that task.

Traditionally, task analysis has been seen as fulfilling a range of purposes, including personnel selection, training and manpower planning, as well as workload assessment and system design, and various analytic procedures have been proposed to meet these purposes. Many purposes are given by Phillips *et al.* [177], who also note that 'systems which are stimulus-intensive, non-sequential and involve many cognitive responses, such as computer-based systems' have been less amenable to traditional methods.

There has recently been a growing body of opinion that styles of task analysis that do not take into account relevant facts about human cognition are less than fully adequate for the analysis of complex tasks. This has led to attempts to describe those principles of cognition which are most relevant for task performance, or to devise task analysis methods that are in harmony with the human appreciation of the tasks. However, the lack of firmly established theoretical principles for such an analysis has meant that various authors have taken, or suggested, different approaches to this goal of a cognitive task analysis (CTA).

To take stock of this situation, we consider three issues in this chapter. Firstly, we ask what it is about Human-Computer Interaction (HCI) in com-

plex systems that requires a *cognitive* task analysis. Secondly, we look at
a number of approaches, taken from the HCI literature, which either have
claimed, or could be claimed, to be contributions to CTA; and we ask how
these various approaches relate to one another, and how they would need to
be complemented to produce a useful CTA. Thirdly, we briefly consider the
possibility of an approach to a CTA other than the ones discussed.

2   Why 'cognitive' task analysis ?

Task analysis has many possible objectives, and we need to be clear about the
objectives of performing the analysis if we are to arrive at any conclusions.
For example, if analysing tasks to be performed by a fully automatic system,
which did not need (or did not support) direct human supervision, there would
be little motive in designing the system with reference to how a human might
perform it. In contrast, there is a range of complex industrial or commercial systems (including power plants, chemical works, aircraft, ships, traffic
control systems, and possibly aspects of organisations themselves) which are
unlikely to be fully automated in the foreseeable future. There are a number
of reasons why not. Firstly, we would not generally like to entrust decisions
that can affect the lives of people to an automatic system which does not
have human accountability, nor the sense of responsibility that comes with
that. This may or may not be backed up by legal requirements or licensing.
Secondly, there is the need to be able to cope with situations where the control system, for whatever reason, stops working, or malfunctions in a way not
explicitly allowed for in the design. Thirdly (a related point), there is a level
of complexity beyond which it is impractical to design automatic responses
to all possible fault combinations. When something anticipated goes wrong,
perhaps some automatic system could deal with it, but if something truly
unexpected should happen, the system may well not be programmed for that
eventuality. Fourthly, in any system in which people are involved, there are
likely to be factors relevant to a decision which are not directly available to automatic sensing or interpreting. In this category would come the personal, the
inter-personal, and the social factors, as well as the apparently unmediated
pickup of information from aspects of the system which were never designed
for that purpose. There is much anecdotal evidence about the ability of main-
frame computer operators, for example, to deduce all kinds of things from the
rhythmic noises of disk drives, teletypes, etc. [5].

In these cases, and for these reasons, there are many instances in which we
would like to have one or more humans involved with the computer system,
either sharing the control of the complex system, or supervising the computer
system's decisions. Clearly, if a human in this situation is to be effective (not
merely a token presence), he or she needs access to whatever information is

necessary to take decisions. The supervisory task needs to be analysed, and the computer system designed, taking into account the human's information needs. A CTA will properly involve an analysis of the information flow and the required knowledge states throughout the entire system.

This much would probably be familiar and accepted background for most people who have considered these problems, but unfortunately there is no commonly agreed way of proceeding beyond traditional task analysis, and determining what the human's information needs are. In more traditional clerical and manual jobs, the information needs have often been straightforward and easily defined. The skill in clerical jobs was maintaining accuracy in tasks that were logically simple; in manual tasks the skill comes from the learning of how to co-ordinate a psychomotor response to achieve a simply specifiable goal. In contrast, the information requirements for a managerial or supervisory control job are not easily specified. Much of the skill of such a job lies in information control and processing, and a task analysis in this field should at least contribute to defining the information requirements of a human performing a task, and thus answering a practical need of systems analysts and designers.

3   In what way are current approaches 'cognitive'?

Cognition is about information flow and usage, and therefore we could term a task analysis which deals specifically with information issues a CTA. However, not all analyses of complex system control could be called cognitive. It is possible to concentrate on other issues, like the necessary sequencing and interrelationship of different operations, and when it comes to information needs for decisions, simply to assume that all the necessary information is available. The result of largely ignoring cognitive issues is demonstrated by the still-current design approach of 'one data point one display element' (Woods, Chapter 7) for control rooms, where all the information is presented with equal availability, and little or no effort is put into integrating or prioritising information. The information management is left as an unanalysed skill which the operators are expected to develop following what amounts to a craft-apprentice paradigm.

Given the widespread side-stepping of the issue of cognition, it may be no surprise that current ideas on CTA are little more than approaches, and are as yet far from a comprehensive methodology. We may identify at least three directions of approach, as a preliminary to discussing examples of them at greater length.

Firstly, there are methods of decomposing a task, or formalisms into which to analyse a task, whose authors hope (explicitly or implicitly) that the formalisms or methods of decomposition match the human's cognitive structure to a useful extent, and thus that a decomposition in these terms could be called a cognitive analysis—an analysis of a task in terms which, it is hoped, relate to human cognition. Secondly, there are theories and models of human cognition, which specify the units and structure of supposed human cognitive methods and resources. This could be characterised as the analysis of (internal) cognitive tasks, which does not, of itself, specify how to analyse and map external tasks into these internal units, but obviously asks to be complemented by such a mapping. Thirdly, there are observations on salient features of human cognition in complex processes that may directly relate neither to current models of cognition nor to current methods of logical analysis of tasks. Here we find the distinctions between novice and expert styles of reasoning, and Rasmussen's distinctions between skill-, rule- and knowledge-based behaviour [185]. We can see these as offering partial specifications of what CTA should cover.

3.1 Decomposition formalisms

As mentioned above (p. 149), there are task analysis techniques that are legitimately not intended to provide a structure similar to a human cognitive structure for that task. In particular, techniques for analysing tasks, so that they can be coded in a program to be executed automatically, have important criteria other than similarity to human cognition. Here, a clear logical structure which conforms to convention is important in coding, testing, validation and maintenance. In contrast, the formalisms presented below have been promoted in the field of HCI, with at least some attention to the idea of matching human cognition.

3.1.1 The GOMS family of models

The analysis given by Card *et al.* [41] is based around a model of task performance, referred to as GOMS, which stands for Goals, Operators, Methods and Selection rules. The Goals are those that the user is presumed to have in mind when doing the task. The Operators are at the opposite end of the analysis from the Goals: they are the elementary acts which the user performs (not to be confused with the human 'operator' who controls a process). The Methods are the established means of achieving a Goal in terms of subgoals or elementary Operators. When there is more than one possible Method for the achievement of a certain Goal, a Selection rule is brought into play to choose between them. The acts are assumed to be sequential, and the authors explicitly rule out consideration of the possibilities of parallelism in actions. They also see the control structure in their model as a deliberate approximation, being more restricted in scope than the production system of Newell and Simon [167].

What is considered elementary for the purposes of the analysis is to some extent arbitrary. The authors give examples of different analyses of the same text-editing system using different classes of elements: possible elementary units range from the course grain of taking each editing task as an Operator, to the fine grain of the keystroke as the Operator (known as the Keystroke Level Model, KLM). At each level, the times to perform each elementary unit operation should lie generally within a certain band, which signifies the grain of analysis at that level [159]. For the course grain, this would be at least several seconds; for the fine-grain keystroke units it would be a fraction of a second.

The predictions made by GOMS-type analyses suggest that there may be a degree of correspondence between a GOMS structure and human cognition *for text editing or relevantly similar tasks.* Text editing, and the use of other similar computer tools, has a certain amount of well-defined structure arising from the fact that what is being 'controlled' is itself a computer program. But there is little likelihood of a GOMS analysis matching human cognition in complex process control: GOMS deals with expert error-free operation, not uncharted anomalies of operations where there are multiple goals and constraints.

3.1.2 Cognitive Complexity

The stated aim of Kieras and Polson's Cognitive Complexity Theory [125] is to provide a framework for analysing the complexity of a system from the point of view of the user, out of which should come measures able to predict the 'usability' of that system. Thus the authors are intending to capture something of the human cognition involved in task performance.

The achievement of this aim is via the provision of two formalisms, intended to interact with each other: one for representing the user's knowledge of how to operate the device (the 'job-task representation'), and another for representing the device itself, the generalised transition network. The first formalism allows a designer to create a model of a user's understanding of a task in context. The second is a representation of the system from a technical point of view.

The formalism for the user's job-task representation is based on the concept of the *production system* [167]. Although the authors cite GOMS as the precursor to their work, they do not follow GOMS in deliberately simplifying the full production system formalism, which is a general-purpose architecture capable of great complexity and power. They do not give any clear argument supporting the inherent suitability of the production system for analysing the appropriate aspects of the user's knowledge, nor do they offer any restrictions which bring it more in line with the capabilities of the human. They consider it sufficient justification to refer to other research which has used, or reviewed the use of, production systems.

Representing knowledge in terms of an unrestricted production system seems to be closer to an exercise in ingenuity (with relatively arbitrary results) than an attempt to faithfully reproduce actual human thought processes. Hence arises one of the doubts about whether the computed values of cognitive complexity bear any necessary relationship to the actual difficulties experienced by users.

It may be that the area they chose for study, which is again in the field of text processing, provided a suitable area for the use of their techniques, because the inherent simplicity and inflexibility of the system (compared to complex industrial processes) means that there is less scope for differences of representation, even though there may still be variations in tactics between individuals.

3.1.3   Command Language Grammar (CLG)

This is a development by Moran based on ideas in the GOMS model [159]. The purpose of Moran's CLG formalism is to ensure that the designer has a framework round which to design. The design is done (generally) on four levels: the Task Level, the Semantic Level, the Syntactic Level, and the Interaction Level. Moran gives guidelines, and an example (a simple mail system), for how to do this.

Moran identifies three important views of CLG. The **linguistic** view is that CLG articulates the structure of command language systems, and generates possible languages. This explains the G of CLG. It may be that the linguistic view is of most interest to HCI researchers and theorists.

In the **psychological** view, CLG models the user's knowledge of a system. This assumes that the user's knowledge is layered in the same way as CLG. Moran suggests ways of testing whether a CLG is like a user's knowledge, but he does not give ways of testing the detailed structure of the knowledge, nor whether the representation is the same in both user and CLG. He has a clear idea that it is the designer's model that should be able to be assimilated by the user, hence the designer should be careful to make, and present, a clear and coherent model. But concentrating on this idea neglects discussion of the real possibility that users may develop their own independent models of a system, which may not be describable in the same formalism. We might fairly say that, viewed psychologically, CLG makes another speculative attempt to introduce a theory explanatory of aspects of human cognition. It is hard to identify any success in this endeavour above that which is achieved by other psychological theories.

In the **design** view, CLG helps the designer to generate and evaluate alternative designs, but does not claim to constitute a complete design methodology. It could aid the generation of designs by giving an ordered structure to the detailed design tasks, and Moran suggests that CLG could provide measures for comparing designs, addressing efficiency, optimality, memory load, errors and learning.

An important question is to what extent Moran's level structure (as mentioned above) is correct as a method of analysis for existing systems, rather than just useful as a design tool for new systems. Is this a good way to go about dividing the specification? In the absence of any arguments, we must say that we do not know. It may well be that there are other good ways of analysing a system into different levels, and a different system of levels would give rise to possibly quite different analyses or designs. The most important point to be made here, however, is that it is presumptuous to suppose that the levels given here actually correspond in all or most cases with similar levels in human representations. We can imagine (or perhaps some have experience of) analysis based on other characterisations of level. Would analysts all feel that one particular level model is natural and all the others artificial? So as far as the psychological view goes, we have to say no more than that CLG gives a guess at a possible level framework for human knowledge about a system, and that this guess has no more empirical support than a number of alternative ones.

It may be that there is some definite and constant basis for human cognition in the context of interactive systems, in which case we need to find it and make it the basis of any CTA for HCI. If there is no such basis, we would need to find a more flexible approach to analysis than is offered by the likes of CLG.

3.1.4   Task-Action Grammars (TAG)

The idea of a grammar model of a task is that it is possible to represent tasks, or complex commands, in terms of the basic underlying actions necessary to perform those tasks, and this can be done in a way that parallels the building up of sentences from words, or the building up of programs from elementary commands in a programming language. Grammars which describe the structure of programming languages have often been formalised in Backus-Naur Form (BNF), which is a relatively straightforward formalism.

When a grammatical model has been made of a 'language', two measures are of interest: the total number of rules in the grammar is some measure of complexity of the language, and therefore potentially related to the difficulty of learning it; and the number of rules employed in the construction (or analysis) of a particular statement, command, or whatever, is a measure of the difficulty of executing that command, and therefore potentially related to the difficulty of comprehending it.

Green *et al.* [92] argue convincingly that representing task languages in terms of BNF must miss something of human comprehension, because in many cases the measures of complexity in BNF do not tally with experimentally derived or intuitive human ideas of complexity. Payne and Green's Task-Action Grammars (TAGs) [175] set out to provide a formalism in terms of which simple measures correspond more closely with actual psychological complexity.

A TAG analysis is done by considering important abstract 'features' of the task (i.e., dimensions or attributes on which there are distinct differences between commands), which are assumed to be apparent to a user, and analysing the task language in terms of those features, by enabling rules to be written in terms of the features, as well as in terms of instantiated feature values. The simplest example of this that Payne and Green give concerns cursor movement. Instead of having to have independent rules for moving a cursor forwards or backwards by different amounts, TAG allows the rule

$$Task[Direction, Unit] \rightarrow symbol[Direction] + letter[Unit]$$

provided that the available actions support such a generalisation. An important point made by these authors is that the consistency that allows such schematic rules makes command languages easier to understand and learn, compared to languages whose inconsistency does not allow the formation of such general rules.

Payne and Green themselves admit a lack of empirical data on perceived task structure (perceived by users or operators, that is), and therefore the way in which a task is formalised is up to the judgement of the analyst. Here again we have the problem that the formalism is of such a power as to permit varying solutions. How are we to know whether a particular formalisation is the one that most closely corresponds to a practical human view of the task? Only, it would seem, by experiment, and that would make it impossible to use TAG with any confidence without also performing psychological experiments on perceived complexity of a task from a human point of view. It is to be expected, again, that for inherently well-structured tasks (such as text editing), the representation is fairly self-evident, and therefore a guess at an appropriate formalisation may well be near enough to get reasonably close to human cognition. But as with the other formalisms, there is plenty of room to doubt whether using this technique for analysing the control of complex, dynamic systems would produce anything remotely like a natural human cognitive structure.

3.1.5   General points about formalisms for CTA

No doubt it is already clear that formalisms such as those described above may work reasonably for the analysis of simpler systems, and for systems where the tasks have no latitude for variability. Currently there are no generally known examples of such analysis being performed on a complex system. In this context, we need to distinguish between ease of analysis of a task, and the ease by which the task may be performed. Sometimes a task can be easily defined, but still difficult to perform, because the difficulties occur at a level 'lower' than the level at which the task is easily defined. This could be the case in, for example, tasks with a high motor skill component, or in cognitive tasks which must be performed very rapidly, or where working memory capacity might be exceeded. Such tasks might be perfectly straightforward to analyse. A similar point could be made even of some tasks performed by machine. As Young points out [255], it is reasonable to model what a calculator does as calculating 'the answer according to the rules of arithmetic', without dwelling on the processes that underlie that calculation. We would not expect this difficulty of execution to present a problem to formalisation in the way that system complexity does. If there is a unique clearly defined hierarchical task structure, formal analysis is not compromised by a large number of nodes in that structure.

3.2 Models of cognition

Providing a model cognitive architecture does not in itself present a CTA technique. But if one wishes to perform such an analysis, a cognitive model will define the terms in which the task has to be analysed.

A useful model here would be one which dealt with the aspects of cognition relevant to interacting with complex systems. The main issue is that of relevance. There are many aspects of theoretical cognitive psychology that will not have the slightest impact on predicting the performance of an operator of a complex system. Nevertheless, to the extent that realistic, relevant predictions *can* be made on the basis of tested theory, then such a theory should underpin the whole enterprise of modelling.

3.2.1 The Model Human Processor (MHP)

The simplest 'framework' architecture to consider is MHP (Card *et al.* [41]). This is not closely related to GOMS or the KLM, despite appearing in the same book. The authors attempt to bring together many results from cognitive psychology which they see as relevant to HCI design. The mind is seen as being made up of memories and processors, which have parameters for (memory) storage capacity, decay time and code type, and (processor) cycle time. They give estimates for general values of these parameters. Thrown in with these values are a number of other general principles (e.g., Fitts's Law, and the power law of practice). Taken together, what these parameters tell us is clearly more relevant to short-term simple tasks (and laboratory experiments) than to longer-term subtler cognitive abilities involving problem solving or decision making.

Card *et al.* give several examples of the kind of question which could be answered with the help of the MHP. The questions mostly are about how quickly things can be done (reading, pushing buttons or keys, etc.) in different circumstances. There are no examples of applying the MHP to problem solving or decision making.

What the MHP does in terms of task analysis is essentially to set bounds on what is feasible for a human to do (cognitively). Thus a matching analysis would have to show what items were in what memories at what different times, and to take account of the times required for motor actions. What the MHP does *not* do is to set a limit on depth or complexity of information processing, nor to other values which may be of interest in analysing complex control tasks.

3.2.2 Programmable User Models (PUMs)

The PUMs idea described by Young *et al.* [256] potentially takes the modelling of cognitive processes much further, though its implementation is still thought to be several years in the future. That idea is to represent the user of a system by a program, interacting with another program that represents the system. The purpose of a PUM is to benefit a designer in two ways: firstly, by making the designer think rigorously about how the system requires the user to interact; secondly, if such a program were ever constructed, by enabling predictions of users' competence and performance on a given system in the same kind of way as other analytical methods, but with improved accuracy because of the closer matching of mental processes by PUMs than by simpler formalisms.

What language would the program be written in? How would knowledge be represented and manipulated in that language? They give no definitive answers, but suggest progress towards answers by considering fundamental facts about human cognition: e.g., that working memory is limited (so you can't just reference global variables from anywhere at any time), and that there is no default sequential flow of control in humans, as there is in many programming languages.

Because there is not yet any explicitly decided architecture for PUMs, it is easier to imagine the approach being used in the course of design, rather than analysis. But the potential is there to provide a detailed language and knowledge structure which would constrain the analysis of a task more closely and helpfully than the MHP. In the meantime, using the PUMs concept in analysis could be a way of testing the plausibility of hypotheses about the mechanisms of task-related cognition: one could attempt to fit a task into the constraints selected, and if the performance was similar to that of a human, that could be said to corroborate those constraints.

3.2.3   ACT*

Anderson's ACT* [11] is a much more specific implemented architecture that aims to model human cognition generally. It deals with three kinds of cognitive units: temporal strings; spatial images; and abstract propositions. Anderson does not discuss in detail the cognitive processes that convert sensory experience into these units.

There are three distinct forms of memory dealing with cognitive units: working memory, which, as its name suggests, stores directly accessible knowledge temporarily; declarative memory, which is the long-term store of facts, in the form of a tangled hierarchy of cognitive units; and production memory, which represents procedural knowledge in the form of condition-action pairs.

Factual learning is said to be a process of copying cognitive units from working memory to declarative memory. This is seen as quite a different process from procedural learning, which happens much more slowly, because of the danger of very major changes in cognitive processes, which may be produced by the addition of just one production rule.

Procedural learning is the construction of new productions, which then compete for being used on the same terms as the established productions. ACT* allows procedural learning only as a result of performing a skill. First, general instructions are followed (using established general-purpose productions), then those instructions are compiled into new productions, which are then tuned by further experience in use. Compilation happens through two mechanisms: first a string of productions is composed into a single production (a mechanism called 'composition'); then this composite production is proceduralised by building in the information which had previously been retrieved from declarative memory.

Anderson illustrates the operation of learning by ACT* simulating the acquisition of early language, specifically syntax. Many assumptions are made for this purpose, including the assumption that words and parts of words (morphemes) are known and recognised. More important, the meaning of complete utterances is assumed to be understood.

From this brief description, we may see that ACT* is designed to emulate human learning, among other things. However, it is very difficult to see how, for the kind of complex systems that we are considering, ACT*'s mechanism for procedural learning could work. Where would the initial 'general' productions come from, which would be needed to guide the initial experience?

The question of whether ACT* serves to guide a task analysis in a useful cognitive way is a separate question. Since the knowledge which results in action in ACT* is implemented in a production system, it would make sense to analyse tasks in terms of production rules, and there is no reason to suppose this is a difficulty, since this is the formalism adopted by Kieras and Polson. The problem is not that production rules are difficult to create, but rather that it is possible in general to analyse a task in terms of production rules in many widely differing ways—just as it is in general possible to find many algorithms to solve a particular problem. The ACT* model does not help to focus an approach to analysis, but rather leaves this aspect of the analysis open. ACT* does not seem to pose the right questions, or offer useful guidance, for the practical problem of analysing a task in terms that are specifically matched to actual human cognition.

The same criticism could be made of SOAR [132] (also cited by some HCI authors), which is an architecture for general intelligence also based on a production system, similar in some ways to ACT*, but with less explicit attention given to correspondence with human cognitive processes.

What both SOAR and ACT* need, to complement them in providing guidance for task analysis, is (at least) a way of finding those production rules which best represent a particular human approach to a particular task. Analysing a task in terms of goals and rule structures is simply not a strong enough constraint to specify a method of cognitive task analysis.

3.2.4   Interacting Cognitive Subsystems

Recently, Barnard [19, 20] has described an original and ambitious approach to CTA that is rooted in cognitive theory. This approach is based on Barnard's own theoretical cognitive framework which he terms 'Interacting Cognitive Subsystems' (ICS) and which itself is an attempt to satisfy 'the need for applicable theory', i.e., a theory that is applicable to real-world problems, to operator error and to the design of systems. To produce such a theory, or even a framework for such a theory, represents a major departure from the cognitive science tradition of isolating the component processes of cognition for study in highly constrained laboratory tasks. In contrast, Barnard's focus is on their co-ordination and integration. Barnard also argues for the need for explicit mapping between cognitive theory, user performance and system design. Barnard's approach may be regarded as a development of the GOMS model, in which, Barnard argues, the key theoretical connections for relating the 'model human information processor' to the higher-level descriptions of tasks and knowledge are missing.

Barnard's approach represents a fusion between two rather different traditions within cognitive psychology. The first of these attempts to describe the general architecture of cognitive resources (the stores, processors, types of coding, etc.) and the control processes which govern the flow of information. This is the approach which has dominated the study of memory and attention and which essentially views the cognitive system as a general-purpose computer, with a central operating system controlling resource allocation. In contrast, the approach of psycholinguistics has emphasised the meaning of information being processed and has focussed on the underlying knowledge and the content-specific nature of processes required for language understanding. The emphasis here has been on computation and on rule-governed processes.

Barnard proposes a distributed architecture for human cognition. A number of processing modules or 'cognitive subsystems' are functionally independent and perform their operations in parallel. There is no general-purpose 'working memory' or 'central executive'. There are, however, interactions between the subsystems over a data network which permits integration and co-ordination to occur. Each subsystem has the same internal structure. It can compute, by performing some recoding process on input, and it can copy incoming information into an 'image record' or episodic memory. Barnard has worked out the details of a distributed architecture for perception, cognition and action and has applied this to various phenomena in verbal information processing. In the more recent version [20], eight subsystems are proposed. Two are sensory subsystems, acoustic and visual; four are representational subsystems, morphonolexical, propositional, implicational and object; and two are effector subsystems, articulatory and limb. Each is constrained by a list of operating characteristics which are capable together of accounting for many of the phenomena of information-processing psychology, such as selective attention, serial recall, etc. An important distinction is made between episodic memory and procedural knowledge. Barnard [20] shows how this model can be applied by performing an analysis of word processing and by accounting for the results of a number of experiments in the learning of HCI dialogues.

Most traditional task analysis starts with a description of the structure of action, or of the knowledge underlying those actions. A CTA in the style of Barnard starts with a specification of the constituent processing resources of cognition. It proceeds by trying to establish general relationships between the properties of the mental code (associated with a particular subsystem) and the characteristics of overt behaviour. These relationships form the analysis which is a description of the interplay between pre-existing procedural knowledge, the accessing of memory records, and the dynamic control of processing activity in the various subsystems. Most of Barnard's examples are drawn from experimental cognitive psychology or from HCI. Nevertheless a general applicability is claimed. While the nature of the representations involved would differ, the basic operation of the interacting cognitive subsystems should remain the same across tasks.

Barnard himself proposed that the form and content of CTA might be represented in the knowledge-base of an expert system. Thus, CTA would be developed by simultaneously top-down (development of the theoretical framework) and bottom-up (evidence from attempts to apply the system) approaches. Wilson *et al.* [238] have reported one attempt to develop a dynamic tool for CTA, constructed using an expert system shell (Xi) with the knowledge-base cast in the form of production rules based on Barnard's model. The knowledge-bases have been developed for command name types, for strictly ordered sequences of several commands and for verb-object selections in a menu dialogue. This work demonstrates the formidable problems to be overcome and the large amount of knowledge needing to be compiled if we are to develop truly generic tools of this kind. Despite these shortcomings it does, however, represent an impressive start.

3.2.5   Comparing cognitive models : a trade-off analysis

In an attempt to reveal the scope of cognitive (or 'user') models in HCI, Simon [216] has produced a kind of taxonomy based on the various trade-offs employed in their development. The models he considers include some of the formalisms, and some of the architectures, discussed in this chapter, and he places them in a trade-off 'space', thereby allowing the models to be distinguished along a number of dimensions. This is a useful framework for, among other things, revealing the partial nature of all existing models and for clarifying their purposes. Previous distinctions had only attempted to classify such models in terms of gross categories, such as the distinction (by Green *et al.* [92]) between competence models, which simply predict legal sequences of behaviour, and performance models, which attempt to describe the knowledge requirements of the user. Simon's classification scheme places each model at a point along at least four dimensions.

First, each model is classified by the nature of its output. These are either : primarily time ; or the computed complexity of output or cognitive acts ; or the predicted effects of interaction. Then, Simon compares the representations employed within each model by plotting them in a three-dimensional space. Two of the axes plot a trade-off. There is first a trade-off between degree of idealisation and the qualitative representation of processing. Degree of idealisation refers to the extent to which there is some variability built in, ranging from fixed and/or errorless behaviour at one extreme to entirely adaptive behaviour at the other. Against this is a dimension measuring the qualitative representation of processing, the extent to which the model specifies the actual mental operations involved in performance. Thus, we see that if a model represents behaviour in some kind of idealised way then it does so at the expense of being able to detail the mental operations involved in the predicted behaviour. Similarly, there is a trade-off between the extent to which the mental representation is parameterised and the degree to which the model operationalises knowledge. A model which sets numerical values for such constructs as the capacity of memory, or reaction times, will tend not to be specific about the content of the knowledge users will need to employ in the tasks. (It is not clear that this is a necessary trade-off.)

Finally, Simon further classifies the models in terms of the processing resources represented. Here he offers a rather limited distinction between the kind of behavioural elements focussed on by the model in question. These cover motor actions, perceptions and, set between these, 'cognition'.

Although it is possible to suggest other dimensions of comparison, and to criticise some of the details of Simon's trade-off space, the overall effect of his analysis is to provide a framework within which we can make some informed judgements. One immediate insight is revealed: most of the model space is uninhabited. Thus we see that the GOMS family of models, Cognitive Complexity Theory, CLG and TAG (Section 3.1) are all classified as favouring idealisation in the trade-off against the actual specification of mental operations. The clustering makes it quite clear that two models differ fundamentally from all the others. These are PUMs, which, as we have have noted (Section 3.2.2), do not yet properly exist, and Barnard's ICS architecture (Section 3.2.4). Both these architectures combine strong representations of the nature of processing with high levels of knowledge operationalisation.

Simon also makes use of Card and Young's [42] distinction between two ways of carrying out a task analysis: task space analysis and task instance analysis. In the former an analysis of a whole range of tasks is carried out. Most of the models require this kind of analysis to be carried out first, followed later by the input of particular task instances for prediction. The kind of model represented by ICS is intended to require much less effort on the part of the task analyser. One version of this has been implemented in the form of an expert system which guides the analyst in a kind of knowledge elicitation process. This is likely to be useful for the interface designer who needs detailed guidance about user characteristics.

3.2.6 General points about models of cognition

Simon's trade-off analysis suggests that Barnard's ICS model fills a gap. Certainly we would agree that it is different from the other architectures and formalisms, and thus could be expected to fit a cognitive task analysis better than other models, in cases where an analysis in terms of cognitive subsystems was relevant to task performance. On the other hand, for a task where the difficulty was focussed elsewhere, or where the analysis in terms of subsystems was not consistent across different instances of performance of the same task, the ICS model may not have any advantage, or even may be at a disadvantage.

Barnard makes specific assumptions: firstly that 'perception, cognition, and action can usefully be analysed in terms of well-defined and discrete information-processing modules', and secondly in the way that he specifies those modules. Other authors make assumptions that are often less explicit. Many of the older forms of analysis of cognitive tasks seem to rest greatly on the analyst's intuitive understanding of the domain, and of how people think and act in that domain. This may be successful insofar as the analyst has a rich, but informal, model that is not made explicit. However, where the assumptions are formalised and written down as a cognitive model, they tend to appear arbitrary, capturing perhaps something of the essence of the examples familiar to the theorist, but failing to be comprehensive. In no case do we consider that the assumptions made are both justified, and broad enough to cope with the generality of situations involving the control of complex systems.

3.3   Important features of cognition in complex systems

There are certain intuitively obvious features of human cognition in complex systems, which a good CTA should be able to deal with effectively. For example, many authors have acknowledged the fact that individual human operators have different strategies and different views of any particular task. This may well have a bearing on the information requirements and priorities, and thus it should be reflected in any comprehensive CTA. We may here make a useful distinction between individual variation in Intelligent Tutoring Systems (ITS), and in complex system control. For ITS, it is not difficult to imagine the production of models of complete and incomplete knowledge of a domain, and expert and 'buggy' performance strategies. In contrast, in complex process control it is much more difficult to define what would comprise 'complete' knowledge, and what (if anything) is an optimum strategy for a given task, since, although there is usually much that is defined in procedures manuals, this is never the whole story. Hence, for complex systems, it is implausible to model individual variation as an 'overlay' on some supposed perfect model. In current approaches to cognitive task analysis, individual variation is often ignored, and analysis simply performed in terms of a normative structure, often justified simply by the observation that it is plausible to analyse the task in this way. But, considering the reality of complex process control, to ignore differences is highly implausible, since there are apparent obvious differences in the way that, for example, novices and experts perform tasks.

3.3.1   Skills, rules and knowledge

Rasmussen and various co-workers wished to have a basic model of human information-processing abilities involved in complex process control, including (particularly, nuclear) power plants and chemical process works, in order to provide the basis for the design of decision support systems using advanced information technology techniques. The analysis of many hours of protocols from such control tasks has led to a conceptual framework[1] based around the distinction between skill-based, rule-based and knowledge-based information processing. This is presented as a 'step ladder' diagram, showing the progression of the steps of an idealised decision process, which can be shortcut

---

[1]See [187] for a summary.

by rule-based reasoning, or completely by-passed by subconscious skill-based decisions.

Rasmussen refers to Fitts and Posner's [77] distinctions in the phases of learning a skill: the early or cognitive phase; the intermediate or associative phase; and the final or autonomous phase; and he identifies these with knowledge-, rule- and skill-based cognition respectively. Thus a novice would use predominantly knowledge-based cognitive processes, and an expert would use many skill-based responses. Of course the expert will still revert to rule- and knowledge-based response in the many situations where skill-based responses have not had a chance to develop.

Although Rasmussen presents his stepladder model as a framework for CTA, he suggests neither an analytical formalism, such as a grammar, nor any explanation of the framework based on cognitive science. In a later report [188], he does give examples of diagrammatic analysis of a task in terms of his own categories. However, this is neither formalised nor based on any explicit principles.

Clearly, what Rasmussen gives does not amount to a complete cognitive task analysis technique. Writing in the same field, Woods [244] identifies the impediment to systematic provision of decision support to be the lack of an adequate *cognitive language of description*. In other words, neither Rasmussen nor anyone else provides a method of describing tasks in terms that would enable the inference of cognitive processes, and hence information needs. What Rasmussen does provide is an incentive to produce formalisms and models that take account of the distinctions that he has highlighted. Any new purported CTA technique must rise to the challenge of incorporating the skill, rule and knowledge distinction.

3.3.2 Mapping cognitive demands

Roth and Woods [201] base their suggestions on experience with numerous successful and unsuccessful decision support systems designed for complex system control. They see the central requirements for CTA as being, firstly, analysing what makes the domain problem hard, i.e., what it is about the problem that demands cognitive ability; and, secondly, the ways people organise the task that lead to better or worse performance, or errors. Once the errors have been understood, it should become possible to design a support system to minimise their occurrence.

The central requirements of CTA are referred back to Woods and Hollnagel [247]. They recognise three elements basic to problem-solving situations: 'the world to be acted on, the agent who acts on the world, and the representation of the world utilised by the problem-solving agent'. Before considering the interrelationship of all three elements, their proposed first step in the analysis is to map the cognitive demands of the domain in question, independently of representation and cognitive agent. This implies that any variation between cognitive agents (people, computers, etc.) will not feature in this first stage of the analysis. We may expect this to capture any necessary *logical* structure of a task, but this is not the cognitive aspect in the sense related to actual human cognition. The only variation they allow at this stage is between different 'technically accurate decompositions' of the domain. For these authors, 'determining the state of the system' is an example of this kind of cognitive demand. The difficulty with this mode of analysis is, given the possibility of variant human strategies and thence representations, that the human description of the 'state of the system', and the method for determining it, may indeed vary both with the individual operator and with the representation that they are currently using.

To try to retreat into technical descriptions at this point is only further to side-step the cognitive issue, and evade the question of whether there is any *cognitive* analysis at all that can be done independently of the agent and the representation. A possible reply might be that it is necessary to abstract from the influence of the agent and the representation in order to make progress in task analysis, since these factors are difficult to capture; however, this does no more than beg the question of the possibility or ease of finding out about the agent and representation—and that question has not been opened very far, let alone closed.

Inasmuch as some analysis is done without reference to the agent and the representation, we could see this as compromising the cognitive nature of the analysis, taking it further away from a full treatment of cognitive issues, back towards the a priori formalisms of Section 3.1. Woods and others' approach still has some advantage over such formalisms, by taking the operational setting into account, but this trades off against simplicity, and means that their approach is harder to formalise.

In essence, the approach to CTA advocated by these authors falls short of a detailed methodology, because there is still uncertainty about how the domain problem is to be described in the first place. Of course, for systems which are not especially complex, there may be a certain amount of cognition-independent task analysis based on the logical structure of the task. For more complex tasks, it is difficult to see how cognitive aspects of the task could usefully be analysed without a concurrent analysis of the actual cognitive task structure that the operators work with.

3.3.3 Quasi-independent subsystems

Moray [163], following systems theorists, suggests that humans naturally think about complex systems in terms of quasi-independent subsystems. In the absence of a strictly hierarchical decomposition of a system into subsystems, the quasi-independent ones are those which are near enough independent for many practical purposes, and Moray suggests that the development of skill amounts to the discovery of a suitable mental model comprising these subsystems, in terms of which rules for the operation of the plant can be formulated. Such rules, although less accurate than they could be, would be sufficiently accurate to allow a reasonable degree of control while at the same time being simple enough to understand.

Moray furthermore claims that there are methods which could automatically discover the plausible subsystems of a complex system. This would mean that CTA could proceed by identifying these subsystems, and using them as basic terms in the language describing the task from a cognitive point of view. The same subsystem structure could also be used as the basis for organising the information to be displayed to the operator.

We should note that Moray offers no evidence about the extent to which actual models of operators match up with the methodical analyses. Furthermore, it is not clear to what extent individual operators can or do develop their own models, differing from those of others. It would be surprising, though far from incredible, if a methodical analysis could show up a range of possible subsystem decompositions to match a range of individual models. If these questions are taken as challenges to further work, particularly towards discovering actual human mental models and representations, Moray's suggestions could be forerunners of a task analysis approach that was cognitive without being arbitrary or irremediably intuitive.

4 Another approach to cognitive task analysis

A broad overview of our three categories of approach suggests that none of the approaches given above are fully adequate for a CTA in the context of complex systems. The task-centred approaches lack sufficient input from cognitive psychology; the cognitive models lack sufficient relevance to the realities of complex tasks; and the current formalisms lack both. For another approach, we propose focussing on the original definition of cognitive task analysis: that is, an analysis dealing with information flow and usage. In cases where the task is logically defined in a simple way, a formal analysis will tell us all we need to know about information needs at that level. In cases where the complexity of the task lies in the degree of internal mental processing necessary, models of cognition in the style of Barnard may tell us what we need to know about information flow. In cases where the task has a necessarily hierarchical structure, hierarchical task analysis will reveal that structure, along with the implied information requirements; and so on.

But, in general, in the kind of complex systems we have in mind, a task may have many of these features. In this general case, we cannot currently do better than to investigate the information requirements of specific operators in specific situations. We may or may not discover variation across the different situations, or across individuals; but in any case, the results of this investigation would provide insight necessary for the construction of theories, formalisms, and other task analysis methods, suited to the domain investigated.

The issues that naturally arise here can be separated into two complementary questions. Firstly, for any particular situation, task and operator, what is the specific requirement for information that will provide the necessary basis for the operator's cognitive task execution in that situation? In other words, how is the system best represented to that particular operator at that time? The answer to this question must fit in with the rules, or whatever method, that the operator uses to make decisions in that context. Secondly, how are the various different representations articulated? What are the criteria for changing, and how is the decision made to change from one to another? When a change is made, what, if any, information is transferred to the new representation? If methods were found for answering these questions, they would provide the basis for a useful CTA, since the operator's representation of the current task at any time would specify what information is necessary.

Answers to both questions must have an empirical content, that is, they must be a *posteriori* rather than a *priori*, because of the inherent underdetermination of how to represent a complex system. The methodology for answering these questions is the necessary complement to current approaches, to obtain an effective CTA technique. This invites the development of automated or semi-automated tools, perhaps along the lines developed for knowledge elicitation [206]. Following sufficient empirical investigation, we may hope to formulate more general principles governing representations, which would be useful in early design, as well as in analysis of systems not yet mastered by people.

5   Conclusions

At this stage, we are presented with a two-dimensional framework for cognitive task analysis. The first dimension concerns where the emphasis lies: whether with the task (Section 3.3), or the cognitive psychology (Section 3.2). Investigation of the cognitive processes involved in complex control tasks would appear to be valuable and necessary, but does not in itself constitute a CTA methodology, since it is quite possible to model inessential cognitive processes while neglecting aspects that are important in real-life tasks. On the other hand, investigation of tasks independently of human cognition incurs assumptions; and subsequent investigation of the consistency of those assumptions with human cognition may show that an analysis based on them is of little relevance to people involved in complex tasks with complex systems. Current formalisms fail to bring the two sides together effectively, as there is much on both sides that they cannot encompass. Looked at in this dimension, the aim of CTA must be to integrate more of both emphases.

The second dimension concerns the progression from *a priori* theory and formalism to approaches based on the empirical investigation of the relevant realities of human cognition. There are plenty of examples of the *a priori* (Section 3.1), but these seem able to capture little of the richness and potential variation inherent in tasks involving complex systems. Their effective application is limited to simpler systems. Cognitive task analysis now requires the identification, and empirical investigation, of the areas of intersection between the task-oriented and the psychology-oriented approaches. Theories are required that are much more comprehensive, and are designed to account for empirical observations that will be made, as well as setting out a basis for what those empirical studies should be. This chapter is a first step towards the latter aim.

Chapter 7

The Cognitive Engineering of Problem Representations

David D. Woods

1   Introduction

There are a variety of studies and demonstrations in both human and machine problem solving which establish that *the representation of the problem domain provided to a problem solver can affect his/her/its performance* (cf. [147, 48, 135]). In this chapter I will explore the consequences of this basic finding in cognitive science for human-computer interaction in complex systems. As a result, questions about display/interface/support system design are types of representations vary in their effect on the problem solver's information processing activities and problem solving performance.

In many naturally occurring problem solving domains (air traffic control, process control, etc.), a large amount of data about the state of the underlying process is sensed and made available to people who are responsible to monitor, troubleshoot, supervise and control these worlds through *media* such as hardwired instruments, sets of VDU displays, decision-support systems.[1] The observability of the state and behaviour of the underlying process depends on how domain data is mapped into these media to produce a dynamic representation of that process. I will define some of the dimensions of this mapping that can affect the domain practitioner's information processing activities and strategies and therefore can impact on performance.

---

[1]The domain practitioner may also extract data about the domain through direct perceptual channels in addition to indirect processed channels, e.g., a pilot's view out of the window or tactile cues available when an anaesthesiologist manually ventilates a patient during surgery.

HUMAN–COMPUTER INTERACTION
AND COMPLEX SYSTEMS: ISBN 0-12-742660-4

2   Elemental data display

Data presentation in industrial control rooms is dominated by a one data point/one display element philosophy. While there has been a revolution in the media used for the display of data in industrial control rooms (the shift from hardwired displays to CRT and other VDU technologies) and in other domains (the shift from paper to computer data-handling systems), the almost universal display philosophy remains the same—what can be termed elemental display of data.[2] Individual pieces of data are the units of display, although they now appear cloaked in more various guises (for example, digital values distributed on a background of a system mimic drawing) and can be manoeuvred more elaborately (e.g., via windowing techniques).

The inability to abandon the elemental data display philosophy inherent in older representational media as technological developments have provided new representational powers has greatly constrained the way display and interface systems have been designed and their effects on user performance. To see this and to see an alternative philosophy, we will refer frequently to some of the properties of the field of data available to a problem solver and to the information processing activities required to build and maintain a situation assessment [245].

The field of data consists of some baseline data units about the underlying process. Ultimately, the base data units for display to domain practitioners consist of the elemental data which are directly sensed, measured or counted quantities—the 'raw' observations. Typically, baseline data units are are very close to the units of measurement. But baseline data units in some domain can be higher-order data that are built up from more elemental units. In a particular domain the baseline data unit could be individual sensor values, e.g., fluid level in a tank. One can always decompose a base unit into more elemental data, e.g., the sensor actually measures fluid level in an annulus outside the tank in question which under most circumstances is equivalent to tank level. Similarly, one can always combine a data unit with other data to produce a higher-order datum. For example, tank fluid level in a thermodynamic system is a measure of volume not mass and could be used with other data to derive an indication of the fluid mass in the tank. Or, for example, redundant sensor channels can be combined into a single 'best' estimate. The basic data unit in some domain is in part a product of the history and conventions of that domain as well as measurement constraints (e.g., it is much easier and cheaper to measure fluid volume rather than fluid mass in large thermodynamic systems).

In human interface design, the philosophy of elemental data display fo-

---

[2]This philosophy has sometimes been called separable display of data. I have used a different term so as to avoid confusion with Garner's concepts of separable and integral perceptual dimensions.

cuses on the availability and accessibility of base data units for the domain practitioner—*design for availability* [242]. It is the responsibility of off-line domain experts to determine what data units should be made available. The domain practitioner then must *gather and process* subsets of these basic data to answer questions during the problem-solving process such as situation assessment, disturbance/fault identification, goal setting, response planning (cf. [251]). Inadequacies in carrying out these cognitive functions are interpreted as requiring remedial aiding—cognitive prostheses (e.g., [200]).

2.1   Problems in design for availability

When interfaces are designed only for data availability, there are a variety of hidden assumptions and unaddressed issues in Human-Computer Interaction (HCI).[3] Note that all of the issues which follow involve how the data available through an interface inform the domain practitioner and how the practitioner uses available data to track and control the state of the underlying process.

Base data units are assigned to one 'home' in the virtual or physical data space and presented in one form. Display system design focusses on the layout of the data elements themselves. The base data units do not appear in multiple places and forms, each adapted to the question the user is trying to answer. Instead, the domain problem solver must decide what data to acquire when. When the user decides to check a datum, he or she must navigate to the *one* home that the data point resides in. When this datum needs to be combined with other data to reach some judgement about domain state, the user must acquire each base datum in series and then integrate them (see Mitchell and Saisi [154] for a description of one such system in the domain of satellite communication control centres). This means that the flexibility of the computer medium to bring data to the user, to organise the data in different ways for different purposes, and to show data in different forms is under-utilised.

Interfaces designed only for data availability do not address the problem of data overload. In fact, the computer medium's ability to make more and more data available tends to exacerbate data overload. There is nothing in the interface *per se* that supports the user's cognitive task of deciding what is the right data at the right time, when there are large amounts of potentially relevant data available [243]. For example, the investigations of the Three Mile Island accident concluded that, 'it seemed that although the necessary information was, in general, physically available, it was not operationally effective. No one could assemble the separate bits of information to make the correct deductions' [122]. The practitioner must filter available data to focus in on the relevant subset for that stage in an unfolding problem, and what

---

[3] What follows is a description of a pure type; individual cases will vary in their fit to this exemplar.

subset is relevant varies with context. (In the words of Sherlock Holmes, 'It is of the highest importance in the art of detection to be able to recognise, out of a number of facts, which are incidental and which are vital.')

I have pointed out elsewhere [242, 243] that the significance or meaning extracted from an observed datum depends on the relationship of that datum to a larger set of data about the state of the domain, goals, past experience, possible actions, etc.—the context in which the datum occurs. This means that processing of an observed value or change on one data channel depends on contact with a variety of other information derived from checking or remembering or assuming the state of other data (cf., [49] for examples from the medical domain). In elemental data display, available data is presented as individual signals to be processed and interpreted. There is no concern with communicating what is signified by the data (or aiding the observer in this process) by relating a signal to its context. The observer must acquire, remember or build the context of interpretation datum by datum with the associated possibilities for incompleteness or error and with the associated mental workload.

Elemental data display also fails to address a related factor that is critical in HCI and decision support. Not only does a datum gain significance in relation to a set of other data, but also what data belongs in this relevance set will change as function of the state of the domain and the state of the problem-solving process. The above points—(a) a subset of the available data is actually relevant at a given point in the problem solving process, (b) a set of contextual data is needed to extract meaning from a datum, and (c) the fact that these data sets change with context—define the *context sensitivity problem*. The degree of context sensitivity is a major cognitive demand factor of a domain which has profound implications for representation design and human performance.

Since the user must move about the display space collecting the subset of relevant base data units, navigation in the data space becomes an important cognitive task and difficulties in navigation have become a major class of high-level interface problems [241]. Getting lost problems have occurred with large display networks designed only for data availability in event-driven tasks (e.g., [73, 131]).

As the user must gather a subset of base data units to address domain issues, he or she may not gather all of the data needed to completely assess that aspect of the state of the domain. This could take several forms—keyhole effects [241], tunnel vision [161], stereotypical routes through the display space, increased emphasis on familiar shortcuts in evidence processing [187]. The point is that interfaces designed only for data availability do not attempt to help users make judgments based on the full pattern of evidence and may increase any tendencies to make judgments based on only partial state information. For example, in many domains where engineered processes are involved (power plants, aircraft systems, chemical process control) one property of the data field is that individual sensor values, considered alone, are uncertain indicators of process state and that there are usually diverse sources of evidence on an issue (information redundancy across data channels). Evaluation of the full set of evidence is important especially in unusual incidents [245], and practitioners frequently use redundant data channels in order to cope with data uncertainty [57]. How the interface as problem representation affects the completeness with which a practitioner gathers data for judgments about process state is an important HCI issue.

Finding and integrating a series of base data units can affect user information processing depending upon the levels of mental workload involved. If the mental activities required to locate base data units are not automatic but require mental effort or capacity, they may disrupt or divert mental resources from the main line of reasoning [241, 155, 204]. If a series of base data units must be gathered to reach a judgment, excessive working memory loads can be imposed on the practitioner unless the interface can function as an external memory. The number of mental steps involved in finding and integrating base data units (or the associated workload) creates the possibility of trade-offs between effort and accuracy [118]. Finally, there can be information processing consequences that depend on the workload that is involved in mentally integrating the subset of base data units once they are acquired.

Design for data availability addresses the sequence of actions required to manoeuvre through the data space (in order to ensure accessibility). But, because the focus is on providing homes for base data units, it tends to ignore how the behaviour of the underlying process is captured and reflected in the behaviour of the interface. Domain 'events' that is, behaviours over time, are captured only by happenstance in the dynamics of the interface.

Subsets of base data units are generally available within a single view due to the characteristics of the medium itself (e.g., a single display frame). However, organisational criteria are chosen simply to meet the inherent constraints of the medium—physical space for conventional control panels or display pages in conventional CRT-based display systems. Typically, the organisational criterion is some variant on the physical structure of the underlying process, e.g., systems, subsystems. However, the layout is in terms of the data elements themselves. For example, one sees a profusion of system mimic diagrams where a version of the physical topology is used as a frame on which to hang a variety of sensor measurements, frequently in digital form. And one sees both designers and human-computer specialists attempt to specify what form data should be displayed in (iconic, analogue, digital) independent of what the data signifies or what it is used for.

In effect, the one datum/one display element philosophy is based on the assumption that any datum that is available in the external data base should be found and used whenever it is needed in domain problem solving. This is a parallel to the equi-availability assumption in teaching which assumes that, if a person can be shown to possess a piece of knowledge in any circumstance, then this knowledge should be accessible under all conditions where it might be useful. In contrast, a variety of research has revealed dissociation effects where knowledge accessed in one context remains *inert* in another [29, 83]. Thus, Gick and Holyoak [85] found that, without explicit prompting, people will fail to apply a recently learned problem solution strategy to an isomorphic problem (cf. [128] for another of many cases where human performance varies on problem isomorphs that differ only in representation).

Evidently, the fact that people possess relevant knowledge does not guarantee that this knowledge will be activated when needed. The critical question is whether or not situation-relevant knowledge is activated and utilised under the conditions in which the task is performed. Similarly, in HCI, the critical question is whether or not the data relevant to the current situation is examined under the conditions in which the task is performed—assisting the practitioner in finding the right data at the right time.

3   HCI as problem representation

3.1   Design for information extraction

After Gibson [84], one can define a display as

> a surface shaped or processed so as to exhibit information about more than just the surface itself.

Given this definition,[4] informativeness is not a property of the data field alone, but is a relation between the observer and the data field (cf. [243]), the design of displays/interfaces/aids is shaping or processing display surfaces (the medium, e.g., VDUs, and the elemental domain data) so as to exhibit information for a domain practitioner (the problem solver who is also the problem holder). One can term this approach *design for information extraction*. It is important to emphasise that, in this view, display/interface design cannot be separated from the design of decision aids.

3.2   Interfaces as representational systems

Design, evaluation and research in HCI and HICI (human-intelligent computer interaction) should be seen in terms of representational issues. The display/interface is a referential medium where visual (and other elements) are signs or tokens that function within a symbol system [87, 113].

---

[4] And given a specific view of information where information is not a thing-in-itself, but rather a relation between the data, the world the data refers to, and the observer's expectations, intentions and interests.

Again, the representation of the domain provided to a problem solver can affect his/her/its problem-solving performance. The physical form of a code does not in itself define or even indicate the mode of symbolising [87]. How the code is *used in a symbol system* determines the type and effectiveness of the symbolising, i.e., its semantic properties. As Paul Kolers has remarked in summarising the results of his research program in cognitive psychology, "...cognitive operations are not independent of the symbols that instigate them and that 'information' is not wholly separable from its embodiment in a symbol system" (Gonzalez and Kolers [86, p. 319]). This point emphasises that performance is a joint function of the nature of the cognitive demands posed by the domain, the nature of the representation of that domain available to the problem solver and the characteristics of the problem solving agent [245].

There are no *a priori* neutral representations which one can retreat to in order to finesse the issue. The central question is what are the relative effects of different forms of representation on the cognitive activities involved in solving domain problems. HCI research then needs to investigate *representational form* as opposed to merely visual form, to investigate the *referential functions* that are performed by HCI tokens within a symbol system, and to investigate the interface as an *coherent representational system* rather than as a collection of independent parts, e.g., display pages.

3.3   Representational form

Display design questions often have been framed in terms of visual forms, particularly the advantages or disadvantages of different visual forms such as bar charts versus geometric patterns or digital values versus analogue meters.

However, visual appearance *per se* does not define the representational form. *Representational form* depends on how data is mapped into the features and behaviour of a visual form to influence information extraction by an observer [249]. Bar charts, trends and other visual forms can be used to create the same representational form (or variants on a representational theme). Conversely, a single visual format such as a bar chart can be used in many representational forms.

The design challenge for creating effective representations is to set up this mapping so that the observer can extract information about task-meaningful semantics. Becker and Cleveland [21] call this the decoding problem, that is, domain data may be cleverly encoded into the attributes of a visual form, but, unless observers can effectively decode the representation to extract relevant information, the representation will fail to support the practitioner.

In HCI, visual form is often confused with representational form. A frequent example occurs in the design of object or integrated displays [249]. To create an integrated display from the point of view of design for information extraction, the designer must decide what higher-order properties are to be communicated to the domain practitioner, choose the specific domain data that is evidence for these properties, and map the data into the properties of a visual form so as to make the domain properties visible to an observer. The representational form results from how this mapping is carried out and can include steps such as making disparate data comparable (e.g., how to integrate data from two different physical dimensions), setting scale resolution, and identifying reference and boundary conditions as a function of context. The *mapping*, not the visual form *per se*, is the critical aspect. However, integrated displays are frequently classified according to their visual characteristics, e.g., geometric patterns displays, face displays, etc. (but cf. [249]).

3.4 Referential functions in HCI

Design then addresses the question: what is the function of the visual elements (the signs or tokens) in this symbol system? I will briefly note some of the referential functions of HCI tokens.

Different representational forms can vary in what information (and how much information) can be directly extracted, how directly this information specifies actions in the domain, how broad or narrow are the uses that the directly available information can be put to [249].

Representations can support effective performance in more ways than just the direct read out of significant information. Lesh [136] suggests and illustrates that the power of a representation is a function of the ability of agents using it to go *beyond the information given*, in the sense of discovering new relationships or generating significant new questions or solving new sophisticated problems. The observer goes beyond the information given in the sense that he or she extracts information beyond the data immediately available and directly specified in the representation.

General attributes of skill can be affected as well. For example, an essential attribute of skill is the flexibility to adapt strategies and resources to a changing world in the pursuit of goals. Some representations may support the flexibility of skilled performance better than others, even when both directly provide useful information.

The concept of inert knowledge mentioned earlier shows another function of an external representation. Characteristics of the representational system can help or hinder problem solvers recognise what information or strategies are relevant to the problem at hand. For example, Fischoff *et al.* [76] and Kruglanski *et al.* [130] found that judgmental biases (e.g., representativeness) were greatly reduced or eliminated when aspects of the situation cued the relevance of statistical information and reasoning. Thus, one dimension along which representations vary is their ability to provide prompts to the knowledge relevant in a given context. The behaviour of the interface does more than act as a repository of domain data: it provides retrieval cues to relevant knowledge given the context of the current situation assessment and past experience [155].

Other referential functions related to memory are the degree to which the representational system serves as an external memory and the degree to which it produces reminders for monitoring checks or actions [98, 138, 155]. For example, a return-to-normal alerting signal functions as a reminder to power plant operators about when to throttle back a system that automatically comes on at maximum capacity when the controlled parameter violates low limits. The reminding cue changes the practitioners cognitive activities. Without the reminding cue, when the practitioner observes the low-limit violation, he or she needs to remember to check parameter recovery and to throttle back the system in the future. The presence of the reminding cue eliminates any memory requirements and converts the task into a simple stimulus-action packet. Note how reminders can be particularly important in domains where practitioners interweave multiple activities.

Representations differ in the degree to which domain *events* are recognizable [246]. Domain events are defined in terms of how *data has changed over time*. This presupposes a concern with how the representation of the domain portrays changes over time. Events include such things as set-point crossings, state changes, qualitative behaviours (e.g., a parameter value could be stable, moving away from target or returning toward target). Emphasising how a representation affects the observability of domain events focusses HCI on the dynamic behaviour of the interface system. One implication of this is that static evaluations are inadequate tests of the ability of an interface or graphic form to support user information extraction in the course of cognitive tasks such as situation assessment and fault management. Very little research is available about dynamic symbol-referent relationships to provide a source of guidance for designers. However, studies of movement perception show that a great deal of information unavailable (or available only with great difficulty) from static representations is immediately extracted from dynamic stimuli [117].

To see another referential function, consider the case where an incident is underway and the problem solver has several information processing activities which he or she should be engaged in (e.g., confirming automatic system responses to disturbances, diagnostic search to determine the source of the trouble). An event occurs on a data channel which the problem solver detects. Should he or she interrupt ongoing lines of reasoning to evaluate the information provided by that event (it could indicate that something new has occurred in the incident—a new fault, or it could be relevant to the lines of reasoning that are ongoing)? Or should the problem solver defer processing of that channel until there is a pause in the ongoing lines of reasoning (e.g., the event is about an issue that is not important in this context, the event is a domain behaviour that is expected for these circumstances, being distracted to pursue every signal in a signal-rich domain would prevent coherent fluent responses in complicated incidents)?

The cognitive demand for control of attention given a limited resource problem solver in a dynamic incident can be influenced by the properties of the representation. When a signal is noticed on a data channel, does the problem solver have to fully process the signal in order to understand its relevance to the current situation (all or none processing of new data signals)? Can the problem solver know something about the signal through a partial evaluation, such as which data channel it occurred on or the general nature of the signal, in order to decide whether to shift attentional resources to more fully evaluate the import of this signal (analogous to preattentive processing in perception). Just knowing what the signal is about in general can help the problem solver to decide whether it is or is not important in this context and whether or not to interrupt ongoing processing for a more complete evaluation. In addition, there is the issue of whether or not the partial processing is economical in terms of mental resources. The partial evaluation could be carried out by processes that are automatic or effortful (consume mental resources), or by processes that tap either the same or different resources than those tapped by the main lines of reasoning (multiple resource theory).

Several results [129] (summarised in [249]) suggest that spatial dedication of data channels helps experienced practitioners to partially evaluate new signals via processes that do not interfere with ongoing lines of reasoning and to control allocation of attention—what one might term *preattentive reference*. In spatial dedication each potential signal event defines a data channel which occupies a fixed location so that whenever a change such as a light going on or off is noticed in that physical area, the experienced observer knows what has occurred without fully processing the signal, i.e., reading the message. When data channels are not spatially dedicated, pictographs (icons) may help perform the same function for low interference, partial evaluation of new signals.

Analyses similar to the above can be made for referential functions related to landmarks and other orienting cues relative to navigation and search in large display networks (cf. [241]).

The diversity of cues provided by a representation may also be an important property. A diversity of cues should tend to expand the retrieval cues available to activate relevant knowledge, to increase the representational system's ability to capture domain events (even if serendipitously), and to increase the reminders available to recall previous states or to trigger courses of action. One example of a serendipitous relationship between the form and content of a representation (serendipitous in the sense that the relationships were not intentional design choices) that was noticed and utilised by the human problem solver occurred in a process control application. The position of a device usually controlled by an automatic system was indicated via hardwired counters that presented a digital position value. These counters happened to make clearly audible clicks when device position changed. Operators were able to make use of the clicking sounds to monitor this system because the clicks and click rate contained information about the behaviour of the automatic controller.

4   Properties of representational systems

I have already alluded to two basic referential properties of representational systems given the kinds of data fields that occur in complex dynamic domains such as process control and flightdecks. One concerns how base data units are collected into groups and how *collection* interacts with properties of the domain and properties of the observer to influence performance. The second concerns the issue that the data collected can be more or less elemental ranging from the raw measurements to higher-order properties. The base data unit available for display can built by integrating lower-order data to directly indicate higher-order properties. This factor is the level of *integration* of data and how it interacts with properties of the domain and properties of the observer to influence performance.

To illustrate these concepts of data collection and data integration, consider the case of a datum about a thermodynamic system which indicates that valve x is closed. In isolation from other data, this datum simply signals a component status. Other data about system state and knowledge about domain structure and function is needed to determine whether valve x should be open in the current context, i.e., that the datum signifies a misaligned component. Given further data and knowledge, the datum could signify that, with valve x closed, the capability to supply material to reservoir H via path A is compromised. Furthermore, the significance of any of the above interpretations depends upon the state of other parts of the domain (Is an alternative available? Is reservoir H inventory an important issue in the current context?) and the person's expectations about domain behaviour. The point is that, to determine the significance of a datum, the problem solver must collect and integrate other data.

HCI research is interested in how the representational system affects user performance of the collection and integration activities as a function of the characteristics of the agent using the representation and the characteristics of the problems the domain poses, e.g., the properties of the data field. It is the mapping of the data field into a representational system for an observer that is critical in assessing the ability of the interface to support domain tasks.

The properties of the implementation technology (the medium) force a designer to partition the field of data into collections (e.g., screens or windows within screens in CRT media).[5] The grouping is based on some type of criterion such as device geography, physical system boundaries, time (e.g., chronological lists of messages) and occasionally domain goals to be achieved or the function performed by parts of the device.[6]

The collection of base data units into groups affects user information processing depending on on the criterion used to set the boundaries, whether the collection boundaries are *fixed or adaptive*, and on how both interact with characteristics of the problems the world poses. Data collections can be either *fixed or adaptive*. In *fixed collection*, the representation designer pre-selects the collections of data by which the user can examine the domain. The effect of a particular definition of fixed collections of data on user performance depends on the amount of across-predefined boundary search that results. In *adaptive collection*, how data is collected into groups is a parameter that changes as a function of the state of the domain in question or as a function of inferred user intent. Machine power is applied to manipulate the representation as a function of the semantics of the domain.

4.1 Fixed collection of base data units

When the representation designer pre-selects fixed collections of data, the effect of a particular definition of collection boundaries on user performance depends on the *amount of across-predefined boundary search* that results. This quantity is a function of three factors.

The first factor is the degree to which the designer's choice of criterion for collecting data anticipates the questions that must be answered to perform domain tasks. An example is that collecting data along physical system boundaries will not support collecting data to answer questions about the status of a function when the domain contains a many-to-many mapping between systems and functions [187, 249].

In a satellite communications control centre investigated by Mitchell and Saisi [154], one criterion for collecting data was classes of hardware. They investigated performance with the original interface in use in actual centres and with a redesigned interface that collected data along criteria of operator

---

[5] Note that there also can be collections of collections. As a result, users often have an information-processing task at the level of collecting collections of data as when the user has available two or more independent VDUs or can assign collections of data to multiple independent windows. Moray [162] contains an example where a significant error occurred in domain task performance due to the user's decision about how to collect data collections.

[6] In data collections, the elements of the collection are distinct. There is nominal depiction of the relationships among the elements of the collection or across collections and no emergent features. Emergent features are part of the defining characteristics of analogical integration. Of course, both collection and integration can be combined and often should be combined in creating a representational system.

functions.[7] One operator function is to ensure that data flow and data quality from each transmitting satellite. To do this, operators are interested in data about the set of hardware that supports a particular satellite transmission. To do this with the original interface required a great deal of display page thrashing because a variety of equipment types support each satellite. Performance assessments by Mitchell and Saisi (op. cit.) showed large and significant performance improvements (both error and productivity measurements) with the new interface.

Collection boundaries can be defined so that each datum occurs embedded in the field of data from which it derives significance—the display of data in context. Note that one can index data based on individual data points (e.g., [246]) or based on higher-order issues (e.g., system functions) or both. In any case the point is that the datum is observed in the context of other relevant data [49]. Collection boundaries defined in this way shift the representational orientation from the display of signals to be interpreted to the display of the significance of the signals. Another result is that individual data can appear in more than one home and in more than one form, e.g., as the focal point or as a contextual datum for another focal point.

There are two paths that can be followed to match collection boundaries to meaningful questions and to define the context relevant to individual data points. One is an empirical path, as in Henderson and Card [102], where you look for patterns in the data search behaviour of people performing the task and then use those patterns to define collections. In Henderson and Card's system the resulting collections define a working set or a room, i.e., collections of windows). An alternative path is to analyse the domain problem-solving demands to determine what issues must be addressed or what questions must be answered and then to collect the data that is relevant to that issue or question. (This analytical route is exemplified by [152, 154, 243, 247].)

The second factor is the characteristics of the representation in which the search occurs that affect search performance across the predefined boundaries. An example of this is the changes in search performance (e.g., getting lost, keyhole effects) that occur depending on the availability of spatial cues to provide a link between data collections [241, 152, 151, 73]. In dynamic worlds, this is called the issue of parallel versus serial display (and it is one of the important cognitive issues behind the medium-oriented question of window management tactics such as tiled versus overlapping windows). The question is, given that there is too much data too be seen at once (note that physically parallel display does not mean all the data can be taken in one glance), how can the representation design be manipulated to help the problem solver decide what data should be examined at this point in the unfolding incident?

---

[7]The new interface also included adaptive collection, computational integration and analogical integration.

Woods [241] extensively discusses this issue and proposes a variety of psychologically based techniques to aid search across fixed collection boundaries (see also [171]). One example is techniques such as the use of landmarks to maintain orientation in a large data space (one kind of referential function). (Empirical results that indicate the utility of these techniques include [152, 151, 73, 154, 235, 227].)

The third factor is the degree to which the links between data sets and questions vary with context for a particular world and for a particular collection criterion. Seeing the collection property of representational systems leads to the HCI concept: when displaying a datum to an observer, also display its context of interpretation. However, another part of the context sensitivity problem is that the interpretative field can change with context. This is one factor that leads to the need for adaptive collection.

4.2   Adaptive collections: the display of data in context

Frequently, what data is relevant depends on the state of the domain or the intentions of the problem solver. In these cases, decision support can be based on adaptive collection. In adaptive collection, how data are collected into groups is a parameter that changes as a function of the state of the world in question or as a function of inferred user intent. This can be manifested in many ways depending upon the complexity of the contingencies involved. In one case, the set of data that occur within a collection boundary may be adapted to the current context. For example, the data used to answer the question 'Is there adequate material inventory inside a container?' may need to change depending upon whether the material is in a liquid state or a gas/liquid mixture. Similarly, to extract meaning from a given value of a parameter (e.g., the pressure in a thermodynamic system is 2235) requires an interpretative context which depends on the past history of the value, how fast it is changing, alarm limits, automatic system activation/deactivation set-points, overall plant status, among other factors [246].

Another case is to adapt the set of collections based on expressed interest, the domain semantics and the current state of the domain. Consider the example of a domain problem solver who expresses interest in a domain goal such as controlling pressure in a control volume within certain constraints in a thermodynamic system (cf. [243, 247]). Based on the domain semantics one can parse the field of available data into collections with respect to:

- Data about the goal—what evidence specifies the state of constraint satisfaction for the pressure quantity within this control volume.

- Data about active processes that affect pressure behaviour—what evidence specifies the state of these processes, their relationships, potential future behaviour, or disturbances in these processes.

- Data about the processes that could be active which affect pressure behaviour—what evidence specifies whether these processes could function if required.

- Data about the side-effects of the current state or state changes of the above processes—what evidence specifies how changes in the processes which are or could affect pressure will affect other goals (e.g., temperature, level).

Within each of these categories one can adaptively collect relevant data based on current plant state. For example, which constraints on pressure are relevant varies with plant mode, or the currently active processes can be shown in more detail than standby processes [241, 80].

Mitchell and Saisi [154] describe another HCI project that used this form of adaptive collection. They used a model of the control tasks, system constraints and operator procedures as a domain semantics. When the operator made a display request, collections of data relevant to that aspect of the system were selected and positioned across windows and screens based on the semantic connections and the current state of the domain (see [237] for another example of adaptive collection).

Note how the above type of adaptive collection changes the selection process for the data search/display frame. The domain practitioner can acquire data by specifying areas or levels of interest in terms of the domain semantics. The data field made available contains items of high potential relevance for that request [243]. The presentation of a bounded set of relevant data provides retrieval cues and supports the practitioner recognising interesting or important conditions to focus on or pursue. In the terminology of Hutchins *et al.* [108], the articulatory distance is reduced.

Adaptive collection requires the use of machine power to manipulate the representation. This can be algorithmic computations where the designer determines in advance the conditional relationships between data collections and the states of the world or more 'intelligent' machine power where the designer provides a description of the functional possibilities which the machine uses to infer the particular data subset to gather in a particular situation. Regardless of the type of computation used, there are several common elements in developing this type of 'intelligent' interface. First, adaptive collection requires a model of domain semantics that specifies the meaningful contexts of interpretation (e.g., [153, 102, 247]). Second, there is a need to compute an assessment of domain state on which to base adaptive collection.

Given context sensitivity as a property of the domain data field, adaptive collection must occur (a cognitive demand factor). The question is how does the design of the interface as a representational system affect the domain practitioner's information extraction activities and performance in the face of this demand—e.g., does a representation reduce the number of information-processing activities, increase their mental economy, reduce their disruptive-ness on other information processing activities. The possibility for adaptive collection with new computational powers introduces new challenges for effective HCI. By definition, adaptive collection means that the display field which the observer sees will change automatically based on the context. This can be done in ways that enhance human information processing or in ways that exacerbate data overload and increase mental workload.

To see one difficulty, imagine that you are monitoring a display when a change occurs automatically—one display frame has been substituted for the page you were examining. You do not know why the display changed, or which pieces of data in the new display you should pay attention to, or why the machine thought that these data were important for the current situation, or what is the interface's perception of the current situation. Following the automatic changes in display can raise the user's mental workload even though it appears that the computer is performing the work for him. This is a result that occurs frequently with increases in interface automation. Woods and Elias [246] describe one intelligent interface that uses adaptive collection in ways to display data in their interpretative context without creating new information-processing burdens. Again the issue is how the interface functions as a representational system that determines the impact on user information processing and performance.

4.3   Computational and analogical integration

Lower-order data can be integrated to directly indicate higher-order properties. Note that this involves a shift from an organisation in terms of the base data units themselves to an organisation based on higher-order domain issues. As was the case with determine effective collections of data, the ability to do this depends on an understanding of domain semantics. For instance, in the satellite communications control centre example mentioned earlier, one base data unit in the original interface is total data block counts (a count of the data blocks transmitted is tabulated). However, to determine software failures the skilled practitioner extracts information about data flow (a rate on data block counts) and moreover compares the observed flow to expected flow. The latter illustrates that integration often involves a shift in dimensions from numerical scales to qualitative scales such as normal-abnormal or expected-unexpected (e.g., [246]).

Integration can be either *computational or analogical*. This is a distinction between data represented as descriptions (i.e., linguistic or digital form) and data represented in depictions (graphic or analogue form). In computational integration the new datum results from direct combination of lower-order data via calculation, inference (e.g., the combination of uncertain evidence into an overall result in expert systems), logic or algorithm. Examples in process control include calculated variables, system availability computations, sensor quality algorithms of varying complexity where multiple redundant and/or diverse sensors that measure a single quantity are combined into a single 'validated' value, inference rules to determine the status of higher-order units. In all of these, the occurrence of a relevant pattern in lower-order data is explicitly computed and noted.

Computational integration is presumed to aid performance by shifting the cognitive activities involved in collecting and integrating lower-order data from the human domain practitioner to the machine.[8] Computational integration can be applied to tasks ranging from simple overhead information-processing tasks up to attempting to generate complete problem solutions. For example, computational integration can be used to recognise domain events. This intermediate-level computation (i.e., a computation that falls short of solving the problem for the user) can then be used in representation design in order to organise data display at the level of events rather than at the level of base data units. The point is that computational integration is one of many techniques that can be used together to create a representational system.

In analogical integration, higher-order properties are represented by de-picting the *relationships among the lower-order data* that define the property. Instead of directly noting the state of a higher-order datum as in computa-tional integration, it is represented as an emergent property of the structure and behaviour of lower-order data. In analogical representation *the struc-ture and behaviour of the representation (symbol) is related to the structure and behaviour of what is represented (referent)*. This means that perceptions about the form of representation correspond to judgements about the un-derlying semantics, for example, a relationship between two elements of the representation corresponds to a relational semantic property of the world. Analogical representation has a variety of potential advantages for user in-formation processing (cf. [87, 218, 243]). In part, these advantages derive from the power of visualisation as an aid to comprehension and conceptu-alisation (e.g., [48]). The priority of space as an organising principle is so compelling that non-spatial data are often given a spatial representation to improve human comprehension (e.g., [94]). And it is the power of analogical representation that undoubtedly contributes to the appeal and effectiveness of direct manipulation interfaces [108].

Because the symbol and referent are not related on all dimensions, the

---

[8] Computational integration is often carried out assuming that there is fixed set of cog-nitive activities involved in carrying out tasks in some domain so that introducing new machine functions does not impact on the human role except to reallocate the automated elements. However, Woods and Roth [249], among many others, note the problems with this assumption.

difficult and critical design problem with this kind of integration is to determine what is a useful *partial isomorphism* between the form and the content of a representation. To accomplish this the designer must determine what constraints between the symbol and what is symbolised should be established via techniques for analysing the domain semantics (e.g., [153, 247]).

A second design problem is how to map the chosen aspects of domain structure and behaviour into characteristics of the representation so that the domain semantics can be easily extracted by the human problem solver (the decoding issue). This includes issues of selecting, scaling and assigning lower-order data to characteristics of the representation. Careful assignment of data is necessary because there are inherent relationships in the graphic format that must be related to and not conflict with the data relationships to be portrayed. For example, Brown [32] and MacGregor and Slovic [144] found that in the faces object display form the data mapped into the mouth feature dominated the data represented on the other facial features. In addition, the mapping of domain semantics into representational form effects also how visible they are to the user. For example, Kleiner and Hartigan's work [126], and the accompanying commentary by Wainer, contains three different solutions to these problems for a single visual form (faces) that visibly change the salience of a single underlying data pattern. On the other hand, irrelevant characteristics or behaviour of the visual form (irrelevant to the designer in the sense that domain information is not mapped into these characteristics or behaviours of the visual form) can be interpreted as carrying domain information by the user and interfere with extraction (decoding) of the relevant domain information. This over-interpretation is one kind penalty that can occur with analogical representations in general [166, 96]. For example, for the observer of a faces visual form data encoded in the mouth feature is a dominant cue, but this may be entirely unintentional from the designer's perspective [144].

Finally, there is the question of what amount and type of training and experience with the representation as window on the domain is needed with representational systems that use analogical integration.

The weak form of analogical integration is to provide structure to a collection so that relationships among the elements of the collection carry information. Not any structure counts, if the representation is to be more than a pictograph. The relationships must be related to domain semantics. The strong form of analogical integration uses machine power to manipulate the behaviour of the representation in ways that directly correspond to domain semantics. Note that in strong analogical integration, as in adaptive collections, it is the representation that is manipulated through the use of machine power. With computational integration, the machine power is applied to the evidence itself and is independent of questions about how to represent the result and the basis for the result.

Given that evidence is integrated and that there are uncertainties in the available evidence, there is the need for the information-processing activity of *decomposition*. In the case of computational integration this corresponds to issues about explanation (what is the basis for the result). In analogical integration the lower-order elements should remain directly visible to the problem solver so that he or she can see in parallel the higher-order property and the lower-order patterns of evidence that signal it [250]. When individual data points considered alone are uncertain indicators of states of parts of a domain, the decomposibility of higher-order data seems to be an important factor in how practitioners will use the aid that provides the intergrated data (or even if he or she will use it). For example, in patient-monitoring systems in anaesthesiology there is considerable concern about whether a signal is reflecting actual patient state or artifact. Sophisticated new monitoring systems seemed to have succeeded or failed depending in part upon whether they provided an immediate, direct and mentally economical way to check for artifact. Several successful monitoring devices display both the waveform and the specific value of interest (e.g., end-tidal carbon dioxide concentration) in parallel. When an anaesthesiologist checks for this value he or she also sees the waveform, whose shape economically communicates whether the value is suspect or not.

5 Resumé: representational systems

One can reinterpret questions about the display of data through media as questions about how types of representations vary in their effect on the problem solver's information processing activities and problem-solving performance. The question for cognitive engineering is what are the important dimensions of problem representations, or, more specifically, how data is mapped into a representational systems for a kind of cognitive agent. It is important to emphasise that representation design involves an orchestration of various techniques to create a total representational system. Again, it is how a code functions within a symbol system that determines the type and effectiveness of the symbolising.

The concepts articulated here show how representations can shift the information-processing activities of the user. For example, when elemental display of data is abandoned, no longer is the problem solver searching a layout of the available base data units to collect and integrate the data sets relevant for the current context. No longer are base data units available in only one home and in one form. The collection and integration activities reveal possibilities for base data units appearing in more than one place and in more than one representational form.

I have only briefly covered the concepts related to HCI and HICI as problem representations. The chapter is intended as the start of an all-encompassing framework of interpretation for HCI. Interface examples are referenced or briefly noted throughout the concepts described. However, the concepts proposed here support much more in-depth analysis of specific HCI and HICI cases.

Is the theory of HCI sketched here descriptive or normative? The conception of HCI as representational systems is intended as a descriptive framework, a set of concepts for analysing reference across interface media. One benefit is that one can have independent description of the interface as a representational system as well as the more usual descriptions in terms of implementation technology and in terms of the language of the domain. Having such a descriptive framework then allows one to begin to research and understand the factors that contribute to effective problem representations. This will enable designers to better create and evaluate new and imaginative interface systems that aid practitioner performance.

Acknowledgements

This work was supported by the Human Factors Aerospace Division of the NASA Ames Research Center under Grant NCA2-351. The conceptual development of the ideas in this chapter began during the New Control Room Concepts project sponsored by the Westinghouse Electric Corporation. I would like to thank all of the colleagues in Westinghouse's Man-Machine Functional Design group for their stimulation and contributions. Emilie Roth, Kim Vicente, Bruce Coury, Chris Mitchell, Erik Hollnagel and Richard Cook provided very helpful critiques on earlier drafts of this chapter.

Chapter 8

Multiplexed VDT Display Systems: A Framework for Good Practice

Lisanne Bainbridge

1 Introduction

Operating a large, complex and changing system such as an industrial process, using an interface of computer-generated displays on VDT/VDU screens, is a complex task. The flexibility of the interface technology means that many types of display format are possible, so these formats may be designed specifically to support the user. But there are disadvantages to this technology as well. Typically, a computer-based display system has three screens. In a multiplexed system, the user has to choose the three display formats to look at, from perhaps 300 potentially available different formats. The user therefore has only a small 'window' on all the data about the present state of the system. And the user has the extra task, in addition to operating the process, of operating the display system.

This chapter concentrates on the design issues involved in minimising the difficulty of the extra tasks given to the user by this type of interface. The main theme will consider the features of a display system which make it possible to use the most efficient human cognitive processes for doing a task, that is, which encourage the development of skill. A subsidiary theme considers whether skills are best supported by using a minimum number of different display formats and, if so, what these formats should be.

In complex modern systems, most of the simpler well-understood tasks of operating the process are done automatically. The human operator is expected to deal with unanticipated situations. These require understanding and problem solving, rather than following predetermined sequences of ac-

HUMAN–COMPUTER INTERACTION
AND COMPLEX SYSTEMS: ISBN 0-12-742660-4

tivity. Classic ergonomics principles for interface layout are concerned with minimising the physical effort of doing prespecified tasks. Different principles for organising interfaces are needed to support user understanding and problem solving. Unfortunately most of the studies which have been done of real complex interface systems are confidential. An interesting exception is Kautto [123].

The question of designing optimum display formats for complex tasks is also discussed by Woods (Chapter 7). In general, this chapter will discuss interfaces displaying basic data, but will not cover displays which depend on computation or on intelligent decision-support systems. The aim of the present chapter is to provide a framework within which good ergonomics practice in the design of multiplexed display systems can be understood.

1.1   The general tasks in using such a system

When discussing how to support an operator's tasks by interface design, it is useful to have a simple framework for the types of task involved, because different design principles are relevant to different aspects of the overall task. This chapter will refer to the following:

- Operating the process plant.

    o understanding the present plant state from the displays.

    o choosing a response.

    o understanding and using knowledge about the underlying system function, in unanticipated situations.

- Using any one interface format.

    o identifying a particular display or control.

    o finding the source of information required.

        ⋆ assigning meaning to the display.

    o finding the means of control required.

        ⋆ executing the action chosen.

- 'Navigating' in the 'library' of alternative display formats.

    o choosing the next format required.

    o finding the next format required.

    o making the action to obtain the next format required.

The main focus of this chapter is on how to design a multiplexed interface so that the main tasks, of operating the process, are not disrupted because the operator has problems with the subsidiary tasks of using the interface. The approach is to ensure that the interface tasks can be done by simple skills.

1.1.1 Types of skill

The general notion of 'skill' is that, after practice, people come to use behaviour which is most appropriate to the context, and most efficient in its use of mental information-processing resources. This chapter suggests four main ways in which human information processing can be more efficient, which are summarised by the schema in Figure 1 [17]. These types of skill will be described in increasing order of cognitive loading.

Perceptual-motor skills. Here, responses are made 'automatically'/'unconsciously'. These responses do not need conscious attention so do not use working memory, which is limited in capacity. So these skills make minimum cognitive demands. For someone to be able to develop this type of skill the environment must be consistent, there must be a 1:1 mapping between display and meaning, display and response, or action and result. And these skills can only be learned by doing them. This chapter will distinguish for convenience between perceptual skills and motor skills, but they both depend on this basic consistency.

Familiar cognitive skills. For these, a well-established successful and goal-related strategy, and the information which it needs for reference, are already available. Familiar cognitive skills can develop when there are stable task situations but not a 1:1 mapping between stimulus and response, so the person has to compare, collate, calculate or choose to find the response. Once a standard strategy for doing this has been learned, the person no longer needs to devise new working methods by problem solving, which is the slowest and most capacity loading type of information processing.

'Prototype'-using skills. A person uses this type of skill when they respond to a situation by referring to what is done in a typical situation of the same general type, or by referring to memories of what was done in a previous similar situation. So this is a type of analogical reasoning. Although people do frequently use this method of dealing with new situations it will not be discussed further here. Computer-based displays are not typically designed to support this type of thinking. Perhaps developments in object-based programming and interfaces will give some insights in this area.

Problem-solving skills. These are used when someone has to devise a new method of working, or to understand some unfamiliar information. People solve problems by working in a 'problem space', the knowledge-base used in devising a new method or understanding. So problem solving can become skilled, that is, more efficient, when someone has adequate knowledge, organised and accessible in a way appropriate to the type of problems.

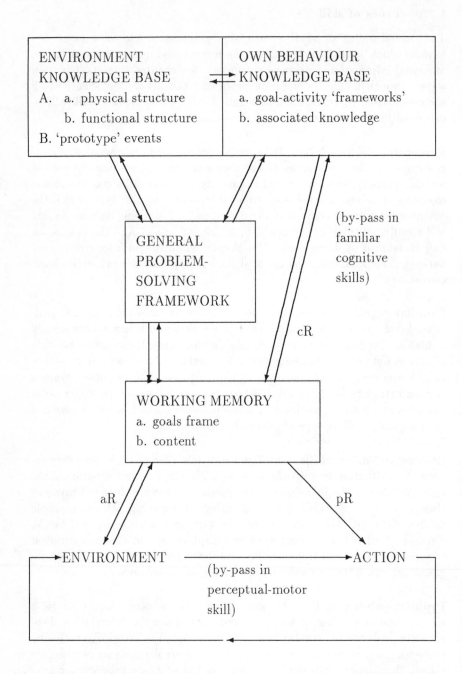

Figure 1 : A schema for the main mechanisms underlying skill (see text)

Problem solving is not an independent type of cognitive activity, in the sense that it is only involved in distinct types of task. Problem solving may be needed at any level of task complexity, when the person does not know what to do. So it might be used by someone searching for a particular display on an unfamiliar interface, or by a commissioning engineer controlling a new process on the basis of fundamental factors underlying process behaviour. The need for problem solving depends on how stable the environment is, and how familiar the person is with the structure and variability of the working environment, the task, the device, and the interface.

Problem solving is a high-workload activity, using limited capacity serial processing. It is also most needed in unfamiliar or unexpected situations. So it is important to minimise workload in these situations by maximising the amount of the task which can be done by perceptual-motor or familiar cognitive skills.

Maximising the possibility of developing one of the first two types of the skill is the basis underlying most ergonomics/human factors interface design principles. The next two sections of this chapter will discuss the nature of these two skill types more fully, and the practical implications for good design of multiplexed display systems to support these skills. The final section of the chapter is concerned with supporting the operator's knowledge-base used in problem solving.

2 Perceptual-motor skills

Automatic skills can only develop when there is a 1:1 mapping between a 'code' and its meaning, using the word 'code' to refer to anything, other than language, which has meaning. This means that, for a user to be able to develop perceptual-motor skills, all codes on an interface should be unambiguous (only one code per meaning) and consistent (only one meaning per code). This principle affects all the task types listed in the introduction. These tasks will be discussed in increasing order of complexity, considering first simple one-dimensional codes, then the multidimensional coding involved in locating items and in pattern recognition.

2.1 Assigning meaning to a simple display code

Interpreting the meaning of a simple code can be done automatically, as a perceptual skill, if there is a 1:1 mapping to its identity. There are many reasons why it is difficult to maintain this 1:1 mapping in a complex interface.

Simple codes can be used with many types of meaning. The meaning of a code may be an identity:

e.g.,	pale blue	steam
	light blue	water,

or a level of importance:

e.g.,	red	danger
	blue	emergency services,

or a size of value:

e.g.,	red	high temperature
	blue	low temperature,

or a state:

e.g.,	red	shut
	green	open,

or guidance about the interface:

e.g.,	light blue	'click' here for more information.

Interface users will not be able to interpret an interface automatically if a code has several potential meanings. For example, if the meaning of a shape depends on the particular context, a user has to remember this context before they can interpret the shape, and error rates may be high. This interpretation uses working memory, and so will interfere with other task thinking.

Colour in particular is much over-used as a code. It also introduces another problem. Red and orange appear brighter than other colours (in daylight), and brighter lights attract attention. If these colours are used simply to attract attention, this will detract from their interpretation as having meaning. Inversely, when easily seen colours are used with unimportant meanings the eye will be attracted to these colours first, rather than to the more important meanings of less intense colours.

multiplexed displays systems can increase the coding problem. In these systems there is usually a large number of different display formats, each of which may use shape or colour with a different meaning, or even with several meanings on the same format. Increasing the number of different formats increases the difficulty of using codes with unique, or even few, meanings, and so reduces the possibility of the user learning to make automatic interpretations.

In practice, a table should be made which lists all the meanings of each code used. The aim is to minimise the number of meanings for each, especially for codes which can indicate danger, urgency or importance. When a code is used with multiple meanings then if possible there should be other information which makes it clear which of the alternative meanings is intended.

2.2   Executing an action to change the process or the interface format

People learn to make actions automatically, by motor skill, by learning the relation between the effect of an action and the visual, heard or feel and touch information they get while making the action. Again learning involves a consistent 1:1 mapping, between the information received while making the action and the result of the action (the display/control ratio). After learning, people know what sensory information implies what result, so they can make effective actions with the minimum of checking and correction. This greatly reduces both their workload and the disturbance to the system being acted on. But, again, maintaining the 1:1 mapping necessary for the development of these skills may not be simple in practice.

Some computer-based interfaces do not have a consistent mapping between an action and its effect. Suppose the same physical device (mouse, trackerball, keys) is used both to make control actions on the process, and to access the display system. There is then no consistency, either in the identity of an action, what type of action has what type of effect on the system, or in the size of the effect of an action, the mapping between the displacement, friction or force of an action and its effect. So none of these dimensions can be unambiguously assigned to a meaning in terms of the effect of the movement. The user is unlikely to be able to develop automatic motor skills in using the interface, and the main task thinking will be interrupted by thinking about how to make actions.

A frequently used solution to this problem is to use conventional controls (i.e., physically unique controls in fixed position) for the main process variables, with computer-based displays. This is a compromise solution, as it is difficult to make the layout of display and controls compatible (as discussed in the next section). Choosing conventional controls as part of the interface design depends on whether it is important for the operator to have well-developed skills for controlling some part of the process, even though these skills may be used rarely.

2.3   Finding the display or control required, finding the next format required

Looking to the display from which information is required, or reaching to the control to be moved, can be done automatically after learning, if each display and control is always in the same place. These 'acquisition' movements again are motor skills, which can develop when there is a 1:1 mapping between location and identity.

This 'location coding' is possible on conventional hardwired interfaces. On computer-based display formats, there is flexibility in the position of items, which has advantages which are discussed below. But this flexibility may be paid for by loosing the advantage of automatic search and acquisition. If each item is in a different position on each display format, then it is not possible to develop the motor skills of automatically looking to or reaching to the display or control needed. Instead the user has to search for an item, keeping in working memory the name of the item wanted, and comparing it with items seen until the required item is found. So working memory for the main task items can be interrupted.

There is a long history of ergonomics studies which have shown that if two layouts which are used together are not the same ('compatible'), then the user takes longer to find an item, and makes more errors in doing so. For example, Lazzari [133] asked people to search for an item on one VDT graphic format, and then to find the same item in a different position on a different format. People took on average 24 seconds to find the second item in a format which had a structure which was not clear to them.

If the item which varies in position is a control then reaching to it, once its position has been found, is an action whose accuracy has to be checked visually, so the eyes have to look away from the main task information.

These effects suggest the practical recommendation that, when stable positions of items cannot be maintained, then at least items should have consistent relative positions in as many formats as possible. In this way, they have a stable topological relation to other items, being consistently above or below another it, or to the right or left of it. So it is possible for the user to search automatically for the required item in the appropriate direction.

The same reasoning leads to practical recommendations about how an interface user should tell the computer which display format they want next. To be able to use the interface system, the operator needs to know what other display formats are potentially available, where the current format is in relation to the other formats, and how to get to the other formats [171, 38, 212].

Suppose the user wants more detailed information about some part of the process. If they indicate this by moving a cursor on the existing display format to where it shows some information about this item, or by touching this item on a touch panel on which the items are in the same relative positions as on the display formats, then there is a consistent mapping between the layout of the existing displays and the layout of the set of alternative displays. So asking for another display format can be done with the minimum of cognitive effort.

If instead the user has to ask for another display format by pointing to an alphanumeric menu on which items are in an arbitrary order, or by typing in some (perhaps arbitrary) alphanumeric code, then they will have to 'think about' what they are doing, which will disrupt the main task thinking. Any alphanumeric menus which are used should be explicitly displayed, obvious in meaning, and laid out in a consistent order.

2.4   Pattern as an aid to interpreting present system state

People, as compared with computers, have a high capacity for parallel processing of information presented in patterns. In patterns of items, not only individual items but also the items together have meaning. Patterns are especially good for displaying relational information. Two types of multidimensional meaning are important in interface design : interpreting the present system state, and understanding the underlying system function. People can learn to identify the present system state by pattern recognition, even when the interface has not been specifically designed to support this. Helping people to understand how the process works does require special layouts.

People can learn the meanings of arbitrary patterns of information. Items can be interpreted as a pattern even when their relative positions do not have any meaning. For example, the layout of labelling can affect the ease of searching an alphanumeric format [145]. Or suppose that in some industrial process each type of fault appears as a unique pattern of pointer positions on the instruments on a conventional interface. Then there is a 1:1 mapping between a pattern of pointer positions and a process fault, and the operators can learn to do fault diagnosis by perceptual-motor skill [208]. In general, when a process is sufficiently simple for each of its different states to appear as a unique combination of its variable values, then state identification can be done by perceptual-motor skill. Computer-generated displays should be designed so that they are not too cluttered for this pattern recognition to be possible.

Although people can learn the meaning of arbitrary consistent patterns of information on a process interface, studies show that operators can identify the overall state of a process plant more easily if information about individual variables is presented in the context of a mimic/schematic of the plant. The parts of the plant are represented by simple symbols, shapes which either look somewhat like the part, such as distillation columns or heat exchangers, or whose meaning has been established by convention, such as pumps and valves. (These symbols should also be well designed [68, 114].) The symbols on a mimic are connected by lines representing the flows through pipes between the parts of the process. So the mimic, as a background to the display of process variables, provides a context of reminders about what the parts of the plant do, and how they are connected together.

This display method of providing a context for interpreting information about the present state of a process is, within limits, much easier to achieve with computer-generated graphic displays. It is important to remember however that understanding a mimic has to be learned. To someone who does not know how a process works and what its parts are, a mimic is simply confusing [133]. The pattern recognition involved, the perceptual skill, is learned after, and still underpinned by, a stage of understanding the separate parts. It does not start by being automatic, but it can become the basis for automatically interpreting the state of the process, or automatically finding the value of a particular variable without searching for it. Only a person who is familiar with a mimic and with what it represents can interpret it easily, especially when mimics are distorted to fit them onto a computer screen. A person with this perceptual skill has developed a 'frame' for interpreting the meaning of patterns.

More usually pattern recognition is not sufficient for understanding the process state, and a process operator can only identify the present process state after doing some 'thinking', comparing and collating data, etc. This involves familiar cognitive skills, as discussed in the next main section.

And in more complex plant, fault diagnosis can only be done by reference to some understanding of how the process works. A pattern-based interface can support this underlying understanding of the general functions of the process, as well as aiding identification of its particular state at any one time. The relative layout of items, and the type of representation, can give information about relationships underlying the variables displayed. For example, a layout to support understanding might be:

cause-effect relation   oil heating affects steam-generation rate,
layout   oil   steam.

Compare this with a layout the support following a given sequence of behaviour:

task   if steam flow changes, use oil flow control,
layout   steam   oil.

This issue of design to support understanding will be approached in the final section of this chapter.

2.5   The number of different display patterns/formats

Although people can learn to deal with pictorial formats automatically, by perceptual skill, we do not know how many different formats people can handle automatically. It is unlikely that the number is large, another reason for reducing the number of different formats. In a display system with 300 different formats, it is unlikely that the users can learn each sufficiently well to be able to:

- Automatically find a required item without search.

- Automatically remember the correct way of interpreting the codes used.

- Automatically integrate the given information into an overview of the system state.

But how many formats can people learn to use easily, is it five, ten, twenty? and how does this change with experience? This sort of information would be very useful, but is difficult to study experimentally.

One aim of increasing the number of different display formats is to make each format task specific. If each subtask has a specific display, then the argument is that each format can be specially designed so that what to do is 'obvious', i.e., it should be possible to do the task automatically, by perceptual-motor skill.

But if it is not possible to learn a large number of formats sufficiently well to respond to them all using perceptual-motor skill, then many of the formats can only be used by searching and thinking about them, that is by problem solving. Ironically, increasing the number of different formats, with the aim that the task can be done by perceptual-motor skill, actually has the opposite effect. The approach of increasing the number of formats considers the mental workload of doing each subtask in isolation. If, however, one considers the cognitive processing required by the subtask done within the context of a complex display system, this suggests the opposite conclusions about interface design.

At present it seems that the best recommendation is to avoid these problems, of reducing the possibility of using an interface by perceptual-motor skill and increasing conscious attention or problem solving. The main approach would be to use a minimum number of different formats, on which codes have consistent meanings and items are laid out so they have a consistent topological relation to each other.

For example, in displaying plant with a relatively simple structure, it may be possible to represent the process at different levels of detail. (In a complex interacting plant it may be difficult to divide the process into relatively independent parts.) As formats should be similar, to maintain perceptual skills, so displays at different levels of detail should have the same general topographic layout. The question of the best basic format to use is addressed in the final section of this chapter.

3   Familiar cognitive skills

Operators use well-established strategies to understand and control industrial processes in familiar situations. This chapter will not discuss decision-support systems, in which the computer does the computations and displays the result (see Hollnagel *et al.* [105], Lehner and Zirk [134], Rouse *et al.* [202] and Woods (Chapter 7)).

The cognitive strategies use working memory. The problem is that working memory is easily disrupted. The key recommendation for minimising this disruption is to ensure that all the information needed in any one decision is displayed at the same time, and within the same perceptual interpretation. This has several implications for display system design.

Figure 2 shows an example strategy. The task structure is a hierarchy of goals, and the subgoals for meeting them. Such a strategy can be thought of as providing a 'framework' in working memory, which structures the task information processing, by:

- Structuring the task goals and subgoals.

- Structuring the mental picture of the current state of the task and the plant, relative to the task goals.

- Specifying the information processing to be carried out.

- Directing attention to which information is needed.

This structure could also be called a 'frame', but to clarify the argument this chapter will use the term 'frame' for the structures of pattern recognition done by parallel processing as an automatic perceptual skill, and the term 'framework' for the structure of task goals and ways of meeting them which is built up in familiar cognitive skill.

The practical problems with supporting familiar cognitive skills are that such multilevel frameworks and the data remembered with them are easily disrupted.

3.1   Data disruption

The data is easily disrupted. Suppose that an interface user has to remember something from a previous format, which they will compare with something on the next format, when they have found it. Search studies (e.g., [133]) show that people take 20–25 seconds to find something on an unknown format. Classic memory studies (e.g., Posner and Rossman [180]) show that if a person has to remember an item for 25 seconds, during which time they are doing something else (in the display case—searching for another item), they will make about 30% errors in remembering the first item. So it is important that all the information needed in one decision can be identified quickly.

3.1.1   Mental task structure disruption

And the mental picture of the task structure is also easily disrupted, particularly by having to use poorly designed interfaces. Operators do not seem to have much difficulty with keeping track of these multiple levels of task goals and information if they are using an interface on which:

- All the information needed when working through one strategy is available at the same time.

- The information and controls are in fixed positions, so can be acquired by perceptual-motor skill.

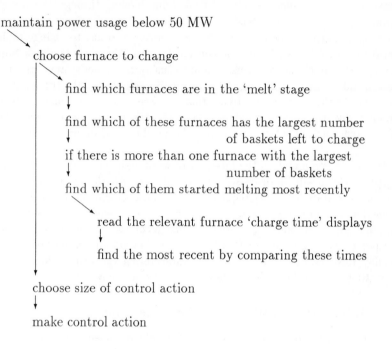

maintain power usage below 50 MW

choose furnace to change

find which furnaces are in the 'melt' stage

find which of these furnaces has the largest number
of baskets left to charge
if there is more than one furnace with the largest
number of baskets
find which of them started melting most recently

read the relevant furnace 'charge time' displays

find the most recent by comparing these times

choose size of control action

make control action

*Figure 2: An example strategy. In a steelworks, as part of the task of
allocating electric power between five steel furnaces, an operator works out
which furnace will be least affected by a power change.*

- The displays are in an unchanging format, so can be interpreted automatically using a single perceptual 'frame'.

But suppose the operator doing the task described in Figure 2 is using a multiplexed interface on which:

- one format shows the electrical power usage;

- another format is used for making control actions;

- there are five furnace formats, one for each furnace;

- to get from one format to another it is necessary to type in an arbitrary code number, which is not given on the format which can be seen.

An operator using such an interface has several difficulties which are added to the difficulties of meeting the main task goals. The operator has to remember charge times (which are trivial from the point of view of the main task decisions) for extended periods of time while looking through the furnaces formats. This puts an unnecessary load on the limited capacity of working memory for arbitrary data items. The operator also has to change rapidly between task frameworks and perceptual frames. There are two task frameworks, for controlling the furnaces and for using the menu system, and three perceptual frames, for finding the data required on each of the three different formats. As the operator has to alternate between these it is difficult to maintain a stable overview of the main task. For other discussions of the problems of keeping track of where one is in a large library of different formats see [241, 18].

Designing to maintain the integrity of working memory therefore has two aspects, which will be discussed in more detail. All the information about the process state which is required in any task should be available at the same time, to minimise the data load on working memory. And supporting familiar cognitive skills leads to the same recommendation as for supporting perceptual-motor skills: there should be a minimum number of different display formats, and the 'frames' for interpreting the display formats and operating the interface system should as far as possible be the same.

3.2 Information available at the same time

If all the information about the process state which is needed in a given task is not available at the same time, the effect of delay and interference on working memory data capacity means that there will be a high probability of human error.

If the information needed at one time is incomplete this is also a source of task stresses, particularly in fault situations, from:

- not knowing what is happening in all parts of the process;

- the risk of giving up the information which is currently available, in order to find out something else;

- the time costs, as well as the disruption, from having to change display formats.

There are two practical aspects to making all the required information available at the same time: what information actually is required at the same time, and how many screens are needed to convey this information.

3.2.1 Information needed at the same time

This chapter suggests three approaches to identifying and grouping task information, which depend on the extent to which the task strategy can be prespecified.

If the task strategy can be prespecified, as in Figure 2, then classic ergonomics Task Analysis techniques may be used to identify what information is needed for any one subtask. These displays will be working-method specific.

If what needs to be done cannot be prespecified, then the operators instead need help with knowledge about how the process works, from which they can think out what to do. For purposes of the present discussion, there are two main ways of grouping information which are not specific to a particular working method:

- Displays which give information about all the parts of the process which might be used in meeting any one main task goal/process function, such as maintaining cooling or pH.

- Displays which give general information about the plant, not related to a particular goal or working method.

There are some situations in which the choice of display type is clear:

- When the operator must do specific operations, perhaps in a particular order, as in start-up or shut-down, then method-specific displays are appropriate.

- In a fault situation, once the main function contributing to plant integrity which has failed has been identified, then it is appropriate to use function-specific displays, to support achieving that function in other ways.

Otherwise there are good reasons to ask whether it is a good idea to use several different approaches to grouping the information on displays. It does, for example, increase the number of different display formats, and so the number of different perceptual frames needed.

The operator of a complex industrial plant is usually part of the control system to deal with unanticipated situations, which essentially require problem solving, thinking of new approaches. If method-specific displays are used for tasks which can be prespecified, then the operator will have little practice with using the device-specific displays supplied for problem solving, and so will not develop the perceptual frames for interpreting them automatically. Thus when the operators have the most difficult type of process operating task, they will also have problems with using an unfamiliar interface. Also it is often not possible to predict when someone in a complex situation will need to change from using familiar strategies to problem solving.

Another argument in favour of method-specific displays is that people make errors when they think for themselves. But people also make errors in following instructions, and people are only good at recognising and recovering from their errors if they have sufficient task information and understanding to know that the result of their actions is not what it should have been. And people who follow instructions are frequently given the higher-level instruction that they should assess whether it is actually appropriate to follow the given instructions in this particular context. So people who are following instructions actually need to understand their task in order to do so effectively.

Both these arguments suggest that it is better to use a more general display format, even in situations for which task-specific displays could be developed, so that the user develops the perceptual-motor skills of accessing and interpreting this information.

3.2.2   Minimum number of display screens needed

Previous sections discuss the importance of displaying at the same time all the information about process state which is needed in one subtask. If this information will not fit onto one computer screen, then sufficient display surfaces are needed to display all the information. This is not the only reason for increasing the number of screens. The operator may need to refer to more than one type of information, and these types of information may be sufficiently different to be best displayed by different formats (see next section).

The number of VDTs needed can be reduced when any of this information can be displayed in printed form rather than on screens. This is particularly appropriate for alphanumeric information and for stable reference information. When alarm lists are on paper, the whole of the alarm list can be looked at, particularly if the typeface on the printer is easier to read than the typeface on the screen.

Operating procedures are one type of reference information. But there are advantages in using computer-based displays for these. Variable values, and facilities for making control actions or accessing other display formats can be included in the listing. The procedures may also be updated relatively easily. The disadvantage is that this does require at least one screen, during fault situations when much other information is needed, and one screen gives access to only a small part of the procedure at any one time. Useful guidelines for displaying procedures can be gained from other work on displaying sequences of instructions, such as Green [90] and Dewar and Cleary [64].

Also, people operating complex systems often do more than one task at a time, such as diagnosis and control during fault management (Reinartz and Reinartz [197] found up to ten task goals being considered at the same time). This means that screens are needed to display all the information needed for all these tasks, for example:

- To cover the number of simultaneous and independent faults which can occur. The basic number of screens needed to describe one part of the process needs to be multiplied by this number.

- To be able to sample information about other parts of the process, which may change while one part of the process is being displayed.

This multitasking is another argument for using general-purpose rather than task-specific displays. A general-purpose display gives the information used in several tasks, and provides a context for seeing any interdependencies between the tasks.

Some of the problems of keeping track of several parts of the plant can be resolved by providing an overview mimic. This could be a dedicated VDT or a wall mimic. A wall mimic has the advantage that it can be hard-wired so larger. An overview mimic may also help with the general question, whether operators using an interface of a small number of screens, and therefore having a small amount of information about the total state of the process at any one time, can develop an integrated mental model of the whole process.

If the interactions in the process are such that it is not possible to display simultaneously all the important influences on, or effects of, a particular event on the available VDTs, then it is necessary to consider whether this type of display technology will lead to too high a probability of human error.

And if the number of screens needed is too high for one operator to keep track of simultaneously, say four, then it is necessary to increase the number of operators.

4   The knowledge-base for problem solving

To support problem solving, thinking of new working methods in unusual situations, the operator needs to know how the process works, presented in displays which do not constrain the type of thinking used. These displays cannot be based on a classic type of Task Analysis which concentrates on working methods. Instead it is necessary to analyse the required structure of information about the plant and the operating goals. A major practical problem is that there is a large number of different types of knowledge which could be displayed to the operator. If the aim is, as suggested in previous sections, to reduce the number of different formats, then it is important to ask which formats would best support the operator.

4.1   Types of device-task knowledge

A list of the different types of knowledge that an operator uses is quite long, and makes it clear that it is not practical to display all the potential information about how the process works. Figure 3 shows some of the knowledge structures that a low-level part of a process, such as a pump, can be involved in. The knowledge involves several 'hierarchies'/networks of networks, which do not have a simple relation to each other.

1. There are at least six hierarchies of parts, 'part-of' hierarchies:

- the task goals and subgoals: the reasons for using the process, the product criteria, and the human activities by which these are met;
- the process goals and constraints which arise for reasons of safety or efficient productivity;
- the operating procedures.
- the physical structure of the plant;
- the functional structure of the plant: in terms of cause-effect relations and whether these are implemented mechanically, chemically, or by electronics/software means;
- the fault tree: and associated failure probabilities.

There are well-known techniques for representing most of these types of hierarchy, and for identifying subgroupings of items which work together and so must be displayed at the same time. There has been recent interest in describing functional effects in a process. Cause-effect relations can be described by signal-flow graphs, as in Systems Theory textbooks on network theory. The technique includes methods of mathematical simplification, for identifying the subgraphs in a process, and the interactions which cannot be further simplified. Mass-energy flow techniques (e.g., Chapter 10; Duncan et al. [66]) may be useful to simplify the description of the functions in a nuclear power station, which essentially consists of a series of heat transfers, but are not rich enough to describe chemical plant in which aspects such as pH, concentration or physical state must be maintained.

In addition, most of these hierarchies are not simple trees. Items at a higher level are not a simple concatenation of items at the next lower level. Instead their organisation is essential. For example, within a cooling circuit there is only a limited range of places where a pump can be located for it to carry out its function adequately.

2. Categories of item:

Most items are also members of another type of hierarchy, an 'is-a' hierarchy. They are members of a general category, such as 'pump' or 'turbine'. The category contains general information about this type of item. This sort of information is usually assumed to be supplied by the operator from memory, and is not displayed.

3. Information about the state of the process:

- the actual variable values, or multidimensional states, in the past, present and predicted future;

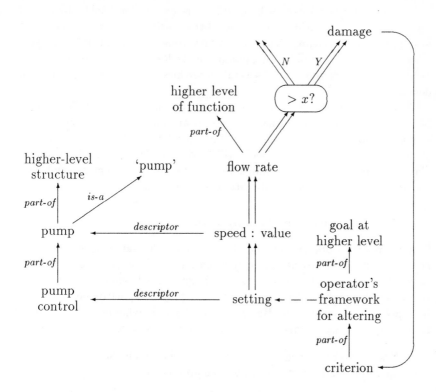

Figure 3: Some of the links in the knowledge structure about a small part of a complex process. (Double line = cause-effect relation)

- patterns of changes over time, the parameters of transient and steady-state responses;

- sequences of events: process phases, event trees.

4. The physical properties of an item:

The colour or geographical position of an item may have nothing to do with its function in the process, but may still be useful to know, if it helps in identifying or finding the item.

5. Events (not represented in Figure 3):

Memories of past events and typical incidents, which are referred to in thinking about unfamiliar situations.

Obviously Figure 3 cannot be used as a framework for display design. Although it is complex, it does not show all the possible types of complexity. It does illustrate the complexity involved. Any one component of the process, whether at the level of individual pumps, or the level of major groupings such as heat exchangers, is a part of several hierarchies, or networks of interdependent items.

The display problem is that there is not necessarily any simple mapping between these hierarchies. That means that any one two-dimensional display format can only show a small slice through all this information. So what should be displayed? Two aspects will be discussed: what need not be displayed because it can be supplied from the operator's memory, and what should be emphasised in the primary display formats.

4.2   Use of high-capacity long-term memory

Compared with working memory, the capacity of human long-term memory is huge, and access to the stored information is relatively good, if it is accessed fairly frequently, and the person is given cued reminders. Obviously the present state of the process has to be displayed explicitly, people cannot be expected to remember it. But providing the underlying information about how the process works might be approached in three different ways:

- Using 'external' memory: displaying explicitly all the information the operator might need about how the process works.

- Using 'cued' memory: giving sufficient reminders on the displays, so that experienced users can remember relevant back-up information.

- Using 'recall' memory: expecting the user to remember without help everything about how the process works, what the operating constraints are, and so on. This is the approach on most conventional interfaces.

Taking advantage of cued memory access to the users' own knowledge means that the number of different display formats can be reduced. So the question becomes: which of the above types of information can the display designer expect an experienced user to supply from memory?

4.3   The displays needed by the operator

Any representation of information should make the most important points the most salient (easily seen), should provide a structure for thinking about the related task, should provide cues to remind experienced users about other relevant information, and should handle complexity by providing several levels of detail, and different representations which are optimum for different aspects.

Papers by Shepherd [207], Mitchell and Miller [153], Mitchell and Saisi [154] and De Keyser [55] discuss the information needed by the operator. Papers by Vermeulen [226] and by Chechile *et al.* [46] discuss the usefulness of, and mapping between, different types of knowledge and display. Many studies on how to help people to extract technical information from pictorial representations have actually been done in a different context, that of technical drawing, e.g., Rabardel and Weill-Fassina [182].

In a pilot study of two graphic displays, Brennan [30] asked people to explain events in a complex system. They were given system information either in a mimic or in a signal-flow-graph (SFG) representation. The results suggested that the SFG was more useful to people who did not already know how a particular system worked, and so needed information about the cause-effect links underlying the events. But the mimic display was better for people who did already understand the system represented. The mimic diagram can give many cued reminders about other types of information, while the SFG represents only one of the many possible 'hierarchies' of information, and does not directly give cues about the physical structure of the plant.

There has been little research on how easy operators find it to think in terms of higher-level abstract functions, but it is important to establish this before displays representing abstract functions are used as the operators' primary display format. The above findings suggest that mimics should be used as the primary display, with SFGs or box diagrams, which focus on function, as back-up for dealing with unfamiliar situations. The irony of this suggestion is that while SFGs or box diagrams may be good in principle to support the understanding of unfamiliar situations, in an unanticipated fault situation the problem is that cause-effect relations are unknown, so it is not possible to provide an SFG or other cause-effect display.

The most promising current approaches deal with unfamiliar situations by side-stepping this issue, avoiding expecting the operator to think about diagnosis and fault management from first principles, and concentrating on process behaviour. This is possible because the operators' primary responsibility in fault situations is to maintain process integrity and stability.

'Critical function monitoring systems' identify the critical process functions which maintain system integrity, and then present information to the operator about which methods of maintaining these functions are still available. This is a 'decision-support system' involving sophisticated computing, so is outside the scope of this chapter. Though it is relevant to mention that a complete display system for critical functions may raise the same issues of complexity as have been discussed in this chapter.

The 'state' approach to fault management is based on a system analysis. This identifies all the states which the process can get into which require a different response. It also provides general procedures for identifying which of these states the process is in, and for making the appropriate response. This approach may only be applicable to fairly simple processes, not to ones in which there are complex interactions, such as a train of distillation columns. Earlier this chapter pointed out that it is important not to give a restricted view of the state of such a process. The usual difficulty with complex systems appears—the more complex the process, the fewer methods of aiding someone to think about it there are.

This chapter shows that a few simple principles for using efficient cognitive processes, for maximising the use of perceptual-motor skills, and minimising the disruption to working memory, have wide-ranging implications for many aspects of complex interface design. In summary, these support the use of two to three levels of mimic/schematic displays, giving a permanent overview and more detailed formats with the same general topology of layout, and reminder cues about functions. Subsidiary formats would be used for goal/function integrity checking, and for procedures.

Chapter 9

Ways of Supporting Ergonomically and Technically Correct Display Design

Bernd-Burkhard Borys

1 Introduction

Computer-generated graphical pictures displayed on CRT screens are now common in modern industrial plants. The graphics hardware and software have become increasingly sophisticated during the last decade and, with memory size increases, it is now possible to have a range of different pictures to hand without need for loading from external media. Graphics processors are now fast enough to generate pictures on-line, in accordance with process state and operator demand. Higher resolution allows finer icons and different text styles, while the large number of colour shades available in modern systems even gives scope for an adaptive system capable of tuning display colours to match ambient light conditions.

Such new features promise great advantages for operators working in process control rooms, but only if new features are used in an appropriate way. Presently, despite decreasing prices, the newly available features of modern computer graphics systems are not fully used in process industry [116]. This is especially true for the more conservative arena of power plants. Clearly, prior to the introduction of such features, it is appropriate to evaluate industrial and user needs. This has been done as a basis for ESPRIT project P857, 'Graphics and Knowledge Based Dialogue for Dynamic Systems', called GRADIENT.

HUMAN–COMPUTER INTERACTION
AND COMPLEX SYSTEMS: ISBN 0-12-742660-4

GRADIENT is an on-going 5 year project founded by the European Community within the ESPRIT program. A consortium of five partners from four different European countries aims at improved interfaces for operators of large dynamic systems. The introduction of enhanced computer graphics and knowledge-based systems is central to this enterprise and will be demonstrated in the area of coal-fired power plants and data networks.

One stream of work in GRADIENT is the development of a prototype Intelligent Graphical Editor (IGE) for use by designers of graphical displays for process control systems. Work on the IGE within GRADIENT has followed a modular approach. This began with the development of a conventional graphical editor and a conventional presentation system which are now expanded through the addition of designer support.

In our search for a commercially available conventional graphical editor, a survey [27] indicated that no available editor could form a basis of the IGE. So GRADITOR, the graphical editor for GRADIENT, was developed at the University of Kassel. GRADITOR supports picture element generation and maintenance of picture element libraries as well as picture composition from library elements. Since it must design for process visualisation systems, it also supports connection of process measurements to display items. Pictures composed from GRADITOR's icons will be delivered to the operators' screens by the presentation system.

Display designers will face more problems with the increasing number of plant components while, in parallel, the features of enhanced graphics systems get more complex. Thus, adding an 'intelligent' part for designer support extends GRADITOR to the Intelligent Graphical Editor. This will support the designer in different ways, using available plant data as well as industrial and ergonomic guidelines. In addition, this intelligent support should enable designers to take full advantage of the enhanced features of today's computer graphics systems.

From an examination of the state-of-the-art [8], an urgent need for improvement to the interface between process and controlling operators became evident. Task analyses in power plants [28], confirmed that operators want to be in charge: They even choose to perform some tasks manually, though they have been fully automated, like igniting burners or synchronising the generator. Operators cannot be replaced by sophisticated control algorithms and we do not want to replace them. We want to give them the best support to do their job, this means providing all the necessary process information in a suitable form. Currently, operators must gather such information from control room instrumentation and a growing number of CRT displays.

In the following, the concept of the IGE will be presented and different ways of supporting the display designer will be detailed. All material presented relates to pictures designed for use on graphical CRT displays in control rooms of power plants or similar applications.

2   Conventional display design

During any design, a set of real-world constraints is applied to the huge (possibly infinite) set of desirable solutions. This process needs much knowledge, a high level of intelligence, and creativity. In display design, all of this is mixed with low-level operations such as line drawing, selecting and positioning.

Display design is combinatorial design [222], in which the designer needs:

- knowledge on existing entities (pictures, picture elements);

- knowledge on how to operate the entities and on constraints (like which icon to use for what), and how to resolve constraints;

- knowledge on how to combine the entities (which icon connected to which other icon by which type of line);

- knowledge on how to detail existing parts (whilst satisfying constraints);

- knowledge on how to construct a solution (whilst satisfying constraints).

Experience gained while using our own and several other graphical editors showed that, during picture design, the work of the designer can be separated into creative work and simple tasks. The simple tasks are (1) collection of information, (2) selection of items from larger sets, and (3) arrangement, alignment and positioning.

These three steps will be illustrated in the following example: 'Design a picture showing Device LAC01AP001 with its inputs and outputs.'

Collection of information
We may assume that the designer already knows that he is dealing with a power plant (the application domain) in Germany (standards to be used). From the device code (LAC01AP001), he recognizes that this is a feedwater pump. For this device, the applicable icons are pump icons. The device code also signifies that the pump is part of the feedwater system, thus, transported medium should flows from right to left and top to bottom. This is to maintain consistency with clockwise flow in the conventional process overview picture.

From the plant data and knowledge on how to detail existing parts, the designer finds that the device in question (LAC01AP001) consists of two single pumps (LAC01AP001KP01 and LAC01AP001KP02) driven by the feedwater pump turbine XAA01. This reduces the range of applicable icons to turbine-driven two-stage pumps. The feedwater pump turbine gets its input from pipe LAB11BR01 and delivers output to pipe LAB11BR02, thus the designer has information on the number, type and names of connections to be shown in the designed display.

Selection of items
When the necessary information is collected, item selection is performed using knowledge of existing graphical entities (icons, lines, connections, different end point and other details from the graphical library) Additional knowledge is required on how to operate these entities and on constraints; for example, selection of a the right pump icon fitting on the screen, selection of the right line type for low-pressure (input) and high-pressure (output) process water.

Arrangement, alignment and positioning
In the last phase, picture elements have to be placed on the screen. The pump should be centred and the pipes aligned with the pump. The designer needs knowledge on how to manipulate the graphical entities by moving or rotating them, by changing their size or colour. He needs to know about how to combine them : i.e., where are the points representing output and input of an icon and how should the connections be applied. Finally, the designer must know how to construct a solution by using graphical commands (move, rotate, zoom) while observing constraints (minimum sizes, optimum distances and the appearance of the picture as a whole).

All of this work consists in tasks or subtasks, which can be supported or performed more or less automatically. For example, during selection of items, support can be given by applying constraints, according to ergonomic rules, company or customer guidelines, application domain, national standards, or layout and specification of the plant, to the set of possible selections.

Support can be given through different levels of automation [149], but sufficient room for creativity must always be left. This conflicts with the goal of fully automatic picture generation. In every design, the number of alternatives may be large or possibly infinite. So as not to exclude new or unusual solutions out of hand, we need the creativity of a human designer. Rather than trying to replace him by an automated system we may may confine ourselves to the support of boring and routine tasks, thereby freeing the designer's creativity.

3   Structure of the IGE

In our work on an IGE, two different worlds are combined, namely Artificial Intelligence (AI) and Computer Graphics. From the outset, we kept these worlds apart, and GRADITOR, the conventional graphical editor, was developed independently from the supporting modules. GRADITOR runs on a 4 MB MicroVAX II with one of two Sigmex graphics terminals. In stand-alone conventional mode, GRADITOR is controlled using menus and locator input.

When design support is used, GRADITOR is initiated and controlled remotely through a command interface by programs running on a Symbolics 3640 AI workstation. All designer interaction is effected through the mouse and screen of the Symbolics workstation, the Sigmex is used for graphical output only. The real knowledge-base work is done using the expert system development tool KEE. To get the full support of the Symbolics operating system, all functions handling command and data exchange are written in LISP. These LISP functions are then called by KEE programs ('methods' in the terminology of KEE).

The Symbolics operating system calls a task performed by a remote host a 'service'. The service uses a protocol and a medium. To get into the VMS world of the MicroVAX, the medium is DECnet. Protocols on this medium need a DNA-CONTACT-ID, which is either a code for a service provided by the VAX operating system or the name of a command file. Each time a service is called, a stream is established to a host providing this service. On the Lisp Machine, all information exchange is done by writing to or reading from this stream.

The graphics software (the GKS-like Sigmex WKS) is designed for inter-active use at a graphics terminal. In consequence, starting this software as a non-interactive network process requires that we simulate the interactive terminal. In the monolithic graphics workstation concept provided by Sigmex hardware and software, a locator device (e.g., graphics tablet, joystick, mouse) must be connected to the graphics hardware. Signals are directly processed by the hardware which results in fast close-circuit cursor movements without any user-controlled processing or manipulation in between. In our modular concept, the locator device is not part of the graphics hardware, but a device within the operating system. Fast cursor movements need some additional programming, but we are free to select the source of the locator data and to perform manipulations on this data, for example, to restrict motion, to use a standard graphics tablet in place of a mouse, or even to simulate the behaviour of a locator from a remote machine.

Information exchange between graphics system and the Lisp Machine requires coding and decoding, performed via a command interface on either side. The commands used have the appearance of LISP lists (ASCII character sequences enclosed in brackets). These sequences are treated as objects on the AI side and as strings on the graphics side. (Note that, one layer beneath programming languages, strings and objects are the same, *viz.*, sequences of bytes in virtual memory.)

Figure 1 shows the different modules of the IGE. On the graphics side, below the interface to the designer and the command handler, the graphical editor consists of three parts: Picture Generator, Picture Element Generator and Process Binding Generator. The operation of these parts is illustrated in Figure 2.

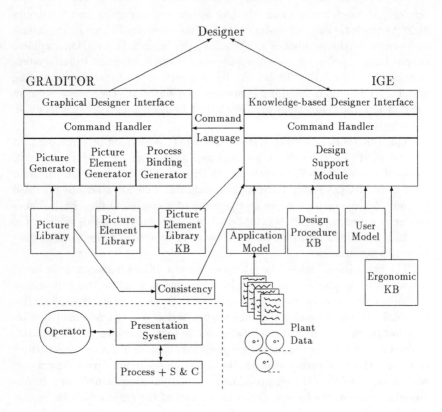

Figure 1 : Modules of the Intelligent Graphical Editor
(KB = Knowledge Base; S & C = Supervisory and Control)

In the initial operation, probably performed only once for several applications in the same domain, essential picture elements are generated. The Picture Element Generator supports creation of icons, lines and text, and also maintains the Picture Element Library. In addition to generation of picture elements, information on each picture element is stored in a knowledge-base. Using the Picture Generator, elements from the Picture Element Library are combined to form pictures. These are subsequently stored in the Picture Library, where information required for checking consistency is also maintained.

The Picture Binding Generator is necessary for connecting measurements displayed in a picture to the corresponding process values. The resultant picture is stored in the Picture Library for use in the Presentation System of

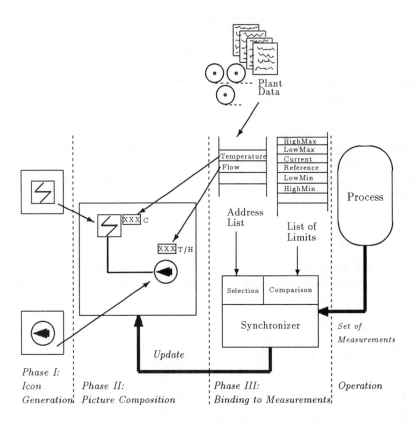

Figure 2: Dynamic picture generation procedure

the final application.

4 Intelligent support for display design

In our present system, the designer-support module has its own interface to the designer. For support, different knowledge-bases are used, containing information on the application, the design process, user needs, and ergonomic guidelines.

The intelligent support for display designers will benefit the designer, as it contributes toward correct display design regarding available data on the plant, and also benefit the operator, as it supports ergonomically sound pictures to serve operators' information needs. The designer will be supported in making sound design choices with respect to guidelines for the application domain. Support will be given by implementing knowledge on perceptual ergonomics and the design process itself, as well as process structure and operator behaviour (see Johannsen *et al.* [115]). Designers will be aided in selecting essential and appropriate picture elements, placing them according to domain dependent rules, drawing the necessary connections, and making pictures consistent throughout an application. Knowledge on operator behaviour will be especially valuable for failure situations, abnormal situations, or status changes, and enable the designer to generate all necessary pictures including all the information the operator needs during these situations. To arrive at all of this information, interviews will be conducted with designers for process control domains, as well as with operators and designers in the graphical arts.

4.1   Example

To elucidate the range of design support, we may review our earlier example: 'Design a picture showing Device LAC01AP001 with its inputs and outputs'.

Collection of information

The designer already knows that he is dealing with a power plant in Germany. Having been in this business for some time, he also appreciates that the device is a feedwater pump. Even so, this information is available from the plant data, keyed in somewhere else in his company, together with information on decomposition of the pump group to single pumps, on the driving turbine, and on the connected pipes. From other work in our project, information will be available about the the operator as the future user of the pictures created, especially his requirements regarding the purpose of this picture, his task, and the plant status. Such information will be drawn from a module called 'User Model'.

Selection of items

Information on applicable picture elements will be available from industrial standards and the knowledge-base accompanying the Picture Element Library. Data on direction of flow on the screen and data for keeping pictures consistent will be stored in the Design Procedures Knowledge-Base and a Consistency Knowledge-Base respectively, and will further support selection of the best picture element. Additionally, selection of picture elements will be supported by rules in the Ergonomic Knowledge-Base with regard to aspects of shape and size, thus, preventing cluttered displays or icons too small to be recognised. Selection of colours will be guided by standards stored in the design procedures knowledge-base.

Arrangement, alignment and positioning

The sequence of picture elements forming a line can be determined from the plant data and simple alignment can be implemented by numerical algorithms. But positioning the picture elements to get a satisfying design must be done by the designer, leaving arrangement proposals and fine tuning to the support system. Thus, support can be given during:

- collection of information from plant data bases;

- selection of picture elements from the library, guided by rules and standards.

Only proposals for arrangement and fine tuning of positioning should be done by the system.

4.2 Technical support

To be technically correct, displays must be consistent with the actual plant structure and plant state. The designer's principal tasks are the collection of information and some selection of items. Display design is performed while the plant is under construction and design data are already available. We expect that all necessary data would be available in some machine-readable format.

From these plant data, the Application Model—a set of three different models—is generated. The different models are the Plant Model, the S&C (Supervisory and Control) Model and the Function Model.[1] The following sections give only an overview over these models. (See Elzer and Johannsen [74], for more information.)

The Plant Model contains a representation of all process-related plant components. These components are separated into aggregates, apparatus, and drives: aggregates doing the work, drives driving the aggregates, and apparatus like piping and tanks in between. Data is structured according the German Power Station Designation System KKS (*Kraftwerkskennzeichensystem*).

Relations between components are indicated by a series of attributes:

- `provides.energy.for` and `receives.energy.from` relate drives to aggregates;

- `successor` and `predecessor` show material flow;

- `is.part.of` points to the next level in the (KKS) hierarchy;

---

[1] Work on this part of the IGE has been the responsibility of Asea-Brown-Boveri, CRH, Heidelberg, FRG.

- `is.controlled.by` and `has.measurements` are used to connect components from the Plant Model to components of the S&C Model.

The S&C Model lists the components of the supervision and control system. This is organised in a block - group - loop hierarchy according to levels of supervision and control systems in power plants, as well as according to types of measurement or control, e.g., closed loop, open loop, measuring circuit. Attributes like `is.controlling`, `is.controlled.by`, `receives.input.from`, `provides.output.for` indicate relations between components. The attribute `is.attached.to` connects components of the S&C Model to the components of the Plant Model. The Function Model is built from information in the Plant Model and the S&C Model and describes the plant on a higher level of abstraction.

4.3   Ergonomic support

Providing all necessary information
Each picture will be designed for a specific task of the operator. From task and knowledge analyses we learn what information the operator needs. These data, stored in the User Model, enable the designer to include all necessary information in a picture. The first step in picture composition will be setting up the Picture Item List from data in the User Model and the Application Model. This list carries all items which must be included in this picture.

Orientation and arrangement
In our sample applications, media, energy, and information all flow through the process. Process elements form lines and the sequence of elements along a line can be derived from the plant data. The Function Model is specially organised in such lines of components.

   Direction of flow on the display will be derived from rules in the Design Procedure Knowledge-Base and the Consistency Knowledge-Base. In power plants, water and steam flow clockwise. The feedwater system is shown at the bottom of the overview picture, thereby, feedwater flow is right to left. Orientation of picture elements reflects direction of flow. Although some rules for graphical arrangement can be implemented as algorithms which assure equal distances, in more complex situations the designer has to indicate positions and only leave fine tuning to the system.

Reasonable shapes and sizes
Selection of picture elements to represent picture items will depend on the meaning of this item as well as the number of other items and available space on the display. Rules from the Ergonomic Knowledge-Base regarding aspects

of shape and size will prevent cluttered displays or elements too small to be recognised.

Applicable picture elements
For each entry in the Picture Item List, one or more picture elements from the Picture Element Library will be permissible. The set of permissible picture elements will be determined from information stored in the knowledge-base accompanying the Picture Element Library. More than one picture element will be permissible if different picture elements are used for different sizes or orientations.

Colour
The selection of the right colour for a picture element is guided by standards implemented as rules in the Design Procedure Knowledge-Base. In enhanced graphics systems, additional fine tuning of the hue will be possible according to background colours or neighbouring picture elements.

5 Further research

The final version of the IGE will enable the designer to create ergonomically and technically correct pictures according to plant structure, plant status and operators' information needs. GRADIENT will demonstrate the functions of the IGE using a small set of rules in our sample application areas. Additional work can be done in finding more rules, rules from other application areas, or additional rules for new features of computer graphic systems (perhaps even for tuning display colours after sensing ambient light intensity and colour, or implementing rules for use of three-dimensional displays). Future development will move away from the special AI hardware and software used in our prototype applications to standard process computers.

In a later phase within GRADIENT, results and modules from the IGE will be implemented as part of a Graphical Expert System which supports online picture composition in a live application and automatically follows plant status or configuration changes.

Acknowledgement

This work is part of ESPRIT project P875 'Graphics and Knowledge Based Dialogue for Dynamic Systems (GRADIENT)' funded by the European Community.

Chapter 10

Representations and Abstractions for Interface Design Using Multilevel Flow Modelling

Morten Lind

1 Introduction

Interfaces for supervision of complex plant are currently designed on the basis of informal approaches and tend to match either the user's more or less well specified needs, design standards or engineering traditions. With the use of modern information-processing systems this approach is unsatisfactory as it leads to inefficient use of processing capability or to an unguided (mis)use of fancy display and presentation techniques. Clearly, more fundamental approaches are required. In the present chapter we will discuss elements of an approach to the systematic development of information interfaces for supervisory control.

Our approach is based on a separation of two issues in the design of such interfaces. These two issues comprise the problem of planning the information content of the interface, i.e., what should be communicated to the operator, and the problem of how to make this information available to the operator using available display techniques. The first issue is a representation problem while the second is a presentation problem. It is clear that the presentation of the system on the display should match the user's understanding (mental model) of the system to be supervised. Thus, the presentation issue relates to various cognitive factors whereas a solution for the representation problem essentially comprises an engineering analysis of the information and control requirements of the supervised system. Both presentation and representation issues are discussed below, with an emphasis on the latter.

HUMAN–COMPUTER INTERACTION
AND COMPLEX SYSTEMS: ISBN 0-12-742660-4

1.1 Background

The background to the present work is the problem of designing human-machine interfaces for knowledge-based systems for plant diagnosis. The complexity of this design problem depends on the nature of the knowledge used by the system. Here we will focus on diagnostic systems using so-called deep knowledge (as opposed to shallow knowledge). The distinction between deep and shallow knowledge is very common in current literature on knowledge-based systems but it is actually not very well defined. For our actual purpose it will suffice to say that shallow knowledge in diagnosis would be represented as rules relating fault symptoms (e.g., instrument readings) to the cause of the fault. Deep knowledge would comprise plant models which represent relationships between plant objects and their physical properties.

A user interface to a knowledge-based system for diagnosis should enable the user to understand the results of the reasoning processes performed by the computer. To this end, explanation facilities are usually provided as part of the user interface. However, early experience with rule-based systems has shown that the explanation facilities commonly provided are inadequate since they present the detailed logic machinery required to derive a certain fault hypothesis. The basic problem with such systems is the lack of separation between the pragmatic meaning of a rule (which is what concerns the user) and the formal logic interpretation of the rule (which the computer is using). Model-based (deep knowledge) systems, which have much more complex representations of knowledge than rule based systems, will suffer from the same deficiencies if the knowledge base is used directly as a basis for explanation, i.e., if no distinction is made between the representation and presentation

The separation of system representation and presentation is not only an issue relevant to the structure of the human-machine interface. It also has implications for the interface development process, as the separation suggests a stepwise development of the user interface. The initial step would be to develop a plant representation as a basis for the design of the knowledge-base. This plant representation should include the knowledge required by the computer to reason about the system and to produce diagnoses. The next step is to relate the plant representation to the user interface so that the conclusions of the knowledge-based system can be presented in a way which is comprehensible to the operator.

Several aspects of this approach to interface design will be discussed in more detail in the following. We will be especially concerned with the categories of knowledge required by a diagnosis system in order to cope with complex plant and with the use of abstraction techniques as a means for managing the complexity of the plant and the interface design process. The discussion of knowledge categories will introduce the types of knowledge required to diagnose complex plant and will relate these types to different phases of the plant life cycle. Given these categories, and provided that our interface design tools (software) support an incremental addition of knowledge elements during the plant life cycle, it is the hypothesis of the present research that an interface can be developed as described above.

2 Categories of plant behaviour

The purpose of information systems for supervisory control is to support operators in understanding plant behaviour so that he/she is able to diagnose faults and to provide compensatory actions. The support of computerised information systems is especially required when operators are dealing with complex plant. The computer has two functions. It should analyse plant events, generate possible diagnoses and propose compensatory actions to the operator. Accordingly, it is important that we know how to characterise behaviour of a complex plant and how different representations provide the basis for understanding the plant behaviour.

Below, we have categorised plant behaviour into four different categories (Figure 1). We distinguish between plant behaviours according to whether they are normal or whether they are categorised as faults. In addition, within each category we have identified the subcategories of intended behaviour and the category of behaviours which are prevented (i.e., measures are taken to avoid this type of behaviour).

It should be emphasised that the categories are not 'crisp', i.e., they do not have sharp boundaries. This is the case both for the boundary between normal and fault behaviour and the distinction between intended and unintended behaviour.

These distinctions are useful as the categorisation of plant behaviour determines the course of action to be chosen by the operator. Thereby, interfaces which enable the operator to make a distinction would be helpful. The importance of these categories for diagnosis can be realised by the following considerations.

2.1 Categories of behaviour and diagnosis

Suppose that the plant is disturbed and it is found that the plant is not behaving as intended, i.e., it is not satisfying design requirements. In such a case we may conclude that the means provided by the designers for achieving plant goals have failed. Clearly, representations of design intentions are useful as heuristic devices for generating fault hypotheses. Furthermore, if the designers have provided alternative courses of action, this categorisation of plant behaviour also suggests remedial action (use alternative).

However, even though the plant is not behaving according to the designer's intentions it may still behave normally according to operating experience.

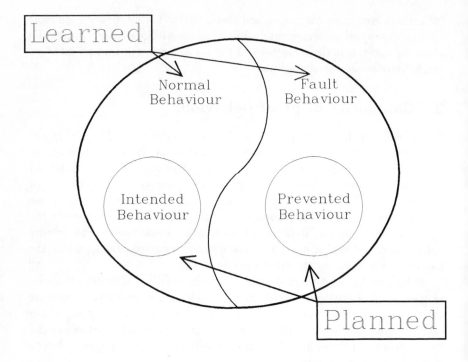

Figure 1 : Categories of plant behaviour

In such situations, remedial actions have been acquired by learning (during plant operation). But if it is further concluded that the plant is not behaving according to operating experience the plant is in a state of emergency (because no remedial action can be provided).

Consider another situation where the plant has failed and is in a state for which the plant designers have provided protective measures. In this case, we can conclude that the cause of the plant disturbance is associated with a defect in the means for protection provided by the plant designers. Again, design intentions prove to be useful heuristic devices for generating fault hypotheses.

Still, the plant can fail in ways not predicted by the designers. In such situations plant behaviour may correspond to fault behaviour which has been experienced before and for which remedial action has been learned.

2.2   Categories of behaviour and the plant life cycle

Evidently, the categories of behaviour relate to different phases of the plant life cycle. Intended and prevented behaviours relate to decisions taken in the plant design phase. Plant goals and functions are defined in the design phase and plant behaviour which conforms with these intentions (i.e., the system doing what it was intended to do) falls into this category. Similarly, in plant design it is decided what types of plant behaviours should be prevented. These decisions are the basis for design of protection systems in the plant.

Accordingly, we can conclude that the knowledge required to diagnose plant disturbances is created in different phases of the life cycle of the system. As operators do not have direct access to the design knowledge, an important role of a supervisory system is to enable the operator to evaluate plant behaviour within the context of what the designers intended the plant to do. If this is not available it will be difficult for the operator to take advantage of efficient design heuristics for state diagnosis and identification of remedial actions.

2.3 Behavioural categories and interface design

For the reasons given above, the representation of plant design knowledge is important for the design of diagnostic systems. We will further stress this point as we argue that representations of such knowledge should be the basis for the design of the interface. Three additional arguments in support of this position can be stated.

First of all, design knowledge is important for providing a context in which plant behaviour can be understood. It is well known that knowledge about the goals or intentions of a purposeful system is valuable for proper interpretation of its behaviour. This is also known to be the case when people interpret the behaviour of other human beings.

Secondly, it is important to consider design intentions for plants which involve economic risks or risks for the environment. Where reliability and safety is a major design goal, such plants are provided with functional redundancy. Redundancy is vital for provision of remedial actions in disturbance situations. Consequently, the human-machine interface clearly present these options to the operator.

Thirdly, a critical part of plant design is the design of the information and control systems. These systems are responsible for the goal-controlled behaviour and recognition of their role in the overall organization and coordination of plant resources is important for understanding plant behaviour.

In the following, we will focus on the representation of design knowledge. We will discuss a method for plant representation called Multilevel Flow Modelling (MFM) which has been developed by the author. The purpose of MFM is to provide a common basis for plant and control systems design and for supervisory system design. MFM, an example of a representation of deep knowledge, has been used as a basis for representation of design knowledge in a knowledge-based system for diagnosis [140].

3   Multilevel Flow Modelling

MFM is a method for representation of complex production plant. The fundamental idea of MFM is to describe a plant in terms of a set of so-called flow structures which represent mass and energy balance functions. With this approach it is also possible to represent information flow. Each flow structure comprises a set of interconnected flow functions. But flow structures can also be related to more global networks representing means-end structures. The fundamental dimensions of representation in MFM are shown below (Figure 2) and the basic modelling concepts are shown in Figure 3. Using the three basic categories of flow (mass, energy and information) MFM makes it possible to describe the interrelations between plant production functions and the functions of the control systems in a unified way.

In MFM a plant is described along two different dimensions (see Figure 2). We describe a plant in terms of different types of representation (i.e., its goals, functions and its physical components) and we can describe each of those entities at different part-whole levels. These types of representation, on different part-whole levels, comprise abstractions of plant properties. But as all types of plant representation are abstractions of some sort we will discuss in more detail below how MFM uses different types of abstraction for managing plant complexity. These abstractions play a crucial role when MFM is used as a basis for interface design.

3.1   Abstraction principles of Multilevel Flow Modelling

The purpose behind abstract descriptions of a plant is to be able to manage plant complexity. However, the type of abstraction applied depends on the use of the description. Thus, some abstractions may be useful for the control room designer planning the display system, whereas another type of abstraction is useful for an operator supervising the plant.

In what follows, we will discuss four different types of abstraction in representing complex systems. These are relevant to different phases of the interface design process and for the operator supervising the plant.

- Levels of system representation
- System aggregation and decomposition
- Semantic subdomains
- Supervisory control task

These types of abstractions are only examples and other categories may be considered. The meaning of these abstractions will be clarified below. We will use an example to show how such abstractions are used to manage different

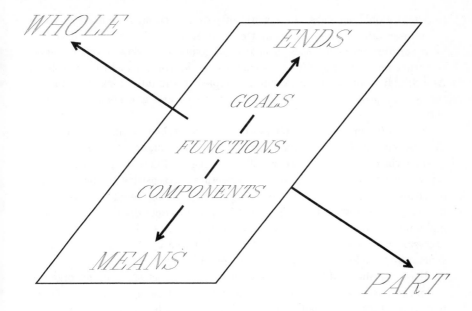

Figure 2: Dimensions of description in MFM

aspects of complexity in system representation and in the development of information displays for supervisory control.

These abstractions have different purposes relating to the tasks before the systems analyst who models the system to be supervised and to the tasks of an operator controlling the system. The problems of the systems analyst and of the operator are not identical and require different strategies for complexity management. The first three strategies of abstraction are relevant mainly to the systems analyst. The last strategy relates to the operator and is therefore important for the design of the interface for supervisory control.

3.2   Levels of representation

The use of different levels of representation is a well-known strategy for dealing with systems complexity in the design of information systems for supervisory control. However, it is often not made clear in what sense representations constitute different levels, i.e., in what way ordering is implied. An explicit formulation of the strategies used in abstraction is often missing.

This difficulty can only be addressed in a meaningful way if the representational problem is discussed within the context of solving a particular problem. It is the structure of the problem which determines the applicable representational schemes. In a world of pure reflection, the choice of levels of representation seems to be a matter of arbitrary choice or taste. However, in a world of action such as in control of complex systems, levels of representation must comply with the structure of the control tasks to be solved. Accordingly, representation is tightly coupled to the intentional structure of the system, possible means of observing system states and possible means of action.

This argument clarifies how system representations, which describe relations between ends and means in the controlled system, are of particular value in supervisory control. However, the ordering of different system representations in levels, i.e., in hierarchical structures, is sensitive to the relativity of means and ends. Thus, the ordering of levels of representation for a system may change when considering categories of system disturbances such as malfunctions during start-up and shut-down. In these situations, it may be necessary to use a system in a way not anticipated by the plant designer, or goals may be achieved using means not provided by design.

If we consider self-organising systems, i.e., systems which either organise system resources as a response to changing goals or change goals as response to changes in system capabilities, the notion of levels becomes problematic. In this case, the ordering of system resources by means-end relations becomes a dynamic feature of the system and the planning of content for the information interface to the system cannot be based on these relations. Accordingly, special consideration should be given to the representation problems of systems with self-organising features. This will not be done here.

Abstractions which make distinctions between means and ends in complex systems are useful for coping with problems of resource management. They lead to a separation of structure, function and goal levels in system representation. The reason why means and ends are important categories is that they provide an understanding of the system which relates to the possible courses of action. (There is not much fun in a representation which does not relate to the courses of action applicable to a decision agent.) Thus, there seems to be strict bounds on the semantics of system representations, if they should be useful for a decision agent.

3.2.1   An example

As an example of using means-ends abstractions in system representation we will consider an MFM model of a central heating system (Figure 4). The corresponding MFM model (Figure 5) represents functions and goals of the central heating system and will be used in the following to illustrate the use of different types of abstraction in development of information systems for supervisory control. The modelling is based on the concepts shown in Figure 3. In order to explain the meaning of the modelling concepts we will provide a short explanation.

First, consider the flow network in the middle section of the MFM model. This part represents the functions related to circulation of mass in the system. These functions represent the means available for the transport of energy provided by the circulation system. This energy transport function is described on the level above and represents the purpose of the mass circulation. If we consider the functional level below the middle level, this represents the means available for achieving the mass circulation. In our example system, we have a lubrication system which maintains a condition for the pump being able to function and a water supply system which is a means for keeping the water level above minimum (a condition for proper circulation). The means-end relations are repeated when a shift is made up the levels or down the levels. Hence, system goals can be identified by searching upwards in the models whereas means for goal achievement are identified by searching downwards.

An MFM model can be used for diagnosis since a search downwards in the model leads to causes for system failure (always related to the failure of means). At the same time, consequences of a failure will show up on the functional levels supported by the failed functions.

The model in Figure 5 provides several levels of representation of the central heating system. These levels are in the specific case organised in a hierarchical structure. As mentioned above, this hierarchical structure may not be valid if the goals of the central heating system change. This is because means and ends cannot be determined independently. Means must be means to achieve something and ends cannot be determined without considering the means. In the same way, the representation will not be valid if the central heating system components are used in a way not anticipated by its designer.

Even though the means-end abstractions result in a considerable reduction of task complexity for diagnosing plant disturbances [140], these advantages are not gained without costs. The difficulty of building an MFM model is one of the main problems. The experience of the present author shows that many people find it difficult to define proper levels of abstraction. These difficulties can in most cases be explained by an incomplete understanding of the concepts of goals and function. Training in the use of these concepts tends to make people better builders of MFM models. A strategy for MFM model building has been developed [141] which supports the user in providing different perspectives on the system during the modelling process.

An MFM model, as shown in Figure 5, can be used as the basis for the development of an information interface to an operator for diagnostic support. But as the model is a highly formalised representation of plant design intentions it may not be directly applicable as a medium for interaction with an operator. The main problem here is that even though the representation reflects plant functional structure it may not match the operator's mental model of the system. One difficulty may be that the iconic MFM representations

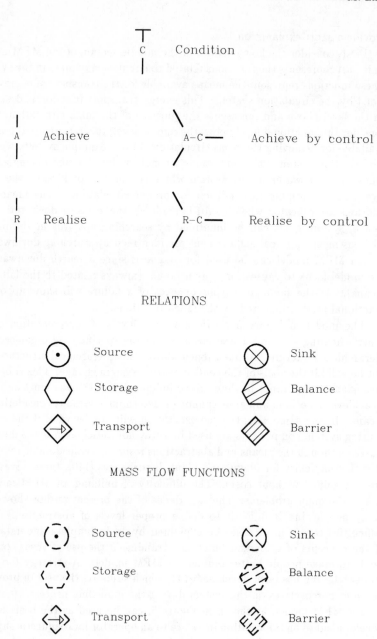

RELATIONS

MASS FLOW FUNCTIONS

ENERGY FLOW FUNCTIONS

Figure 3: MFM concepts and corresponding symbols

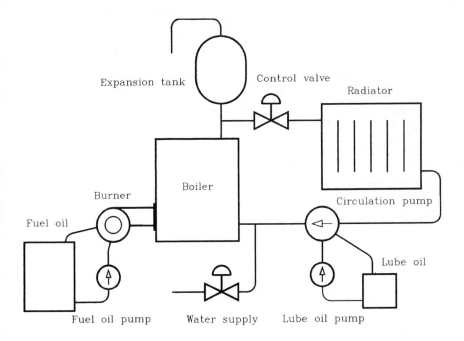

Figure 4 : A central heating system (MFM model shown in Figure 5)

are alien to the operator.

This problem may be solved by development of more adequate icons or simply by training. Another more important problem may be that the operator's functional categories are fuzzy and do not map in a simple way to the formalised MFM concepts. This problem may be solved by providing a mapping between the formal modelling concepts and more informal representation which satisfy the user's needs (such as a mimic diagram).

One possible way to deal with this problem is to use relations between flow functions and the physical levels in the representation. As each flow function is realised by a physical subsystem in the plant, it is possible to map a diagnosis (a hypothesis about the state of one or more flow functions) into a representation of the physical structure of the plant. This approach is illustrated below in Figures 6 and 7. Here it is shown that a set of functions (hatched, in Figure 7) is implemented by a physical subsystem (hatched, in Figure 6).

The advantage of the physical representation in Figure 6 is that it is conventional and can therefore be easily understood. But it has the disadvantage that it does not support the interpretation plant data in diagnosis. Thus, it is not possible to derive the logic dependencies as expressed in the MFM

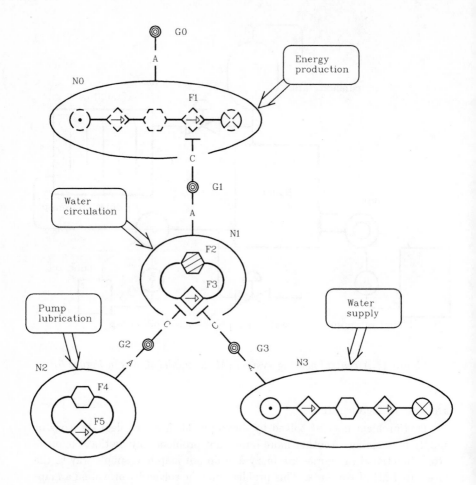

Figure 5: MFM model of the central heating system

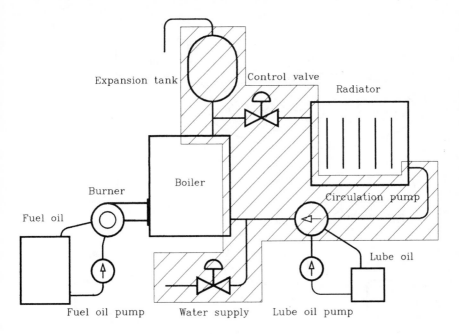

Figure 6: Selected subsystem implementing functions in Figure 7

model. These dependencies have no immediate representation in the physical model. Although the physical representation seems more comfortable than the abstract MFM representation it is not suited as a support in a diagnostic task.

It is worth noting that Duncan and his co-workers [66] have shown that displays based on flow concepts can actually be used by operators properly trained in the concepts of MFM. Their research indicate that operators' diagnostic performance increases significantly when they are supported by this type of display.

3.3 Abstractions for the systems analyst

Building an MFM model is an iterative task where it is necessary to manage a complex information structure. As a MFM model tends to become large and requires work on the detailing of the model in several stages, it is necessary to be able to aggregate parts of the model and to decompose model elements. Thereby, aggregation and decomposition are important strategies for the systems analyst in managing the task of building an MFM model. We will discuss aggregation and decomposition in the next section, once more using the central heating system for illustration.

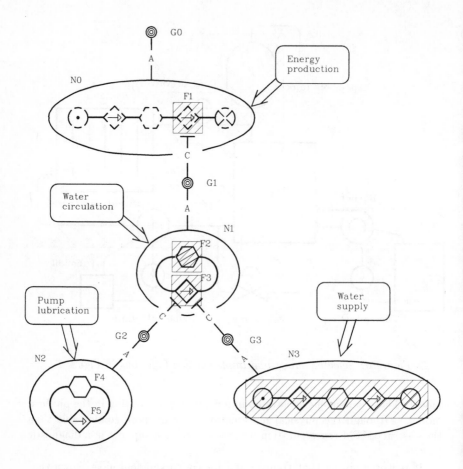

Figure 7: MFM model of functions realised by subsystem (see Figure 6)

3.3.1   System aggregation and decomposition

In the previous section we discussed the use of relations between means and ends as strategies for choice of levels of representation. As explained, this approach serves to provide a system representation which satisfies the needs of an agent in control of a complex system as it represents the system in a way which closely couples to the possible courses of action in the system.

This strategy provides a considerable reduction of the complexity of the system. However, even though the complexity is reduced, system representations can often be changed by aggregation or decomposition. Aggregation serves to maintain an overview of the system by lumping together system elements into super elements. Decomposition is sometimes a necessary stage in model building for clarification of relations between means and ends.

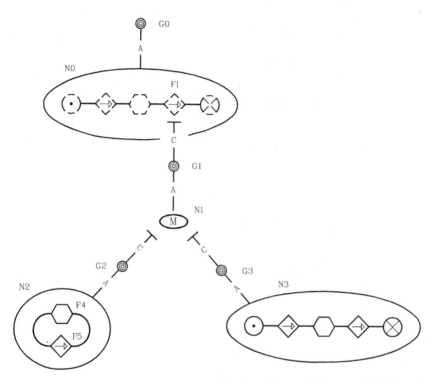

Figure 8 : An aggregated MFM model

Some examples of aggregation in MFM are shown in Figure 8. The functions representing the circulation of mass flow in the central heating system have been aggregated into a so-called support node. Figures 9 and 10 show further examples of aggregation. The resulting MFM model in Figure 10 represents a highly aggregated MFM model.

Even though Figures 8–10 represent stages of aggregation of the model in Figure 5, the model-building process will often be the reverse. Thus, the first stage of the model-building may be to make the overall model in Figure 10 without internal specification of the flow structure nodes. Later stages of the building process may add details by decomposition of the support nodes. The reason for making the decomposition is to represent the linkage of the flow structures with individual flow functions via the condition relations. This detailed information is important for diagnostic and planning applications as it improves the quality of the diagnosis and for making a more explicit

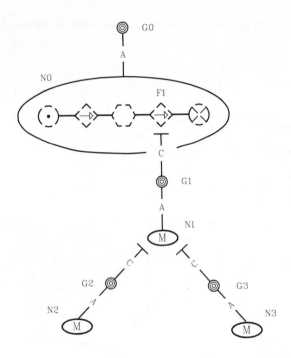

Figure 9: Further aggregation of the model in Figure 8

representation of control task structure.

The purpose of the model building is to provide as much detail as is necessary for diagnosis and for control task definition. But it is often convenient to be able to present the resulting model on different abstraction levels. This is useful for the purpose of model documentation and for the communication of state information. It could also be convenient for the operator to be able to reduce part of the information shown on the display to a smaller area, in order to cope with a restricted screen area. Thus, a flow structure may have two visual representations: one as a support node and another as a blown-up structure with the component flow functions shown.

3.4   Semantic subdomains

Model aggregation and decomposition are the main strategies for the systems analyst in managing the model building task. However, other strategies may also be considered. Thus, for example, the systems analyst may want to make selective investigation of a large model by considering only mass flow functions or energy flow functional elements. This type of model abstraction is based on

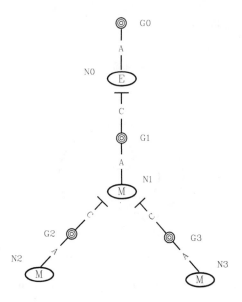

Figure 10: Yet further aggregation of the model in Figure 9

semantic distinctions, i.e., on the meaning of the different model elements, and represents a distinction between different semantic subdomains. Figure 8 is an example of a selective presentation of energy-flow-related modelling elements. Mass flow functions are suppressed in this representation and are only shown as aggregated mass flow structure nodes.

3.5   Supervisory control tasks

Whereas the previous sections considered abstractions which are useful for systems analysts we will now consider model abstractions which determine information structures and can be mapped into display windows. These abstractions define groups of modelling elements which define a set of resources (means) and the associated goals and conditions. This type of abstraction serves the needs of the operator as it defines a context for decision making. Supervisory control tasks can be defined as a specialization of the MFM model added after the model has been defined.

An example of an MFM model abstraction which defines a supervisory control task is shown in Figure 11. The selected MFM flow elements constitute the information structure of a control task. The task is defined by a goal (G1), a network of flow functions (resources; N1, F2 and F3) which achieve the goal, and a set of conditions which should be satisfied in order to maintain the flow functions (G2 and G3).

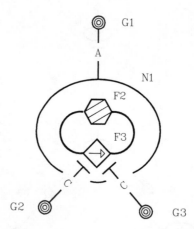

Figure 11: An MFM substructure defining a control task

Supervisory control tasks can be interrelated into task structures as shown in Figure 12. These task structures can be used directly as a basis for planning the structure of the display windows, i.e, the structure of the plant presentation. This structure is obtained by means of a functional analysis and is based on plant design knowledge.

One of the advantages of MFM is, as mentioned before, that it supports diagnostic reasoning. But MFM also supports reasoning about plant control. This can be illustrated by comparison of Figures 12 and 13. In Figure 13 we have indicated the physical components which are involved in the management of the amount of water in the circulation circuit. The same control task is represented in the MFM model in Figure 12 as task 3. Clearly, it is difficult from Figure 13 to identify the tank and the water supply as resources for control of the water content in the circulation system. The role of the circulation system is also very unclear (the vertical hatched area). As the MFM model in Figure 12 directly maps the roles or functions of the different subsystems in the plant, this type of uncertainty is avoided. Thus, the function of the circulation system is to transport water from the supply line to the expansion tank.

4   Outline of a method for interface development

The abstraction techniques described above are parts of a methodology for man-machine interface development. The idea is to conceive interface development as a process with three main stages. The stages comprise an information

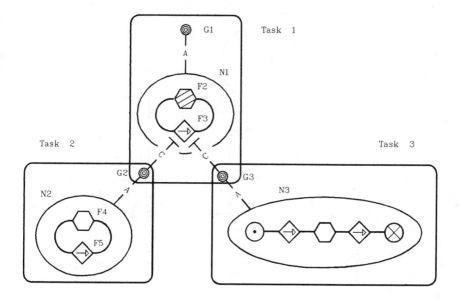

Figure 12 : A set of control tasks

analysis, design of means for generation of required plant information from available measurements and the subsequent planning of how this information should be presented to and manipulated by the operator. We will comment on each of these steps below.

4.1 Information analysis

The purpose of the information analysis is to define the plant knowledge which is required to support the operator in his supervisory task. As mentioned above, the operator needs to consider several categories of plant behaviour in diagnosis. Accordingly, the information analysis is mainly a modelling task.

The basis for the information analysis is to build an MFM model representing the plant in terms of means and ends. The model presents structural relations between plant functions in a highly formalised symbolic language. The model can be considered as a logical structure which describes plant control requirements. But the model is not at this stage a medium for user interaction. To this model should be attached fault information and knowledge of abnormal (not intended) plant behaviour (as mentioned above in relation to the discussion of plant behavioural categories). This coupling of other model categories to MFM models is currently under investigation.

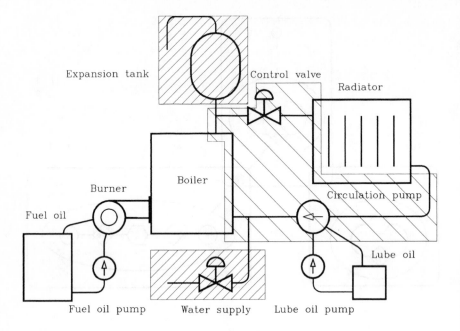

Figure 13: Systems involved in control of water inventory

4.2 Means for information generation

The purpose of this phase of the interface design is to develop the information processes which are required in order to process measured plant parameters into information on the different levels of abstraction, as defined by the models developed in the information analysis phase. This task would comprise the development of diagnostic systems for supporting the operator in interpretation of plant measurements. These systems would use the models generated in the previous phase as a basis for their information processing. The diagnostic expert system in [140] describes strategies which can be used with an MFM model for interpretation of plant data. The result of such an interpretation is a set of plant state hypotheses on several levels of abstraction in the MFM model. Such an expert system would accordingly be required as part of the man-machine interface.

4.3 Means of information presentation and dialogue

The purpose of this phase is to develop displays on the basis of the results of the two previous tasks. Whereas the information analysis defined what items should be presented to the operator, this phase of the development decides how they should be presented and how access should be provided to, e.g., diagnostic support facilities. The focus here is on principles for visual communication, dialogue [231] and on means for management of the screen information.

Note that the planning of the information presentation at the interface may take advantage of the mappings between the different plant representations discussed above. Thus, a physical plant presentation (mimic diagram) may be used to communicate high-level functional state information as derived from a MFM model. In this way, it would be possible to take into account the needs of the operator such as changing the visual representation of concepts or relaxing the formalised structure of MFM by combining information from several abstraction levels or model categories.

Acknowledgement

This work is part of the SIP project, funded by the Danish Research Council (STVF, grant 16-4190.E).

Chapter 11

Cooperation Between Distributed Knowledge-Bases and the User

Ernest Edmonds and Jenia Ghazikhanian

1 Introduction

The exploitation of the knowledge-based approach in the development of technological systems has grown recently. Of particular interest is the development of knowledge-based interactive systems that support users performing complex tasks such as those that arise in command and control. There are two main reasons for taking a knowledge-based approach. Firstly, it enables the use in the system of expert opinion, heuristics and incomplete knowledge, thus extending the scope of applicability of computer support beyond the cases where algorithmic solutions are available. It is, therefore, particularly valuable when dealing with complex systems. The second reason is equally important. In the knowledge-based approach, what is known about the problem is represented in an explicit way within the system. Perhaps the greatest benefit of this is in the cost of maintenance, because it makes it much easier to inspect, consider and modify the knowledge and, hence, the system.

Using knowledge-based systems in practice often requires the use of a number of separate knowledge-bases, as well as conventional components. There may be diverse information sources or components from existing systems that must be incorporated but, in any case, modularity is a general requirement for complex systems.

HUMAN–COMPUTER INTERACTION
AND COMPLEX SYSTEMS: ISBN 0-12-742660-4

The view that the user interface should be a separate software module in a system [69] has grown in its appeal in recent years. The draft ANSA standard [12], for example, identifies it in this way. At the same time, research into the exploitation of knowledge-based techniques in computing has also grown. These two developments have come together in the form of 'knowledge based front ends' (e.g., [240]). Now if a system is, in its core, knowledge-based and it has a knowledge-based front end we must inevitably have a minimum of two knowledge-bases and, of course, a user. Hence, the problem-solving task, whatever it might be, will be distributed amongst a number of knowledge-bases and between the system and the user. Our concern is to investigate how this distribution might take place. The subject of distributed problem solving in general is not new [37, 52, 67, 137, 205, 252]. Davis and Smith [52] in particular have proposed negotiation as an appropriate metaphor. This view corresponds well with the process of user-system cooperation described by Edmonds [70]. In what follows we describe some experiments in extending the earlier work of Edmonds to a distributed problem-solving system that includes a knowledge-based front end. In this work, the notion of a user interface is extended to become the user's personal knowledge-base as well as the module that provides access to the total system. This, in our view, is a natural extension of the notion that the interface must include a model of the application [89].

2   An architecture for cooperation

As a starting point for the investigation we have chosen a centralised approach where the user interface component is given control as shown in the system architecture diagram, Figure 1.

The decomposition and distribution of the task are handled by the user interface component. This is done by direct communication with the knowledge-bases which currently, in our experimental work, do not communicate or share data with each other. This architecture allows the user interface to take a very active part in the system and, as we will see, allows us to minimise communication between system components. In the examples that have been investigated, the intention has been to maximise the amount of processing that can be done on the user's behalf within the user interface component. Cooperation takes place between the elements of the system in a way that enables the user interface to improve its performance in this respect. It is not necessary to initially incorporate all the knowledge in the user interface, it can use and interpret knowledge obtained from the other knowledge-bases appropriately and according to the circumstances, adapting to an individual user requirements. The mechanism that decomposes and initiates the cooperation is the extended NASK system [70] and this is described below.

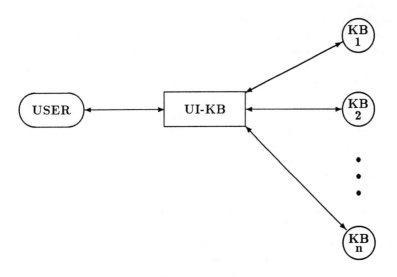

Figure 1: System architecture diagram

3   The NASK concept

NASK is an extension to the Prolog interpreter which incorporates negative knowledge and an automatic asking mechanism. The significance of the introduction of negative knowledge is that the system has three truth values, 'true', 'false' and 'do not know', in contrast to standard Prolog's two, 'true' and 'do not know'. If any time during a proof the extended interpreter has attempted to satisfy a goal and it has not been possible, in other words the result has been 'do not know', its strategy is to 'ask' the user for assistance. The system thus has an inbuilt asking strategy. The NASK system displays that goal and asks the user to respond in one of a number of possible ways. The possibilities are:

- true;
- false;
- sometimes;
- do not know;
- will provide a relevant rule;
- wish to ask a question.

In the first two cases, following that response, the goal, or its negation, is asserted and the proof continues. In the third case, an instance which is true is provided by the user, giving particular values to variables, and that instance is asserted. In the fourth case, the proof simply continues, looking for other ways of proving the main goal. In the fifth case, where the user provides a relevant new rule, it is asserted and then used to explore the new possible proof method provided. Finally, the process can be suspended whilst a new query is responded to, so that the user can freely investigate the rule base before responding to that particular question. In this last case, when a new query has been dealt with, NASK returns to its task, asking the user again about the goal in question. The system always concludes a completed proof attempt with the result 'true', 'false' or 'do not know'.

4   A mechanism for cooperation

In the experiments, each knowledge-base was run under the NASK system, including the user interface. It is the responsibility of the user interface to initiate cooperation. The NASK system user interface component is extended in the sense that prior to asking the user it consults the knowledge-bases of the background system in case the issue can be resolved in that way. In point of fact, so far, the exploitation of NASK is limited in the background knowledge-bases because the power of asking is disabled. However, an added feature is that during the evaluation of a goal it keeps a proof tree, i.e., all the facts and rules used to prove the goal to be either true or false, and this is sent back to the user interface. The user interface module is then able to select the facts and rules that do not exist in its own knowledge-base and assert them.

The consultation only takes place when the user interface cannot prove a goal to be true or false, i.e., it can only conclude 'do not know'. Consultation is done in the experimental system in a sequential manner as follows: if the first knowledge-base returns 'do not know' then the goal is sent by the user interface to the next knowledge-base to be evaluated and so on. If all return 'do not know' then the last resort is to ask the user. The system displays its usual menu to the user, and the process goes on according to the user's response as described above.

As a result of these communications with the knowledge-bases and the user, the user interface gradually extends its knowledge, tailoring itself to the interests and, it is hoped, the requirement of the user. In this way, the knowledge-base in the user interface module evolves and grows from very little or nothing. As it expands it takes more responsibility and often requires less communication with the background knowledge-bases. Little research has been done into precisely what knowledge should be incorporated in the user interface initially. Our approach allows the user interface knowledge-base to adapt to the user requirements.

5   Examples

We consider a simple example in which the user interface cooperates with one or more knowledge-bases and the user to solve a problem in the world of straight lines, in which not more than two lines share any given point (from [70]). Several situations are considered.

The problem is to find a rectangle in Figure 2. The principle rules known to the system, in one sense or another, are (where ~ is the negation operator):

```
rectangle(A,B,C,D):- corner(A,B,C), corner(A,D,C), ~B = D.
corner(A,B,C):- right_angle(A), right_angle(B), right_angle(C),
    line(A,B), line(B,C), ~A = C.
```

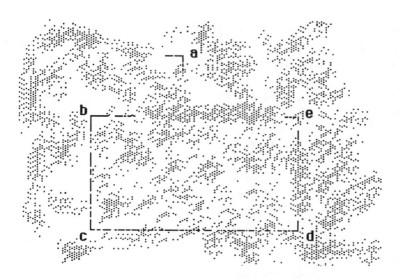

Figure 2: Example problem

Example 1

In this case, the knowledge-base in the user interface (UI) initially contains the principle rules and we will assume that either a signal analysis system or the user has put the following facts into the knowledge base:

```
right_angle(a).
right_angle(b).
right_angle(c).
right_angle(d).
right_angle(e).
line(b,c).
line(c,d).
```

Points at which lines intersect have been labelled, the predicate 'right_angle' asserts that they intersect at 90° and the predicate 'line' asserts that the two points named are joined by a visible line.

The single other knowledge-base, KB1, contains the principle rules and other facts. The responses to the user interface from KB1 consist of a list in which the first element is the answer and the remainder is the proof tree, where appropriate. The consultation starts with the user requesting a solution to:

USER	`rectangle(b,c,d,X)?`
UI to KB1	`line(b,a)?`
KB1	`[false,[(~line(b,a))]]`
UI to KB1	`line(b,b)?`
KB1	`['do not know',[]]`
UI to user	`line(b,b)?`
	`(t) true`
	`(f) false`
	`(d) do not know`
	`(s) sometimes`
	`(n) new rule`
	`(q) question`
	`(e) exit`
	`Select one item:`
User	`n`
UI	`Type in the new rule`
User	`~line(X,X).`
UI to KB1	`line(b,d)?`
KB1	`[false,[(~line(b,d))]]`
UI to KB1	`line(b,e)?`
KB1	`[true,[(line(b,e))]]`
UI to KB1	`line(e,d)?`
KB1	`[true,[(line(e,d))]]`
UI	`rectangle(b,c,d,e) is true, X = e.`

Now, a second question is posed, but this time the UI can bring more knowledge to bear upon the problem.

USER	rectangle(c,X,e,Y)?
UI to KB1	line(c,a)?
KB1	['false',[(~line(c,a))]]
UI to KB1	line(c,b)?
KB1	['true'[(line(c,b))]]
UI to KB1	line(d,e)?
KB1	['true',[(line(d,e))]]
UI	rectangle(c,b,e,d) is true, X = b, Y = d.

Example 2

In this example knowledge-base in UI initially contains no rules or facts about the problem.

USER	rectangle(b,c,d,X)?
UI to KB1	rectangle(b,c,d,X)?
KB1	[e,true,[(~line(b,a)), (~line(b,d)),
	(rectangle(A,B,C,D):-
	corner(A,B,C), corner(A,D,C), ~B=D),
	(corner(A,B,C):- right_angle(A), right_angle(B),
	right_angle(C), line(A,B), line(B,C), ~A=C),
	(right_angle(b)), (right_angle(c)),
	(right_angle(d)), (line(b,c)), (line(c,d)),
	(right_angle(e)), (line(b,e)), (line(e,d))]]
UI	rectangle(b,c,d,e) is true, X = e.

The knowledge-base in UI now contains all of the rules and the facts returned by KB1.

UI	rectangle(c,X,e,Y)?
UI to KB1	line(c,c)?
KB1	['do not know',[]]
UI to KB2	line(c,c)?
KB2	[false,[(~line(A,A))]]
UI to KB1	line(c,b)?
KB1	[true,[(line(c,b))]]
UI to KB1	line(c,e)?
KB1	[false,[(~line(c,e))]]
UI to KB1	line(d,e)?
KB1	[true,[(line(d,e))]]

```
UI          rectangle(c,b,e,d) is true, X = b, Y = d.
```

Note that KB1 in Example 2 solved the problem `rectangle(b,c,d,e)` without having knowledge of `line(X,X)`, by finding other lines of proof. This took approximately 640 goal evaluations. In Example 1, asking to prove the goal `rectangle(b,c,d,e)` takes 450 evaluations and in Example 3 approximately 530 goal evaluations are required.

Example 3

We now introduce another knowledge-base, KB2.

```
USER        rectangle(b,c,d,X)?
UI to KB1   line(b,a)?
KB1         [false,[(~line(b,a))]]
UI to KB1   line(b,b)?
KB1         ['do not know',[]]
UI to KB2   line(b,b)?
KB2         [false,[(~line(A,A))]]
UI to KB1   line(b,d)?
KB1         [false,[(~line(b,d))]]
UI to KB1   line(b,e)?
KB1         [true,[(line(b,e))]]
UI to KB1   line(e,d)?
KB1         [true,[(line(e,d))]]
UI          rectangle(b,c,d,e) is true, X=e.
```

If the user now asks for a solution to `rectangle(c,X,e,Y)` the same dialogue as in example 1 follows.

6 Conclusion

Automatic strategies that can enable the user's personal system, an extended user interface, to cooperate with distributed knowledge-bases has been discussed in relation to certain particular experiments. Much remains to be done, however. In the first instance, the background knowledge-bases might be given the full facilities of NASK and this will open up the question of controlling the asking that might take place. It is clear that a parallel architecture provides an interesting possibility and in future work it is intended to 'broadcast' requests for help in a parallel way. There is no reason why some of the components might not be conventional systems, either databases or algorithms, and this is also under investigation. The most obvious question is: How should the user interface, or the user and the user interface, control the growth of the knowledge-base?

Acknowledgements

The authors are grateful for the advice of Dr Chris Hinde. The work described in the chapter was partly funded by the Alvey Directorate, contract number IKBS//058.

Chapter 12

Human-Computer Interaction Research in the Light of Aulin's Foundations of Mathematical Systems Dynamics

Pertti Järvinen

1 Introduction

Frustration and anxiety are a part of daily life for many users of computerised information systems. They struggle to learn command language or menu selection systems that are supposed to help them do their jobs. Shneiderman [211] proposes that we researchers should take a disciplined, iterative and empirical approach to the study of human performance in the use of interactive systems. Shneiderman's favourite, the controlled experiment, can master simple regularly behaving subsystems like computing systems but may have difficulties with complex ones, e.g., with a self-steering human user. We therefore ask: What is the application domain of the controlled experiment?

Gaines and Shaw [82] estimate that we should move ourselves from the generation of 'human-computer interaction (HCI) rules' towards the generation of 'theory of HCI'. This theory would contain at least theories of software, hardware and human being. The two former in our opinion already exist but we must ask: What is the relevant theory of a human being? Gaines and Shaw also consider rules to be pre-theoretical and therefore prefer a theory proper. We must say that rules also differ from the theory of HCI in such a way that rules emphasise 'how to construct a *good* HCI' but the theory of HCI may say 'what the HCI is'. We must therefore ask: Are the same research approaches valid for construction of HCI systems and for evaluation of HCI systems?

HUMAN–COMPUTER INTERACTION
AND COMPLEX SYSTEMS: ISBN 0-12-742660-4

The mathematical theories both for dynamic systems and the human actor recently developed by Aulin [16] seem to shed a new light on the above problems. Aulin's mathematical systems dynamics will be introduced in the next section. Aulin shows that the same mathematical formalism is valid for technological dynamic systems and for a goal-seeking human being. This is very important, because our computing systems belong to the former and our users to the latter.

The purpose of this chapter is to analyse some recommended research approaches in the context of Aulin's [16] categories of dynamic systems. Weaknesses and restrictions of known approaches will be shown and alternative approaches proposed.

2   On mathematical systems dynamics

Aulin [16] differentiates three primary types of causality: causal relation, causal law and causal recursion, from weakest to the strongest. Causal recursion is the type of causality required at the fundamental level of physical theory, and thus for natural science generally. This implies a complete state-description of the dynamical system concerned, given by a total state x, as a function of which any property x of the system at any moment t can be expressed: $z(t) = z(x(t))$. Causal recursion is defined for the total state x if there is a transitive recursion of $x(t)$ to any past state $x(\tau)$, i.e., if

$$x(t) = \phi^{t\tau}(x(\tau)), \phi^{tt'} \diamond \phi^{t'\tau} = \phi^{t\tau} \text{ for } t > t' > \tau$$

Thus a system having causal recursion is what Ashby [14] called a 'state-determined system'.

Causal recursion is *nilpotent*, if there is such a positive integer s and state x_0 that

$$\phi^s(x) = x_0 \forall x \in X \subset E$$

$$\phi(x_0) = x_0,$$

where E is a Euclidean space and X is a set of states of the system (Figure 1).

The initial state x_0 is called the rest state and the nilpotent dynamical system has the property that it comes back to its initial state after a finite number (s) of units of time. We can say that an external disturbance (or stimulus) occurring at the moment $t = 0$ throws the system out of its rest state x_0 to a perturbed state x, after which the nilpotent causal recursion conducts the total state $xt = u$ along the half-trajectory uT^+ until, at the moment $t = s$, the system is back in the rest state x_0. During its return journey the system gives response to the stimulus. If the same stimulus is

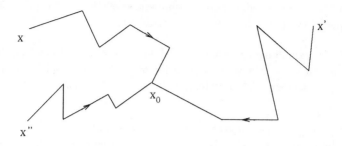

Figure 1: Nilpotent dynamical system

offered again, the system gives the same finite total response. Thus it is a memoryless system that does not learn from experience.

If the nilpotent system contains feedback, it is called a cybernetic nilpotent system. If a computer is programmed to solve a finite problem, i.e., a problem that can be solved in a finite number of steps of computation in the machine, it is a cybernetic nilpotent system. (But computers can also be programmed to simulate systems that have full causal recursion.)

A dynamical system with full causal recursion does not have any rest state to be reached in a finite number of steps (in a finite time). Thus, causal systems can be classified into two categories: nilpotent systems and systems with a full causal recursion (see Figure 2).

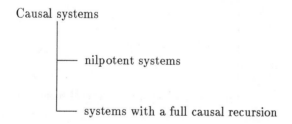

Figure 2: Two categories of causal systems

The mathematical definition of 'goal' is based on an infinite process, and thus on a full causal recursion [16]. To define exactly the difference between a goal and a task, Aulin assumes that an external disturbance throws the system at the moment $t = 0$ from an unperturbed state x to a perturbed state p. Corresponding to the alternative cases, related to the behaviour of the Euclidean distance $\rho(pt, xR^+)$ of the point pt from the half-trajectory

xR^+ and to the boundedness or unboundedness of xR^+ we have the following four types of systems with full causal recursion:

1. If, for a small enough δ neighbourhood $S(x, \delta)$ of x, Euclidean distance $\rho(pt, xR^+) \to 0$ with $t \to +\infty$ for all $p \in (x, \delta)$, and if the positive half-trajectory xR^+ is unbounded, the system is called *self-steering in state x*.

2. If the convergence of $\rho(pt, xR^+)$ is as above, but the half-trajectory xR^+ is bounded, the system is called *self-regulating in state x*.

3. If, for a small enough δ neighbourhood $S(x, \delta)$ of x, Euclidean distance $\rho(pt, xR^+)$ remains finite for all $p \in (x, \delta)$, but does not for all $p \in (x, \delta)$ converge to zero with $t \to +\infty$, the system is called *steerable from outside in state x*.

4. If in any δ neighbourhood $S(x, \delta)$ of x there is a point p for which $\rho(pt, xR^+) \to \infty$ with $t \to +\infty$, the system is called *disintegrating in state x*.

Here $S(x, \delta)$ is the open sphere with centre x and radius δ. The four definitions obviously exclude one another, and together exhaust the class of all the dynamical systems having a full (i.e., non-nilpotent) causal recursion (see Figure 3).

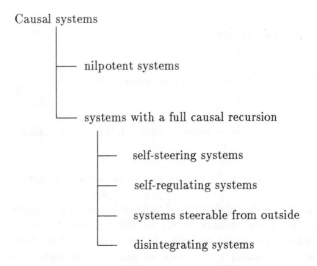

Figure 3: Classification of all non-nilpotent dynamical systems

We may ask whether we find any real systems in every category, for example, which real system belongs to the category of self-steering systems? If the uniqueness of states of mind, along with the goal-oriented nature of thought processes, is typical of human consciousness, the only thinkable causal representation of what takes place in the human mind in an alert state is the self-steering process. It is, however, necessary to limit the interpretation so that what is self-steering in the human mind is the total intellectual process. All the partial processes need not be self-steering.

Real-world examples of self-regulating systems include a ball in a cup that has the form of a half-sphere, a room equipped with a good thermostat (self-regulating equilibrium systems); some living organisms like a heart (periodically pulsating self-regulating systems), etc.

A flying ball (for which the resistance of the air is negligible), a frictionless oscillator, and a robot, are examples of systems steerable from outside. A radioactive atom and a dead organism are disintegrating systems.

3   HCI research and mathematical systems dynamics

Burrell and Morgan [34] distinguish in the case of research methodology two extremes: nomothetic methodologies (formal-mathematical analysis, laboratory and field experiments, field studies and surveys) and ideographic ones (case studies, action research). The ideographic approach to social science is based on the view that one can only understand the social world by obtaining first-hand knowledge of the subject under investigation. The nomothetic approach to social science lays emphasis on the importance of basing research upon systematic protocol and technique. Those two approaches pay attention on an existing reality, but they are not considering how to construct a new reality. Taking into account the special character of computer science as a prescriptive science, I distinguish one more category, constructive methodologies (conceptual development, technical development).

Aulin's theory above is representative of formal-mathematical analysis. Laboratory experiments were traditionally performed for prediction. To this end we shall first study prediction in the context of HCI. It may provide new information of some nomothetic methodologies. Over the last two decades many rules have been derived for guiding the development of human-computer interfaces. For this reason, we also study such rules, since these serve as an example of constructive methodologies. Finally, action research is considered as an ideographic methodology.

3.1 On prediction

Card *et al.* [40] proposed a simple model, called the Keystroke-Level Model, for predicting one aspect of performance: the time it takes an expert user to perform a given task on a given computer system. The model is based on counting keystrokes and other low-level operations, including the user's mental preparations and the system's responses. Performance is coded in terms of these operations and operator times summed to give predictions.

According to Reisner [199], behavioural experiments are currently the primary method of assessing the human factors in end-user systems. Such experiments, however, are time consuming and sometimes come too late in the development cycle to influence ease of use. Analytic tools, which involve an abstract representation of a user interface and some manipulation of that representation to predict ease of use, are potentially faster.

In this chapter I call a combination of an end-user, hardware and software an end-user system. As far as I can see both Card *et al.* and Reisner considered an end-user system as a nilpotent system only. This system comes back to its initial state after performing a task. Users are assumed to be experts who do not make any error. In this context, I would like to ask: Whether their human image corresponds to reality or not? If an end-user system were near to a self-steering one, no prediction is then possible, because an end-user can during the usage period change his/her goals. This means that we cannot express a causal recursion for the end-user's behaviour in the future although we sometimes can derive the causal recursion of his/her past behaviour.

3.2 On rules

In their extensive survey of literature on dialogue design, Alty *et al.* [9] brought to light a lot of rules, which (to mention the five most common) included: 1. Use the user's model, 2. Be uniform and consistent, 3. Allow query in depth, 4. Make the state of the dialogue observable, 5. User should control computer. Rule 2 is self-evident. Rules 3 and 4 emphasise the fact that the software of the end-user system should alleviate the mental load of the user. From our point of view (mathematical systems dynamics), rule 1 and rule 5 are of most interest.

After detailing other researchers' views on rule 1, Alty *et al.* note that

> despite uncertainty both on the degree of user modelling that can be achieved, and the risks of going too far in such modelling, it is safe to say that an effective dialogue system must embody a user model which is able to accommodate and adjust to significant differences between individual users, in a manner that seems natural and comfortable to each user.

These authors did not consider every user as a similar nilpotent system with the same behaviour but accept that there are 'differences between individual users'. To my mind they did not consider an end-user system as a robot (i.e., as a system steerable from outside) either. But if an end-user is considered as a self-steering system, whose prediction was shown above to be impossible, our model (self-steering system) says that such a system never returns to its earlier trail (the same state never returns). This means that user modelling is very difficult, almost impossible.

Rule 5 (User should control computer) was based on such arguments as:

1. in the present state of the art the computer does not have the capability for adequately modelling the user, so the user should dominate the interaction, and

2. unless the computer or the user dominates interaction the results will be unstable [81].

I agree with Alty *et al.* when they said that stable interaction may not require that either the user or the computer dominate all the time. Mathematical systems dynamics says that argument (1) is always valid, for if the computer would dominate over the user, he/she were then considered as a system component steerable by the computer (i.e., steerable from outside and hence human being were then considered as a robot). Rule 5 is in accordance with Aulin's theory of dynamical systems.

3.3   Action research

Oquist [174] defines action research as the production of knowledge to guide practice, with modification of a given reality occurring as part of the research process itself. Within action research, knowledge is produced and reality modified simultaneously; each occurring due to the other. Action research differs from laboratory experiment in such a way that it is based on subject-object (researcher-research object) interaction but laboratory experiment is objectivistic such that a researcher is a neutral observer.

In addition to mathematical systems dynamics Aulin [16] also considered human action and derived the theory of actors and acts based on interaction between a subject (a conscious actor) and an object (some part of the real world at which the act of the actor is directed). According to Aulin every human act has its premises and consequences in the world of objects. But the latter is composed of dynamical systems, in fact is itself a dynamical system defined in a complete state-description of the world. By assuming that the world is a dynamical system it follows that human beings too are dynamical systems, as well as they are actors. Aulin then derives a connecting link between the theory of actors and that of dynamical systems.

Referring to above it seems to me that there is no fundamental or principal argument against action research as methodology for studying an end-user system as a dynamical system. This is very important, if an end-user system is considered to be a self-steering one and hence other methodologies are not valid.

4 Conclusions

Our consideration shows that the traditional laboratory experiment is the valid approach, if our object of study is a nilpotent system, i.e., a user can in a finite number of steps perform his/her task using an interactive computing system. But if his/her tasks in the future are so complex that the required end-user system resembles a self-steering system, no prediction is possible.

The rules intended to guide a development of an interactive system can never be proved to be right or wrong. Mathematical systems dynamics seems to shed a new light when a certain rule is reasonable and when not. I think that the self-steering view would propose such an approach for constructive research that we should build up as flexible software as possible and this software would allow a user him/herself to build a model of the activity being undertaken. If the computing system is intended to support communication between two or more users, they should then describe their common model together.

If users have problems with their interactive systems, action research was with good reason shown to be a right research approach. The link between the theory of the actor and that of dynamical systems also seems to give promising general results as The Law of Requisite Variety [13] and The Law of Requisite Hierarchy [15]. The former says that 'only variety can kill variety'. The latter that 'the weaker the average regulatory ability and the larger the average uncertainty of available regulators, the more requisite hierarchy is needed in the organisation of regulation and control for the same result of regulation'. If we cannot, for example, make changes in our computing system, and if we want to get the same result from our end-user system, we must either improve our users' regulatory abilities or increase the hierarchy by increasing staff and co-ordinating efforts. Should the flexibility of our computing system admit of improvements in its regulatory ability by utilising its new potential opportunities, then the same result of regulation may be achieved without staff increases or additional user education.

References

[1] Alexander, H. (1985). Formally based techniques for designing human computer dialogues. Report RGP 35, Department of Computer Science, University of Stirling, UK.

[2] Alexander, H. (1986). ECS: A technique for the formal specification and rapid prototyping of human-computer interaction. In: Harrison, M. D. and Monk, A. F. (eds), *People and Computers: Designing for Usability*, pp. 157–179. Cambridge University Press, Cambridge.

[3] Allen, J. (1983). Maintaining knowledge about temporal intervals. *Communications of the ACM*, 26: 832–843.

[4] Allen, J. F. (1984). Towards a general theory of actions and time. *Artificial Intelligence*, 23: 123–154.

[5] Alty, J. L. Personal communication.

[6] Alty, J. L. (1984). Path algebras: A useful CAI/CAL analysis technique. In: Smith, P. R. (ed.), *Selected Proceedings from the Computer Assisted Learning 83 Symposium*, pp. 5–13. Pergamon Press, Oxford.

[7] Alty, J. L. and Brooks, A. (1985). Microtechnology and user friendly systems: The CONNECT dialogue executor. *Journal of Microcomputer Applications*, 8: 333–346.

[8] Alty, J. L., Elzer, P., Holst, O., Johannsen, G., and Savory, S. (1985). Literature and user survey of issues related to man-machine interfaces for supervision and control systems. Technical Report ESPRIT P600 Graphical Dialogue Pilot Phase Report, Computer Resources International, Copenhagen.

[9] Alty, J. L., Mullin, J., and Weir, G. (1986). Survey of dialogue systems and literature on dialogue design. Technical Report AMU8701/01S, Scottish Human-Computer Interaction Centre, Glasgow.

[10] Alty, J. L. and Ritchie, R. A. (1985). A path algebra support facility for interactive dialogue designers. In: Johnson, P. and Cook, S. (eds), *People and Computers: Designing the Interface*, pp. 128–137. Cambridge University Press, Cambridge.

[11] Anderson, J. R. (1983). *The Architecture of Cognition*. Harvard University Press, Cambridge, MA.

[12] ANSA (1987). The ANSA reference manual. ANSA, Cambridge. Release 00.03.

[13] Ashby, W. R. (1956). *An Introduction to Cybernetics.* Chapman and Hall, London.

[14] Ashby, W. R. (1972). *Design for a Brain.* Chapman and Hall, London.

[15] Aulin, A. (1982). *The Cybernetic Laws of Social Progress.* Pergamon Press, Oxford.

[16] Aulin, A. (1989). *Foundations of Mathematical Systems Dynamics: The Fundamental Theory of Cybernetic Causality.* Book Series of Systems Engineering. Pergamon Press, Oxford.

[17] Bainbridge, L. (1989). Development of skill, reduction of workload. In: Bainbridge, L. and Ruiz Quintanilla, S. A. (eds), *Developing Skills with New Technology*, pp. 87–116. Wiley, Chichester.

[18] Barker, P. G., Najah, M., and Manji, K. A. (1987). Pictorial communication with computers. *International Journal of Man-Machine Studies*, 27: 315–336.

[19] Barnard, P. J. (1985). Interacting cognitive subsystems: A psycholinguistic approach to short-term memory. In: Ellis, A. (ed.), *Progress in the Psychology of Language*, vol II, pp. 197–258. Lawrence Erlbaum Associates, Hillsdale, NJ.

[20] Barnard, P. J. (1987). Cognitive resources and the learning of human-computer dialogs. In: Carroll, J. M. (ed.), *Interfacing Thought: Cognitive Aspects of Human-Computer Interaction*, ch 6. MIT Press, Cambridge, MA.

[21] Becker, R. A. and Cleveland, W. S. (1984). Brushing the scatterplot matrix: High-interaction graphical methods for analyzing multidimensional data. Technical report, AT&T Bell Laboratories.

[22] Bellotti, V. (1988). Implications of current design practice for the use of HCI techniques. In: Jones, D. M. and Winder, R. (eds), *People and Computers IV, Proceedings of the Fourth Conference on Human-Computer Interaction.* Cambridge University Press, Cambridge.

[23] Bersini, U., Cacciabue, P. C., and Mancini, G. (1988). A model of operator behaviour for man-machine system simulation. In: *Proceedings of the 3rd IFAC/IFIP/IEA/IFORS Conference on Man-Machine Systems*, Oulu, Finland.

[24] Bignell, V. and Fortune, J. (1984). *Understanding Systems Failures.* Manchester University Press, Manchester.

[25] Booth, P. A. (1989). *An Introduction to Human-Computer Interaction.* Lawrence Erlbaum Associates, Sussex, UK.

[26] Booth, P. A. (1990). ECM: A scheme for analysing user-system errors. In: Diaper, D., Gilmore, D., Cockton, G., and Shackel, B. (eds), *Human-Computer Interaction—INTERACT '90*, pp. 47–54. North-Holland, Amsterdam.

[27] Borchers, H. W., Elzer, P., Siebert, H., Weisang, C., Borys, B.-B., Fejes, L., and Johannsen, G. (1986). Survey of existing sets of picture elements and editors. Technical Report Esprit-GRADIENT Report No. 3., Brown, Boveri and University of Kassel, Heidelberg and Kassel.

[28] Borys, B.-B., Johannsen, G., Hansel, H. G., and Schmidt, J. (1987). Task and knowledge analysis in coal-fired power plants. *IEEE Control Systems Magazine*, 7: 26–30.

[29] Bransford, J., Sherwood, R., Vye, N., and Rieser, J. (1986). Teaching and problem solving: Research foundations. *American Psychologist*, 41: 1078–1089.

[30] Brennan, A. C. C. (1987). Cognitive support for process control: Designing system representations. Master's thesis, University of London.

[31] Briggs, P. (1988). What we know and what we need to know: The user model versus the user's model in human-computer interaction. *Behaviour and Information Technology*, 7(4): 431–442.

[32] Brown, R. L. (1985). Methods for graphic representation of systems of simulated data. *Ergonomics*, 28: 1439–1454.

[33] Burns, A. and Robinson, J. (1986). ADDS: A dialogue development system for the Ada programming language. *International Journal of Man-Machine Studies*, 24(2): 153–170.

[34] Burrell, G. and Morgan, G. (1979). *Sociological Paradigms and Organizational Analysis*. Heinemann, London.

[35] Cacciabue, P. C., Decortis, F., Mancini, G., Masson, M., and Nordvik, J. P. (1988). The contribution of cognitive modelling to the development of decision support system technology. In: *Technical Committee Meeting on User requirements for Decision Support Systems*, Vienna.

[36] Cacciabue, P. C., Decortis, F., and Masson, M. (1988). Cognitive model and complex physical systems: A distributed implementation. In: *Proceedings of the 7th European Annual Conference on Human Decision Making and Manual Control*, Paris.

[37] Cammarata, S., McArthur, D., and Steeb, R. (1983). Strategies of cooperation in distributed problem solving. Technical Report N-2031-ARPA, The Rand Corporation.

[38] Canter, D., Powell, J., Wishart, J., and Roderick, C. (1986). User navigation in complex database systems. *Behaviour and Information Technology*, 5: 249–257.

[39] Card, S. K., Moran, T. P., and Newell, A. (1980). Computer text-editing: An information-processing analysis of a routine cognitive skill. *Cognitive Psychology*, 12: 32–74.

[40] Card, S. K., Moran, T. P., and Newell, A. (1980). The keystroke-level model for user performance time with interactive systems. *Communications of the ACM*, 23(7): 396–410.

[41] Card, S. K., Moran, T. P., and Newell, A. (1983). *The Psychology of Human-Computer Interaction*. Lawrence Erlbaum Associates, Hillsdale, NJ.

[42] Card, S. K. and Young, R. M. (1984). Predictive models of the user: A selective review. In: *NATO Advanced Workshop on User-Computer Interaction*, Loughborough, England.

[43] Carré, B. (1979). *Graphs and Networks*. Clarendon Press, Oxford.

[44] Carroll, J. M., Kellogg, W. A., and Rosson, M. B. (1991). The task-artifact cycle. In: Carroll, J. M. (ed.), *Designing Interaction: Psychology at the human computer interface*. Cambridge University Press, Cambridge.

[45] Carroll, J. M. and Rosson, M. B. (1985). Usability specifications as a tool in iterative development. In: Hartson, H. R. (ed.), *Advances in Human-Computer Interaction*. Ablex, Norwood, NJ.

[46] Chechile, R. A., Eggleston, R. G., Fleischman, R. J., and Sasseville, A. M. (1989). Modelling the cognitive content of displays. *Human Factors*, 31: 31–43.

[47] Cockerill-Sambre (1984). Prise en compte des facteurs humains dès la conception et l'installation de la coulée continue de la S. A. Cockerill-Sambre-Chertal.

[48] Cole, W. G. (1986). Medical cognitive graphics. In: Mantei, M. and Orbeton, P. (eds), *Human Factors in Computing Systems: CHI'86 Conference Proceedings*. ACM/SIGCHI.

[49] Cook, R. I. (1988). Scenarios for bedside medical data communication. *SigBio Newsletter*, 10(1).

[50] Coriat, B. and de Terssac, G. (1984). Micro-électronique et travail ouvrier dans les industries de process. *Sociologie du Travail*, 3: 369–397.

[51] Daniellou, F. and Boel, M. (1983). L'activité des opérateurs de conduite dans une salle de contrôle de processus automatisé. Rapport No. 75, Coll. Ergonomie et Neurophysiologie du Travail, Paris.

[52] Davis, R. and Smith, R. G. (1983). Negotiation as a metaphor for distributed problem solving. *Artificial Intelligence*, 20: 63–109.

[53] De Jong, J. and Koster, E. P. (1974). The human operator in the computer-controlled refinery. In: Edwards, E. and Lees, F. (eds), *The Human Operator in Process Control.* Taylor and Francis, London.

[54] De Keyser, V. (1981). La fiabilité humaine dans les processus continus, les centrales thermo-électriques et nucléaires. Report 720-ECI-2651, CEC, Brussels.

[55] De Keyser, V. (1987). How can computer-based visual displays aid operators? *International Journal of Man-Machine Studies*, 27: 471–478.

[56] De Keyser, V., Decortis, F., Housiaux, A., and Van Daele, A. (1987). *Les communications hommes-machines dans les systèmes complexes.* Politique Scientifique. Action Fast, Brussels.

[57] De Keyser, V., Decortis, F., Housiaux, A., and Van Daele, A. (1987). Les communications hommes-machines dans les système complex. Rapport politique scientifique belge, Université de Liège.

[58] De Keyser, V., Masson, M., Van Daele, A., and Woods, D. D. (1987). Fixation errors in complex systems. In: *International Congress of Trieste*, Italy.

[59] De Keyser, V. and Piette, A. (1970). Analyse de l'activité des opérateurs au tableau synoptique d'une salle de contrôle en sidérurgie. *Le Travail Humain*, 33(3–4): 341–352.

[60] Dean, T. L. and McDermott, D. V. (1987). Temporal data base management. *Artificial Intelligence*, 32: 1–55.

[61] Decortis, F. (1988). Dimension temporelle de l'activité cognitive lors des démarrages de systèmes complexes. *Le Travail Humain*, 51(2): 125–138.

[62] Decortis, F. and Cacciabue, P. C. (1988). Temporal dimension in cognitive models. In: *Proceedings of the 4th IEEE Conference on Human Factors and Power Plants*, Monterey, California.

[63] Decortis, F. and De Keyser, V. (1988). Time: The Cinderella of man-machine interaction. In: *Proceedings of the 3rd IFAC/IFIP/IEA/IFORS Conference on Man-Machine Systems*, Oulu, Finland.

[64] Dewar, A. D. and Cleary, J. G. (1986). Graphic display of complex information within a prolog debugger. *International Journal of Man-Machine Studies*, 25: 503–521.

[65] Dörner, D. (1987). On the difficulties people have in dealing with complexity. In: Rasmussen, J., Duncan, K., and Leplat, J. (eds), *New Technology and Human Error.* Wiley, Chichester.

[66] Duncan, K. D., Prætorius, N., and Milne, A. B. (1989). Flow displays of complex plant processes for fault diagnosis. In: Megaw, E. D. (ed.), *Contemporary Ergonomics, 1989*, pp. 199–206. Taylor and Francis, London.

[67] Durfee, H. E., Lesser, V. R., and Corkill, D. D. (1987). Coherent cooperation among communicating problem solvers. *IEEE Transactions on
Computers*, C-36(11): 1275–1291.

[68] Easterby, R. S. (1970). The perception of symbols for machine displays.
Ergonomics, 13: 149–158.

[69] Edmonds, E. A. (1982). The man-computer interface: A note on concepts and design. *International Journal of Man-Machine Studies*, 16:
231–236.

[70] Edmonds, E. A. (1986). Negative knowledge toward a strategy for asking in logic programming. *International Journal of Man-Machine Studies*, 24: 597–600.

[71] Edmonds, E. A. and Guest, S. (1984). The SYNICS2 user interface
manager. In: *INTERACT '84: First IFIP Conference on Human-
Computer Interaction*, vol 1, pp. 53–56, Amsterdam. Elsevier.

[72] Edwards, E. and Lees, F. (1974). *The Human Operator in Process
Control*. Taylor and Francis, London.

[73] Elm, W. C. and Woods, D. D. (1985). Getting lost: A case study in
interface design. In: *Proceedings of the Human Factors Society*. 29th
Annual Meeting.

[74] Elzer, P. and Johannsen, G. (1988). Concepts, design and prototype
implementation for an intelligent graphical editor (IGE1). Technical
report, ASEA Brown Boveri and University of Kassel, Kassel.

[75] Faverge, J. M. (1966). *L'ergonomie des processus industriels*. Presses
de l'Institut de Sociologie de l'ULB.

[76] Fischhoff, B., Slovic, P., and Lichtenstein, S. (1978). Fault trees: Sensitivity of estimated failure probabilities to problem representation. *Journal of Experimental Psychology: Human Perception and Performance*,
4: 330–344.

[77] Fitts, P. M. and Posner, M. I. (1962). *Human Performance*. Brooks/
Cole, Monterey, CA.

[78] Fraisse, P. (1957). *Psychologie du temps*. Presses Universitaires de
France, Paris.

[79] Freud, S. (1922). *Introductory Lectures on Psychoanalysis*. Allen and
Unwin, London.

[80] Furnas, G. W. (1986). Generalized fisheye views. In: Mantei, M.
and Orbeton, P. (eds), *Human Factors in Computing Systems: CHI'86
Conference Proceedings*. ACM/SIGCHI.

[81] Gaines, B. R. and Shaw, M. L. G. (1983). Dialogue engineering. In:
Sime, M. E. and Coombs, M. J. (eds), *Designing for Human Computer
Communication*, pp. 23–53. Academic Press, London.

[82] Gaines, B. R. and Shaw, M. L. G. (1986). From timesharing to the sixth generation: The development of human-computer interaction, part I. *International Journal of Man-Machine Studies*, 24: 1–27.

[83] Gentner, D. and Stevens, A. L. (eds) (1983). *Mental Models*. Lawrence Erlbaum Associates, Hillsdale, NJ.

[84] Gibson, J. J. (1979). *The Ecological Approach to Visual Perception*. Houghton Mifflin, Boston.

[85] Gick, M. L. and Holyoak, K. J. (1980). Analogical problem solving. *Cognitive Psychology*, 12: 306–365.

[86] Gonzalez, E. G. and Kolers, P. A. (1982). Mental manipulation of arithmetic symbols. *Journal of Experimental Psychology: Learning, Memory, and Cognition*, 8: 308–319.

[87] Goodman, N. (1968). *Languages of Art*. Bobbs-Merrill, New York.

[88] Grant, A. S. (1990). Modelling cognitive aspects of complex control tasks. Scottish HCI Centre, Strathclyde University. Ph.D. thesis.

[89] Green, M. (1985). Report on dialogue specification tools. In: Pfaff, G. E. (ed.), *User Interface Management Systems*. Springer-Verlag, Berlin.

[90] Green, T. R. G. (1982). Pictures of programs and other processes, or how to do things with lines. *Behaviour and Information Technology*, 1: 3–36.

[91] Green, T. R. G. (1987). Limited theories as a framework for human-computer interaction. Invited address to the Austrian Computer Society's 6th Annual Interdisciplinary workshop. Mental models and human-computer interaction.

[92] Green, T. R. G., Schiele, F., and Payne, S. J. (1988). Formalisable models of user knowledge in human-computer interaction. In: van der Veer, G. C., Green, T. R. G., Hoc, J.-M., and Murray, D. M. (eds), *Working with Computers: Theory versus Outcome*, pp. 3–46. Academic Press, London.

[93] Guttag, J. and Horning, J. J. (1980). Formal specification as a design tool. In: *Proc. of 7th Symposium on Principles of Progamming Languages*, pp. 251–280, Las.Vegas.

[94] Haber, R. N. (1981). The power of visual perceiving. *Journal of Mental Imagery*, 5: 1–40.

[95] Habermas, J. (1981). *The Theory of Communicative Action: One, Reason and the Rationalisation of Society*. Beacon Press, Massachusetts. English translation 1984.

[96] Halasz, F. and Moran, T. (1982). Analogy considered harmful. In: *Human Factors in Computer Systems: Proceedings of CHI'82*, Gaithersburg, MD. ACM/SIGCHI.

[97] Hansen, S. S., Holgaard, L., and Smith, M. (1988). EUROHELP: Intelligent help systems for information processing systems. In: *Proceedings of the 5th Annual ESPRIT Conference*, Amsterdam. North-Holland.

[98] Harris, J. E. (1984). Remembering to do things: A forgotten topic. In: Harris, J. E. and Morris, P. E. (eds), *Everyday Memory Actions and Absent-Mindedness*. Academic Press, London.

[99] Hartson, H. R. and Hix, D. (1989). Toward empirically derived methodologies and tools for human-computer interface development. *International Journal of Man-Machine Studies*, 31(4): 477–494.

[100] Hayes, P. J. (1979). The naïve physics manifesto. In: Michie, D. (ed.), *Expert Systems in the Microelectronic Age*. Edinburgh University Press, Edinburgh.

[101] Hayes, P. J. (1985). Executable interface definitions using form-based interface abstractions. In: Hartston, H. R. (ed.), *Advances in Human-Computer Interaction*, vol 1, pp. 161–190. Ablex, Norwood, NJ.

[102] Henderson, A. and Card, S. (1987). Rooms: The use of multiple virtual workspaces to reduce space contention in a window-based graphical interface. *ACM Transactions on Graphics*, 5: 211–243.

[103] Henderson, P. (1986). Functional programming, formal specification, and rapid prototyping. *IEEE Transactions on Software Engineering*, SE-12(2): 241–250.

[104] Hollnagel, E. (1989). Action monitoring and plan recognition: The response evaluation system (RESQ). Technical Report P857-WP6-Axion-099, Computer Resources International, Birkerød, Denmark.

[105] Hollnagel, E., Mancini, G., and Woods, D. D. (eds) (1986). *Intelligent Decision Support in Process Environments*. Springer-Verlag, Berlin.

[106] Hollnagel, E. and Weir, G. (1988). Principles for dialogue design in man-machine systems. In: *Proceedings of the IFAC/IFIP/IFORS/IEA Conference on Man-Machine Systems*, Oulu, Finland.

[107] Hollnagel, E. and Woods, D. D. (1983). Cognitive systems engineering: New wine in new bottles. *International Journal of Man-Machine Studies*, 18: 583–600.

[108] Hutchins, E., Hollan, J., and Norman, D. A. (1985). Direct manipulation interfaces. *Human-Computer Interaction*, 1: 311–338.

[109] Ihde, D. (1979). *Technics and Praxis*. D. Reidel, Dordrecht, Holland.

[110] Iosif, G. (1968). La stratégie dans la surveillance des tableaux de commande. I. Quelques determinants de caractère objectif. *Review Roumanian Science and Social-Psychology*, 12(2): 147–163.

[111] Iosif, G. (1969). La stratégie dans la surveillance des tableaux de commande. II. Quelques aspects de l'activité de surveillance chez les opérateurs dans la production semi-automatisée. *Review Roumanian Science and Social-Psychology*, 13(1): 75–94.

[112] Jacob, R. J. K. (1983). Using formal specifications in the design of a human-computer interface. *Communications of the ACM*, 26(4): 259–264.

[113] Janvier, C. (ed.) (1987). *Problems of Representation in the Teaching and Learning of Mathematics*. Lawrence Erlbaum Associates, Hillsdale, NJ.

[114] Jervell, H. R. and Olsen, K. A. (1985). Icons in man-machine communications. *Behaviour and Information Technology*, 4: 239–254.

[115] Johannsen, B., Borys, B.-B., and Fejes, L. (1986). Ergonomic knowledge support in graphical interface design for industrial process operators. In: *Proceedings of the 2nd Symposium on the Human Interface*, pp. 579–584, Tokyo.

[116] Johannsen, B., Rijnsdorp, J. E., and Tamura, H. (1986). Matching user needs and technologies of displays and graphics. In: Mancini, G., Johannsen, G., and Maartenson, L. (eds), *Analysis, Design, and Evaluation of Man-Machine Systems*, pp. 91–97. Pergamon Press, Oxford.

[117] Johansson, G. (1975). Visual motion perception. *Scientific American*, pp. 76–88.

[118] Johnson, E. and Payne, J. W. (1985). Effort and accuracy in choice. *Management Science*, 31: 395–414.

[119] Johnson-Laird, P. N. (1981). Mental models in cognitive science. In: Norman, D. A. (ed.), *Perspectives on Cognitive Science*. Ablex, Norwood, NJ.

[120] Johnson-Laird, P. N. (1983). *Mental Models: Towards a Cognitive Science of Language, Inference, and Consciousness*. Cambridge University Press, Cambridge.

[121] Johnson-Laird, P. N. (1988). *The Computer and the Mind: An Introduction to Cognitive Science*. Fontana Press, London.

[122] Joyce, J. P. and Lapinsky, G. W. (1983). A history and overview of the safety parameter display system concept. *IEEE Transactions on Nuclear Science*, NS-30.

[123] Kautto, A. (1984). Information presentation in power plant control rooms. Research Report 320, Technical Research Centre of Finland, PO Box 516, SF-00101 Helsinki 10.

[124] Kautz, H. (1987). A formal theory of plan recognition. Technical Report 215, University of Rochester, Department of Computer Science, Rochester, NY.

[125] Kieras, D. E. and Polson, P. G. (1985). An approach to the formal analysis of user complexity. *International Journal of Man-Machine Studies*, 22(4): 365–394.

[126] Kleiner, B. and Hartigan, J. A. (1981). Representing points in many dimensions by trees and castles. *Journal of the American Statistical Association*, 76: 260–269.

[127] Knowles, C. (1988). Can cognitive complexity theory (CCT) produce an adequate measure of system usability? In: Jones, D. M. and Winder, R. (eds), *People and Computers IV*, pp. 291–307. Cambridge University Press, Cambridge.

[128] Kotovsky, K., Hayes, J. R., and Simon, H. A. (1985). Why are some problems hard? Evidence from Tower of Hanoi. *Cognitive Psychology*, 17: 248–294.

[129] Kragt, H. and Bonten, J. (1983). Evaluation of a conventional process-alarm system in a fertilizer plant. *IEEE Transactions on Systems, Man, and Cybernetics*, SMC-13: 586–600.

[130] Kruglanski, A., Friedland, N., and Farkash, E. (1984). Lay persons' sensitivity to statistical information: The case of high perceived applicability. *Journal of Personality and Social Psychology*, 46: 503–518.

[131] La Porte, T. (1987). Personal communication.

[132] Laird, J. E., Newell, A., and Rosenbloom, P. S. (1987). SOAR: An architecture for general intelligence. *Artificial Intelligence*, 33: 1–64.

[133] Lazzari, G. (1988). Efficacy of VDU graphic displays measured on variable mappings on two formats. Master's thesis, University of London.

[134] Lehner, P. E. and Zirk, D. A. (1987). Cognitive factors in user/expert system interaction. *Human Factors*, 29: 97–110.

[135] Lenat, D. B. and Brown, J. S. (1984). Why AM and EURISKO appear to work. *Artificial Intelligence*, 23: 269–294.

[136] Lesh, R. (1987). The evolution of problem representations in the presence of powerful conceptual amplifiers. In: Janvier, C. (ed.), *Problems of Representation in the Teaching and Learning of Mathematics*. Lawrence Erlbaum Associates, Hillsdale, NJ.

[137] Lesser, V. R. and Erman, L. D. (1980). Distributed interpretation: A model and experiment. *IEEE Transactions on Computers*, C-29(12): 1144–1162.

[138] Levy, R. L. and Loftus, G. R. (1984). Compliance and memory. In: Harris, J. E. and Morris, P. E. (eds), *Everyday Memory Actions and Absent-Mindedness*. Academic Press, London.

[139] Lind, M. (1988). Diagnosis using multilevel flow models. Technical report, Technical University of Denmark, Lyngby, Denmark.

[140] Lind, M. (1988). Issues in modelling of information flow. Contribution to Bad Homburg Workshop on New Technology, Distributed Decision Making and Responsibility.

[141] Lind, M. (1989). Strategies for building MFM models. IACS lecture notes.

[142] Lowgren, J. (1988). History, state and future of user interface management systems. *Sigchi bulletin*, 20(1): 32–44.

[143] Macar, F. (1980). *Le Temps, perspectives psychophysiologiques*. P. Mardaga, Bruxelles.

[144] MacGregor, D. and Slovic, P. (1986). Graphic representation of judgmental information. *Human-Computer Interaction*, 2: 179–200.

[145] Mann, T. L. and Schnetzler, L. A. (1986). Evaluation of formats for aircraft control/display units. *Applied Ergonomics*, 17: 265–270.

[146] Marsden, P. H. (1990). Modelling the retrieval of incomplete knowledge. PhD Thesis, Department of Psychology, University of Manchester.

[147] Mayer, R. E. (1983). *Thinking, Problem Solving, Cognition*. Freeman, New York.

[148] McDermott, D. (1982). A temporal logic for reasoning about processes and plans. *Cognitive Science*, 6: 101–155.

[149] Medland, A. J. (1986). *The Computer-Based Design Process*. Kogan-Page, London.

[150] Michon, J. A. (1979). Le traitement de l'information temporelle. In: *Du temps biologique au temps psychologique*. Presses Universitaires de France.

[151] Mitchell, C. M. and Miller, R. A. Personal communication.

[152] Mitchell, C. M. and Miller, R. A. (1983). Design strategies for computer-based information display in real-time control systems. *Human Factors*, 25: 353–369.

[153] Mitchell, C. M. and Miller, R. A. (1986). A discrete control model of operator function: A methodology for information display design. *IEEE Transactions on Systems, Man, and Cybernetics*, SMC-16: 343–357.

[154] Mitchell, C. M. and Saisi, D. L. (1987). Use of model-based qualitative icons and adaptive windows in workstations for supervisory control systems. *IEEE Transactions on Systems, Man, and Cybernetics*, SMC-17: 573–593.

[155] Miyata, Y. and Norman, D. A. (1986). Psychological issues in support of multiple activities. In: Norman, D. A. and Draper, S. W. (eds), *User Centered System Design: New Perspectives on Human-Computer interaction*. Lawrence Erlbaum Associates, Hillsdale, NJ.

[156] Montangero, J. (1979). La genèse des raisonnements temporels. In: *Du temps biologique au temps psychologique*. Presses Universitaires de France.

[157] Montmollin, M. (1984). L'intelligence de la tâche. In: *Eléments d'ergonomie cognitive*. Peter Lang.

[158] Montmollin, M. and De Keyser, V. (1985). Expert logic vs operator logic. In: *2nd IFAC/IFIP/IFORS/IEA Conference on Analysis, Design and Evaluation of Man-Machine Systems*, Varese, Italy.

[159] Moran, T. P. (1981). The Command Language Grammar: A representation for the user interface of interactive computer systems. *International Journal of Man-Machine Studies*, 15(1): 3–50.

[160] Moran, T. P. (1986). Analytical performance models: A contribution to a panel discussion. In: Mantei, M. and Orbeton, P. (eds), *Human Factors in Computer Systems - III: Proceedings of the CHI'86 Conference*, Amsterdam. Elsevier.

[161] Moray, N. (1981). The role of attention in the detection of errors and the diagnosis of failures in man-machine systems. In: *Human Detection and Diagnosis of System Failures*. Plenum Press, New York.

[162] Moray, N. (1986). Modelling cognitive activities: Human limitations in relation to computer aids. In: Hollnagel, E., Mancini, G., and Woods, D. D. (eds), *Intelligent Decision Support in Process Environments*. Springer-Verlag, Berlin.

[163] Moray, N. (1987). Intelligent aids, mental models, and the theory of machines. *International Journal of Man-Machine Studies*, 27: 619–629.

[164] Moray, N. and Senders, J. (1989). *Why Do Things Go Wrong? A Study of Human Error*. Lawrence Erlbaum Associates, Hillsdale, NJ.

[165] Mullin, J. (1989). *The GRADIENT Dialogue System: User Manual*. University of Strathclyde, Glasgow, UK.

[166] Naveh-Benjamin, M. and Pachella, R. G. (1982). The effect of complexity on interpreting Chernoff faces. *Human Factors*, 24: 11–18.

[167] Newell, A. and Simon, H. A. (1972). *Human Problem Solving*. Prentice-Hall, Englewood Cliffs, NJ.

[168] Norman, D. A. (1981). Categorization of action slips. *Psychological Review*, 88: 1–15.

[169] Norman, D. A. (1983). Design rules based on analysis of human error. *Communications of the ACM*, 26(4): 254–258.

[170] Norman, D. A. (1986). Cognitive engineering. In: Norman, D. A. and Draper, S. W. (eds), *User Centred System Design: New Perspectives on Human-Computer Interaction*. Lawrence Erlbaum Associates, Hillsdale, NJ.

[171] Norman, K. L., Weldon, L. J., and Shneiderman, B. (1986). Cognitive layouts of windows and multiple screens for user interfaces. *International Journal of Man-Machine Studies*, 25: 229–248.

[172] Olsen, D. R. (1983). Automatic generation of interactive systems. *Computer Graphics*, 17(1): 53–57.

[173] Olsen, D. R., Kasik, D., Rhyne, J., and Thomas, J. (1987). ACM SIGGRAPH workshop on software tools for user interface management. *Computer Graphics*, 21(2). Complete issue.

[174] Oquist, P. (1978). The epistemology of action research. *Acta Sociologica*, 21: 143–163.

[175] Payne, S. J. and Green, T. R. G. (1986). Task-action grammars: A model of the mental representation of task languages. *Human-Computer Interaction*, 2: 93–133.

[176] Pfaff, G. E. (ed.) (1985). *User Interface Management Systems, Proc. IFIP/EG Workshop on UIMS, Seeheim, Fed. Republic of Germany, October, 1983*. Springer-Verlag, Berlin.

[177] Phillips, M. D., Bashinski, H. S., Ammerman, H. L., and Fligg, Jr., C. M. (1988). A task analytic approach to dialogue design. In: Helander, M. (ed.), *Handbook of Human-Computer Interaction*, pp. 835–857. North-Holland, Amsterdam.

[178] Piaget, J. (1946). *Le développement de la notion de temps chez l'enfant*. Presses Universitaires de France, Paris.

[179] Polson, P. G. (1987). A quantitative theory of human-computer interaction. In: Carroll, J. M. (ed.), *Interfacing Thought: Cognitive Aspects of Human-Computer Interaction*. MIT Press, Cambridge, MA.

[180] Posner, M. I. and Rossman, E. (1965). The effect of size and location of information transforms upon short-term retention. *Journal of Experimental Psychology*, 70: 496–505.

[181] Potts, G. R. (1975). Bringing order to cognitive structures. In: Restle, F., Shiffrin, R. M., Castellan, N. J., Lindman, H. R., and Pisoni, D. B. (eds), *Cognitive Theory*. Lawrence Erlbaum Associates, Hillsdale, NJ. Vol. 1.

[182] Rabardel, P. and Weill-Fassina, A. (eds) (1987). *Le Dessin Technique*. Hermes, Paris.

[183] Rasmussen, J. (1976). Outlines of a hybrid model of the process operator. In: Sheridan, T. and Johannsen, G. (eds), *Monitoring Behaviour and Supervisory Control*. Plenum Press, New York.

[184] Rasmussen, J. (1980). What can be learned from human error reports? In: Duncan, K., Gruneberg, M., and Wallis, D. (eds), *Changes in Working Life*. Wiley, London.

[185] Rasmussen, J. (1983). Skills, rules, and knowledge; signals, signs, and symbols, and other distinctions in human performance models. *IEEE Transactions on Systems, Man and Cybernetics*, SMC-13: 257–266.

[186] Rasmussen, J. (1986). A framework for cognitive task analysis in systems design. In: Hollnagel, E., Mancini, G., and Woods, D. D. (eds), *Intelligent Decision Support in Process Environments*, pp. 175–196. Springer-Verlag, Berlin.

[187] Rasmussen, J. (1986). *Information Processing and Human-Machine Interaction: An Approach to Cognitive Engineering*. North-Holland, Amsterdam.

[188] Rasmussen, J. (1987). Modelling action in complex environments. Technical Report Risø-M-2684, Risø National Laboratory, DK-4000 Roskilde, Denmark.

[189] Rasmussen, J., Pedersen, O. M., Mancini, G., Carnino, A., Griffon, M., and Gagnolet, P. (1981). Classification system for reporting events involving human malfunctions. Technical Report Risø-M-2240, SIN-DOC(81)14, Risø National Laboratory, Roskilde, Denmark.

[190] Reason, J. (1979). Actions not as planned: The price of automatization. In: Underwood, G. and Stevens, R. (eds), *Aspects of Consciousness, Vol. I. Psychological Issues*. Academic Press, London.

[191] Reason, J. (1984). Lapses of attention in everyday life. In: Parasumanan, R. and Davies, R. (eds), *Varieties of Attention*. Academic Press, New York.

[192] Reason, J. (1987). Generic error-modelling system (GEMS): A cognitive framework for locating human error forms. In: Rasmussen, J., Duncan, K., and Leplat, J. (eds), *New Technology and Human Error*. Wiley, London.

[193] Reason, J. (1989). Cognitive aids in process environments: prostheses or tools? In: Hollnagel, E., Mancini, G., and Woods, D. D. (eds), *Cognitive Engineering in Dynamic Worlds*. Academic Press, London.

[194] Reason, J. T. (1987). Cognitive aids in process environments: Prostheses or tools? *International Journal of Man-Machine Studies*, 27(5–6): 463–471.

[195] Reason, J. T. (1987). The cognitive bases of predictable human error. In: *Ergonomics Working for Society: Proceedings of the Ergonomics Society's Annual Conference*, Swansea.

[196] Reason, J. T. (1990). *Human Error*. Cambridge University Press, Cambridge.

[197] Reinartz, S. J. and Reinartz, G. (1989). Analysis of team behaviour during simulated nuclear power plant incidents. In: Megaw, E. D. (ed.), *Contemporary Ergonomics, 1989*, pp. 188–193. Taylor and Francis, London.

[198] Reisner, P. (1981). Formal grammar and human factors design of an interactive graphics system. *IEEE Transactions on Software Engineering*, SE-7(2): 229–240.

[199] Reisner, P. (1983). Analytic tools for human factors software. In: Blaser, A. and Zoeppritz, M. (eds), *Enduser Systems and Their Human Factors*, pp. 94–121. Springer-Verlag, Berlin. Lecture Notes in Computer Science 150.

[200] Roth, E. M., Bennett, K. B., and Woods, D. D. (1987). Human interaction with an 'intelligent' machine. *International Journal of Man-Machine Studies*, 27: 479–525.

[201] Roth, E. M. and Woods, D. D. (1989). Cognitive task analysis: An approach to knowledge acquisition for intelligent system design. In: Guida, G. and Tasso, C. (eds), *Topics in Expert System Design: Methodologies and Tools*, pp. 233–264. Elsevier, Amsterdam.

[202] Rouse, W. B., Geddes, N. D., and Curry, R. E. (1987-8). An architecture for intelligent interfaces: Outline to an approach to supporting operators of complex systems. *Human-Computer Interaction*, 3: 87–122.

[203] Sanderson, P. (1986). Skills, displays and decision support. In: Hollnagel, E., Mancini, G., and Woods, D. D. (eds), *Intelligent Decision Support in Process Environments*. Springer-Verlag, Berlin.

[204] Schneider, W. (1989). Training models to estimate training costs for new systems. In: Elkind, J., Card, S., Hochberg, J., and Huey, B. (eds), *Human Performance Models for Computer Aided Engineering*. National Academy Press, Washington, D.C.

[205] Shatz, S. M. and Wang, J. P. (1987). Introduction to distributed software engineering. *Computer*, 20(10): 23–31.

[206] Shaw, M. L. G. and Gaines, B. R. (1987). An interactive knowledge-elicitation technique using personal construct technology. In: Kidd, A. L. (ed.), *Knowledge Acquisition for Expert Systems: A Practical Handbook*, ch 6. Plenum Press, New York.

[207] Shepherd, A. (1985). Hierarchical task analysis and training decisions. *Programmed Learning and Educational Technology*, 22: 162–176.

[208] Shepherd, A., Marshall, E. C., Turner, A., and Duncan, K. D. (1977). Control panel diagnosis: A comparison of three training methods. *Ergonomics*, 20: 347–361.

[209] Sheridan, T. B. and Hennessy, T. (1984). *Research and Modelling of Supervisory Control Behavior*. National Academy Press.

[210] Shneiderman, B. (1982). Multiparty grammars and related features for defining interactive systems. *IEEE Transactions on Systems, Man and Cybernetics*, SMC-12(2): 148–154.

[211] Shneiderman, B. (1987). *Designing the User Interface*. Addison-Wesley, Reading, MA.

[212] Shneiderman, B. (1988). We can design better user interfaces: A review of human-computer interaction styles. *Ergonomics*, 31: 699–710.

[213] Shoham, Y. (1988). *Reasoning about Change*. MIT Press, Cambridge, MA.

[214] Sibert, J. L., Hurley, W. D., and Bleser, T. W. (1986). An Object-Oriented User Interface Management System. In: Evans, D. C. and Athay, R. J. (eds), *SIGGRAPH '86*, pp. 259–268, Dallas, Texas. ACM.

[215] Simon, H. A. (1972). *The Sciences of the Artificial*. MIT Press, Cambridge, MA.

[216] Simon, T. (1988). Analysing the scope of cognitive models in human-computer interaction: A trade-off approach. In: Jones, D. M. and Winder, R. (eds), *People and Computers IV*, pp. 79–93. Cambridge University Press, Cambridge.

[217] Skorstad, E. (1988). Technology and overall control. In: De Keyser, V., Qvale, T., Wilpert, B., and Quintanilla, A. R. (eds), *The Meaning of Work and Technological Change*. Wiley, Chichester.

[218] Sloman, A. (1978). *The Computer Revolution in Philosophy: Philosophy, Science and Models of Mind*. Harvester Press, Sussex.

[219] Sufrin, B. (1986). Formal methods and the design of effective user interfaces. In: Harrison, M. D. and Monk, A. F. (eds), *People and Computers: Designing for Usability. Proceedings of the Second Conference of the BCS HCI specialist group*, Cambridge. Cambridge University Press.

[220] Szekely, P. A. and Myers, B. A. (1988). A user interface toolkit based on graphical objects and constraints. In: Meyrowitz, N. (ed.), *Proc. OOPSLA '88: Object Oriented Programming Systems, Languages and Applications*, pp. 36–45, San Diego, CA. ACM.

[221] Taylor, F. V. and Garvey, W. D. (1959). The limitations of a 'procrustean' approach to the optimization of man-machine systems. *Ergonomics*, 2: 187–194.

[222] Tomiyama, T. and ten Hagen, P. J. W. (1987). Organization of design knowledge in an intelligent CAD environment. In: Gero, J. S. (ed.), *Expert Systems in Computer-Aided Design*. North-Holland, Amsterdam.

[223] Trabasso, T. and Riley, C. A. (1975). The construction and use of representations involving linear order. In: Solso, R. L. (ed.), *Information Processing and Cognition*. Lawrence Erlbaum Associates, Hillsdale, NJ.

[224] Turner, J. (1984). Software ergonomics: Effects of computer applications design parameters on operator task performance and health. *Ergonomics*, 27(6): 663–690.

[225] Van Daele, A. (1988). L'écran de visualisation ou la communication verbale? *Le Travail Humain*, 51(1): 65–80.

[226] Vermeulen, J. (1987). Effects of functionally or topographically presented process schemes on operator performance. *Human Factors*, 29: 383–394.

[227] Vicente, K. and Williges, R. C. (1989). Visual momentum as a means of accommodating individual differences among users of a hierarchical file system. In: Pejtersen, A. M. and Zunde, P. (eds), *Empirical Foundations of Information and Software Sciences*. Plenum Press, New York.

[228] Volta, G. (1986). Time and decision. In: Hollnagel, E., Mancini, G., and Woods, D. D. (eds), *Intelligent Decision Support in Process Environments*. Springer-Verlag, Berlin.

[229] Wason, P. C. (1966). Reasoning. In: Foss, B. M. (ed.), *New horizons in psychology*. Penguin, Harmondsworth.

[230] Wasserman, A. I. and Shaw, D. T. (1983). A RAPID/USE tutorial. Technical report, University of California at San Francisco.

[231] Weir, G. R. S. (1989). Dialogue expertise in man-machine systems. In: Lind, M. and Hollnagel, E. (eds), *Proceedings of the 8th European Conference on Human Decision Making and Manual Control*, Lyngby, Denmark. Technical University of Denmark.

[232] Weir, G. R. S. (1989). Varieties of dialogue in man-machine systems. In: *Proceedings of the 2nd European Meeting on Cognitive Science Approaches to Process Control*, Siena, Italy.

[233] Weizenbaum, J. (1976). *Computer Power and Human Reason: From Judgment to Calculation*. Freeman, San Francisco.

[234] Wheeldon, B., Hollnagel, E., Belleli, T., Jepsen, M., and Ravnholt, O. (1988). RESQ report. Technical Report P857-WP6-CRI-089, Computer Resources International, Copenhagen, Denmark.

[235] Wiecha, C. and Henrion, M. (1987). Linking multiple program views using a visual cache. In: *Proceedings of Interact '87*. IFIP.

[236] Williams, B. C. (1986). Doing time: Putting qualitative reasoning on firmer ground. In: *Proceedings of the AAAI-86 National Conference on Artificial Intelligence*.

[237] Williams, M. D. (1984). What makes RABBIT run? *International Journal of Man-Machine Studies*, 21: 333–352.

[238] Wilson, M., Barnard, P., and MacLean, A. (1986). Using an expert system to convey HCI information. In: Harrison, M. D. and Monk, A. F. (eds), *People and Computers: Designing for Usability*, pp. 482–497. Cambridge University Press, Cambridge.

[239] Winograd, T. and Flores, F. (1986). *Understanding Computers and Cognition*. Addison-Wesley, Wokingham.

[240] Wolstenholme, D. E., O'Brien, C. M., and Nelder, J. A. (1988). GLIMPSE: A knowledge-based front end for statistical analysis. *Knowledge Based Systems*, 1(3): 173–178.

[241] Woods, D. D. (1984). Visual momentum: A concept to improve the cognitive coupling of person and computer. *International Journal of Man-Machine Studies*, 21: 229–244.

[242] Woods, D. D. (1985). Knowledge based development of graphic display systems. In: *Proceedings of the Human Factors Society*. 29th Annual Meeting.

[243] Woods, D. D. (1986). Paradigms for intelligent decision support. In: Hollnagel, E., Mancini, G., and Woods, D. D. (eds), *Intelligent Decision Support in Process Environments*. Springer-Verlag, Berlin.

[244] Woods, D. D. (1987). Commentary: Cognitive engineering in complex and dynamic worlds. *International Journal of Man-Machine Studies*, 27(5–6): 571–585.

[245] Woods, D. D. (1988). Coping with complexity: The psychology of human behavior in complex systems. In: Goodstein, L. P., Andersen, H. B., and Olsen, S. E. (eds), *Tasks, Errors and Mental Models*, pp. 128–148. Taylor and Francis, London.

[246] Woods, D. D. and Elias, G. (1988). Significance messages: An integral display concept. In: *Proceedings of the Human Factors Society*. 32nd Annual Meeting.

[247] Woods, D. D. and Hollnagel, E. (1987). Mapping cognitive demands in complex problem-solving worlds. *International Journal of Man-Machine Studies*, 26(2): 257–275.

[248] Woods, D. D. and Hollnagel, E. (1988). Mapping cognitive demands and activities in complex problem solving worlds. In: Gaines, B. R. and Boose, J. H. (eds), *Knowledge Acquisition for Knowledge-Based Systems*. Academic Press, London.

[249] Woods, D. D. and Roth, E. M. (1988). Aiding human performance: II. from cognitive analysis to support systems. *Le Travail Humain*, 51(2): 139–171.

[250] Woods, D. D. and Roth, E. M. (1988). Cognitive systems engineering. In: Helander, M. (ed.), *Handbook of Human-Computer Interaction*, ch 1, pp. 1–41. North-Holland, New York.

[251] Woods, D. D., Roth, E. M., and Pople, H. (1987). Cognitive environment simulation: An artificial intelligence system for human performance assessment. Technical Report Nureg-CRCR-4862, U. S. Nuclear Regulatory Commission, Washington, D.C. Volume 2: Modeling Human Intention Formation.

[252] Yang, J. Y. D., Huhns, M. N., and Stephens, L. M. (1985). An architecture for control and communications in distributed artificial intelligence systems. *IEEE Transactions on Systems, Man, and Cybernetics*, SMC-15(3): 316–326.

[253] Yoshimura, S., Hollnagel, E., and Prætorius, N. (1983). Man-machine interface design using multilevel flow modelling. Report HWR-96, OECD Halden Reactor Project, Halden, Norway.

[254] Young, R. M. (1981). The machine inside the machine: Users models of pocket calculators. *International Journal of Man-Machine Studies*, 15: 87–134.

[255] Young, R. M. (1983). Surrogates and mappings: Two kinds of conceptual models for interactive devices. In: Gentner, D. and Stevens, A. L. (eds), *Mental Models*, ch 3. Lawrence Erlbaum Associates, Hillsdale, NJ.

[256] Young, R. M., Green, T. R. G., and Simon, T. (1989). Programmable user models for predictive evaluation of interface designs. In: *CHI'89 Conference Proceedings*, pp. 15–19, Austin, Texas.

Index

Note: footnotes are indicated by suffix 'n'.